Critical Theory
and the Novel

Critical Theory and the Novel

*Mass Society and Cultural Criticism
in Dickens, Melville, and Kafka*

DAVID SUCHOFF

The University of Wisconsin Press

The University of Wisconsin Press
114 North Murray Street
Madison, Wisconsin 53715

3 Henrietta Street
London WC2E 8LU, England

5   4   3   2   1

Printed in the United States of America

Parts of "Cold War Cultural Theory" appeared as "New Historicism and Containment: Toward a Post-Cold War Cultural Theory," in *The Arizona Quarterly*, 48 (Spring 1992): 137–161, reprinted courtesy of the Regents of the University of Arizona.

Library of Congress Cataloging-in-Publication Data
Suchoff, David Bruce.
    Critical theory and the novel: mass society and cultural
criticism in Dickens, Melville, and Kafka / David Suchoff.
        232 p.   cm.
    Includes bibliographical references and index.
    ISBN 0-299-14080-6.   ISBN 0-299-14084-9 (pbk.)
    1. Dickens, Charles, 1812–1870—Political and social views.
    2. Melville, Herman, 1819–1891—Political and social views.
    3. Kafka, Franz, 1883–1924—Political and social views.
    4. Fiction—History and criticism—Theory, etc.   5. Fiction—Social aspects.
    6. Literature and society.   I. Title.
    PR4592.S58S83   1993
    823.009'358—dc20   93-21116

In Memory of Frances Ehrenthal Suchoff
1896–1986

Contents

Acknowledgments

I would like to thank the scholars and colleagues who preserved the spirit and substance of this book. At the University of California, Berkeley, and beyond, D. A. Miller was a director and friend whose support was unflagging; Robert Alter, Mitchell Breitwieser, Richard Hutson, and Michael Rogin also contributed to the original version with guidance and commentary.

Jon Klancher's colloquy taught me new ways to think about cultural criticism, and Michael McKeon and Patrick O'Donnell made valuable suggestions that materially improved this book throughout. Responses and often much more from Sacvan Bercovitch, Stephen Dowden, Sharon Kinoshita, Alec Marantz, Jeffrey Mehlman, Susan Mizruchi, Leland Monk, Pam Rothstein, Dianne Sadoff, and Carolyn Williams made it possible to continue my work. I am grateful as well to my parents, Sarah and Burton Sukhov, for sustenance that was strong and deep.

I would also like to thank Marjorie Garber, Henry Louis Gates, Jr., Richard Hunt, and William McFeeley, Directors of the Mellon Fellowship Program at Harvard University, as well as the Center for Literary Studies at Harvard, for their support. My colleagues in the English Department at Colby College, and its Chairs, John Mizner and Patricia Onion, provided the best possible setting for concluding this book.

More than thanks are due to Karen, who knows how much I owe her, as do Dani and Jessi. While writing about society and its criticism in the novel, it was the perpetual novelty of their culture that I loved.

Critical Theory
and the Novel

Introduction

This book is a study in the historical origins of cultural criticism in the novel since the mid-nineteenth century. I use the critical theory of the Frankfurt School to examine the critical force of mass culture as crucial to the making of the modern novel. The Introduction analyzes the writing of Walter Benjamin and Theodor Adorno, discussing the contribution it makes to contemporary methods for reading cultural criticism in fiction; the remaining chapters discuss the crucial political novels of Dickens, Melville, and Kafka, and argue for the critical force that problems of mass audience and politics brought to their works. Frankfurt School concepts assist readings that examine the political engagements of their writing, and are used to explore the effective responses of these novelists to the pressures of life in commodity culture.

The first part of Chapter 1 examines the roles played by these novelists in shaping a liberal-modernist paradigm of the critical social novel. American conceptions of cultural criticism, particularly the determining work of Lionel Trilling, were powerfully shaped by liberal readings of Dickens, Melville, and Kafka. This section of the Introduction traces the ways these authors helped to form negative American attitudes toward the critical potential of mass culture in the modern novel. A middle section argues that contemporary criticism of Dickens, Melville, and Kafka, while giving mass culture a renewed critical attention, also shared cold war modernism's limited view of its critical power.[1] The final introductory section explains the contribution of Frankfurt School concepts to a positive view of the critical potential of mass culture in the tradition of the novel. Each subsequent chapter, dealing with an individual novelist, does not "apply" Frankfurt School terms as much as explore the similar approach to cultural criticism Dickens, Melville, and Kafka exhibit in their best social novels.

In reading their fiction and its canonization, I hope to revise New Historical accounts of their work that have either dismissed its engagement with mass culture or, through the category of modernism, denied that connection its socially oppositional force. These writers remain powerful representatives in the ongoing American debate on the political significance of mass culture. Despite the investments of Melville and Dickens in popular fiction, both were often seen as modernist precursors, whose work figured an alienation from modern society and its increasingly commodified culture. Kafka—though his historical concerns were with Czech nationalism, Jewish culture, and Zionism—in turn was considered an ahistorical novelist, whose abstract and formally self-conscious fiction engaged popular movements and totalitarianism at a personal and prophetic remove. Readings of their novels during the 1950s and 1960s complied with a cold war canon of alienated opposition from mass society. Alienation, reflexivity, or psychological complexity became the distinguishing features of cultural criticism in their novels, which were seen as increasingly distant from the mass public for which Dickens and Melville wrote, or as existentially beyond the bureaucratic society in which Kafka lived.

Instead, I stress the ways in which each novelist represents a dialectical and critical involvement with the problems of mass society. Standard literary histories have tended to stress modernist distance when discussing the critical social novel. Most important accounts of the political novel privilege nineteenth-century narrative—typified by Balzac, Dickens, or Melville—as socially critical, while diminishing the social engagement of the tradition of self-conscious fiction, often represented by Kafka or Proust. While differing on the political value of the novel's increasing self-consciousness, important historians of the novel agree on the separation critical social novels establish from mass culture. Liberal critics tend to view this modernist distance positively, as testimony to the novelist's ability to transform the dilemmas of mass society into alienation and art, while Lukács's dominant Marxist perspective defined modernism as the apolitical lapse of liberalism into fashionable angst, or existential despair.[2]

Problems of politics and culture in the era of mechanical reproduction were nonetheless very much the concern of these novelists: Dickens and Melville participated in the origins of mass-market book publishing, and wrote popular political journalism as well, while Kafka produced his greatest fiction while involved with the political mass movements of Czech nationalism and Zionism in turn-of-the-century Prague. I examine the modernist aspects of these novelists as part of their forceful and oppositional engagement with culture and politics. Frankfurt School critics always counted the marketplace and its culture as a factor in the formal development of the novel: Adorno compared the entertainment functions of eighteenth-century fiction with the later development of television and other twentieth-century versions of the entertainment industry.[3] The effects of the Victorian fictional marketplace on Dickens, Melville's critique of his mass audience, and Kafka's criticism of internalized social power, were part of the dialectical engagement of each with the industrial culture of his age.

The Frankfurt School's analysis best resses the novel's relation to these literary and social forces. Benjamin's practice of reading the contradictory meanings of commodity culture and its objects was crucial to Adorno, despite the latter's often pessimistic pronouncements: brushing the text "against the grain" for both meant recognizing the "barbarism" of domination present in modern culture while remaining committed to recovering its oppositional social force.[4] This dialectical approach corrects premature populism, while at the same insisting on the critical, redemptive dimensions of mass culture. Neither a liberatory populism nor a theory of seamless power is adequate to address the issues raised by advertising, music hall culture, mass readership, and social control that these novelists addressed. In using Adorno and Benjamin, I hope to show the kinship of these authors with such an aesthetic of "redemption": Dickens and Melville's involvement with the mass-market novel, and Kafka's internal assault on the ethnic and nationalist ideology, shared the similar perspective of later Frankfurt School writers that the dominating power of mass society was inseparable from the production of counterdiscourses critical of its culture.[5]

It will be helpful to say what I mean by the term "mass culture," given the variety of forms it assumes. Melville's contestatory relations with American popular fiction, the influence of the Yiddish theater on Kafka, and Dickens' complex relations with the Victorian mass audience will color my readings of selected novels by each author. The sources of each novelist were many: Dickens loved and wrote for the Victorian theater and produced periodicals, Melville wrote campaign propaganda that satirized early forms of the media image, while Kafka read popular Czech fiction and knew anarchist and socialist literature as well. Distinguishing genuinely popular material in these novelists from the products of what Adorno later termed the "culture industry" is a difficult problem, well framed by Kafka in a memorable aphorism: "leopards break into the temple and drink the sacrificial chalices dry; this occurs repeatedly, again and again: finally it can be reckoned upon beforehand and becomes a part of the ceremony."[6] It is precisely this task of distinguishing between popular and mass-produced culture that concerned Kafka as a cultural critic, and which makes each of these novelists pertinent to contemporary considerations of cultural criticism. Their novels analyzed the mass-cultural media that constrained the challenging social claims of popular expression, in order to release its socially critical points of view. I have found Frankfurt School approaches valuable because they emphasize mass society's shaping significance to these developments of the modern novel, without prematurely celebrating mass culture's socially oppositional roles.

Much valuable work has been done on the relations these authors sustained with oppositional culture: studies of Melville and the American working class, Kafka's interest in anarchism, socialism, and the Yiddish theater, and numerous works on Dickens' democratic politics have been useful to me and are acknowledged throughout this book. Populist studies of the novel and its culture have also served as useful correctives to the biases of cold war modernism I discuss in Chapter 1.[7] But the idea that Melville's use of popular culture is simply "subversive," as the title of David Reynolds' book on Melville and mass culture suggests, ignores the mass reproduction of resistant effects to which every "popular" gesture was subject in the increasingly powerful American consumer culture that concerned Melville, from his political journalism through *Billy Budd*.[8] Readings of their novels are meant here to evoke a specific sense of "redemption" in the critical-historical context that was Benjamin's: an effort to *recover* the textual complexity of these writers as part of their modernist engagement with mass culture.

Such an emphasis on the "text," to be sure, may not accord for many American readers with the suggestion of cultural criticism. Part of the revisionist effort of this book is to show how this separation of "reading" from historical and cultural criticism arose in the first place in American liberal culture. This split between "textual" and "historical" criticism emerged in all its rigidity in the 1980s as part of late cold war cultural theory's reaction to the liberal-modernist "text." The liberal-modernist movement in American criticism of the 1950s produced Lionel Trilling's emphasis on textual "complexity," as well as New Criticism's practice of close reading. The return of 1980s critics to the historical and cultural contexts of fiction made attention to textuality suspect, and sometimes made it hard to see close textual analysis as anything but a political refusal to face up to mass culture and history.[9] Rejecting the subversive freedom inherent in Lionel Trilling's liberal notion of culture often meant casting aside "close reading" as an impediment to historically grounded study of the novel.

Frankfurt School writers, on the other hand, were unburdened with liberal guilt for having forgotten ideas such as class, buried in the movement of "textual" criticism, and never absolutized the textual/ historical divide in any such way.[10] Adorno's most important essay on cultural criticism criticized this division between "reflexive" criticism and realistic "context" as itself a shadow of the division of labor. "Textuality" should not be seen as a kind of distanced, formalist form of self-reflection, and opposed to the "context," as if the latter guaranteed the solid critical ground of real historical "work."[11] The permanence of this division—and the implied division of critical labor between "textual" and "historical" critics it implies—is illusory, as Adorno suggests, a symptom of reification rather than a concrete set of oppositional critical terms. Instead of splitting textual from historical approaches, Adorno and Benjamin gave attention to the text as a social inscription: reading for both was a way of brushing the commodified object against the grain of its identity with domination to recover its critical social force. Benjamin's Arcades Project, it should be recalled, was a textual reading of the critical potential congealed in the commodity displays of the first Parisian shopping malls, just as Kafka's hermetic modernism was legible as an oppositional account of modern modes of social control. *Reading* the documents of commodity culture—like the *Los Angeles Times* astrology column, which Adorno analyzed, with the same attention he devoted to Heidegger— and arguing their relation to "textual" modernism is central to the practice I develop in this book of reading mass culture in the novel.

It is the response of authors and texts to such objectification that Adorno defined as the substance of cultural criticism. I use the term in the sense outlined in Adorno's essay "Cultural Criticism and Society." There, the critic's recognition of cultural domination is regarded as a moment in a longer critical process: identifying mass cultural domination points to the critical difference a work establishes from within its cultural confines.[12] This dialectical impulse—the identification of oppositional elements in writing that appears critically closed—applies to the cultural criticism of Dickens, Melville, and Kafka studied in this book, and informs my own method as well. Critical theory is meant here to open the question of oppositional criticism in their works anew, and to explore the ways the social novel, by analyzing mass culture's constraints on political action, also provides an enabling vision of the sources of social change.

Finally, this book hopes to emphasize the contribution these novelists have to make to the discipline of cultural studies. New Historicism's reaction against cold war concepts of cultural freedom valuably reintroduced the works of these novelists to history. But the need to debunk the status of Dickens, Melville, and Kafka as oppositional

1

Cold War Cultural Theory
Modernism, Socialism, and Subversion

As part of cold war cultural theory, New Historicism used the notion of "containment" to oppose the idea of a subversive modernism, and read literary works as suffused by power, controlled by mass culture, or subject to the state. This New Historical reaction against the notion of a subversive literary text was framed in opposition to textual approaches, but also to the claims of the "liberal imagination," whose foremost exponent in America was Lionel Trilling. The return to history situated the novels of Dickens, Melville, and Kafka once again in formerly excluded areas of history, and defined cultural criticism itself as subject to the control of social context. But the development of American criticism, as Frank Lentricchia noted in *After the New Criticism,* had already left to one side the Frankfurt School analysis of literature's domination by the marketplace, as well as the common quest of Adorno and Benjamin for a redemptive cultural critique.[1]

Adorno, despite his presence on the American scene through much of the fifties, remained peripheral at best to American novel criticism. American intellectuals were aware of the Frankfurt School, but liberal pluralists looked on Adorno's theory of "mass deception" with suspicion, regarding it as an elitist rejection of the strengths of American democracy.[2] Fears of "McCarthyist attacks" led Adorno to hold back his most optimistic work on the critical potential of mass culture, a book written with Hans Eisler, *Composing for the Films.*[3] As a result, both Adorno and Benjamin remained less than influential in the development of cultural criticism in America.[4] The cold war made ideology a dangerous topic for literary studies, and Trilling argued for a novel free of such "messianic" responsibility, committed to a "complex" and modernist vision instead.[5]

9

In revising the liberal-modernist paradigm, however, New Historicism carried its cold war limitations into new evaluations of the social
novel. Unseating the claimed freedom of Dickens, Melville, and Kafka,
novelists exemplary of a critical, "liberal imagination," meant considering the ideological uses of modernist "subversion." Mass culture
became an important object of study in the new cultural criticism, but
was regarded almost exclusively as a source of social control. This development from liberal cultural theory and its socialist predecessors
took place in the political culture of McCarthyism, liberal pluralism,
and the foreign policy doctrine of containment formulated by George
Kennan in 1947.[6] At the height of cold war culture in America, Fredric
Jameson coined the phrase "strategies of containment," and codified
this cold war conception of politics for the mainstream study of the
novel. At the same time Dickens, Melville, and Kafka became crucial
test cases in the shift from theories of liberal subversion to New Historicism's paradigm, helping to define containment cultural criticism
and its limited view of mass culture. The history of cold war cultural
theory that follows offers a map of the larger cultural politics according to which we have received these authors, against which my own
later argument for the culturally critical force of their novels is meant
to be read.

The Liberal Imagination and Its Discontents

When *Criticism and Social Change* appeared in 1983, Frank Lentricchia
urged the political criticism of literature to avoid the blind alley of
deconstruction and return to history. "Kantian, symbolist, and aes-
theticist patterns of thought . . . all of which father modern political
refusals," Lentricchia argued, had left their traces in poststructuralism's concern with signs, and were to be avoided in favor of attention
to the material functions of literature in society.[7] But Lentricchia's brief
against modernism had its own American cultural history: the cold
war. As liberal cultural theory separated itself from the radicalism of
the thirties and the realist aesthetic favored by the Popular Front, a
notion of modern narrative as subversive had been formed. Dickens,
Melville, and Kafka were used to construct a cultural criticism that
was liberal and modernist, but set socialism aside.

That version of modernism, Lionel Trilling argued, was anticipated
by Freud, who articulated a modern self "submitting to culture and
yet . . . in opposition" to culture's conformist forces. The scope of its
narrative canon was established significantly by Dickens and Kafka,

whose novels were said to show "the perfect continuity of the nineteenth century with the twentieth."[8] J. Hillis Miller's influential *Charles Dickens: The World of His Novels* (1958) would reinforce the connection between Dickens and Kafka as novelists of "metaphysical alienation" and social criticism.[9] But the somewhat obscure work of C. L. R. James, *Mariners, Renegades, and Castaways: The Story of Herman Melville and the World We Live In* (1953) had already placed Melville in the same line of alienated cultural rebellion. An important Caribbean historian and a leader of the Workers Party, James defined Melville as a cultural rather than political opponent of American society.[10] H. Bruce Franklin's New Left revival of James revised his own earlier mythic interpretation of Melville, *The Wake of the Gods: Melville's Mythology* (1963), but saw Melville's class-conscious radicalism without the textual acuity that the contemporary work of Fredric Jameson on the novel would supply.[11] Together with later works, such as Heinz Politzer's *Franz Kafka: Parable and Paradox* (1962), and Pearl Chesler Solomon's *Dickens and Melville in Their Time* (1975), these works helped to construct a cold war definition of modernist radicalism as distinguished from socialism and its ideological concerns.

This notion of narrative modernism as subversive allowed American cultural criticism to move away from Marxism while preserving an oppositional stance. Edmund Wilson's essay "Dickens, the Two Scrooges" (1941) played a crucial role in that process. Wilson defined Dickens for a generation by translating the less nuanced and determinist Marxist interpretation of T. A. Jackson's *Dickens: The Progress of a Radical* (1937) into liberal and Freudian terms. Wilson's highly popular biography of Lenin, *To the Finland Station* (1940), and the socialist commitment it represented, were left behind. Dickens instead was canonized as a smoldering rebel. Childhood trauma in factory work was seen as responsible for his radicalism, and his personality was used to define a realist novel that opposed society in psychologically complex rather than socialist terms. Paul Goodman's work, *Kafka's Prayer* (1947), later followed Wilson's lead in its use of psychology to argue for Kafka as a social critic, and also presaged the frustration of Wilson's investment in psychology as a political stance. Wilson ended his life in bitterness, linking his own position as a cultural critic to the limits of postwar culture in his *The Cold War and the Income Tax: A Protest* (1963), a polemic against American involvement in the Dominican Republic as well as Vietnam.[12] Dickens' reputation as a powerful modernist opponent of mass society, however, had already been established by comparative works. Mark Spilka, in *Dickens and*

Kafka: A Mutual Interpretation (1963), produced an influential argument for both novelists as practitioners of a subversive art of modernist humor, establishing a tradition for Steven Marcus' *Dickens: From Pickwick to Dombey* (1965). James R. Kincaid's *Dickens and the Rhetoric of Laughter* (1971) may have been more systematic in its method, but it shared the propensity of cold war cultural criticism to see rebellion against authority in the novel in modernist and liberal, rather than anticapitalist, terms.

Trilling's work was crucial in making these novelists representatives of a modern, critical liberal culture. The Melville revival of the twenties and thirties had made his novels, along with Dreiser's naturalism, accessible as material for critiques of commercial culture.[13] In stressing Melville's liberalism, Trilling offered the "awareness of complexity and difficulty" in place of the determinism of Progressive critics and later "vulgar" Marxist analysis. Trilling judged Melville's modernist attitude as superior to a cultural criticism that limited its analysis to economic terms.[14] New Critics with their emphasis on the formal self-enclosure of literature, Trilling observed, had delivered the modern novel from such determinism, but had lost sight of the "subversive tendency of modern literature" and its criticism of society.[15]

Trilling's cultural position dovetailed with the work of "consensus" historians like Richard Hofstadter, and with the pluralist premise of "American exceptionalism" that shaped books such as Louis Hartz's *The Liberal Tradition in America* (1955) and Daniel Boorstin's *The Genius of American Politics* (1953). Hofstadter, in a review of pluralist approaches written in 1968, argued as did Trilling for the "complexity" of such anti-ideological modernism and its criticism of culture. The "consensus" approach represented by Hofstadter offered an alternative to the economic analysis of the Progressives, seeing pluralism and status competition as replacing divisive social conflict. Daniel Bell argued that ideology in America had come to an end.[16] Hofstadter's judgment, that "the very idea of complexity will come under fire once again," provided a kind of prophecy of later New Historicist reactions to consensus cultural theory and of the return of ideology to the text.[17] But against the perceived ideological crudity of literary interpretation practiced by Progressive historians of American literature such as Charles Beard and Vernon Parrington, Trilling theorized a literature both formally complex and socially critical. Parrington's method, Trilling wrote, "amounts . . . to not much more than the demonstration that most writers incline to stick to their own social class."[18]

This hostility to the Progressives led to the canonization of an official, subversive modernism. A concept of radical modernist culture, detached from socialism, developed in the circle that surrounded *Partisan Review*. These New York Intellectuals, as they have come to be called, included former and present socialists and communists, among them Trilling, Philip Rahv, Edmund Wilson, and Dwight Macdonald. Together, they opposed the limits of the Popular Front and the Stalinist taste for leftist realism and formulated a notion of aesthetic modernism, hostile to mass culture and detached from any ideological program.[19] In 1940, Van Wyck Brooks, an inheritor of the socialist legacy, came out in a famous lecture against T. S. Eliot, Proust, Joyce, and Stein as creators of "coterie literature," obsessed with "form." *Partisan Review* invited Trilling, William Carlos Williams, and others to respond.[20] Trilling scorned Brooks's hostility to modernism, but carefully differentiated his response from Dwight Macdonald's socialist attack, entitled "Kulturbolshevismus Is Here."

The dispute over "coterie literature" foreshadowed the later cold war splitting of liberal modernist from socialist approaches. "Macdonald's article on Brooks is very just as far as its literary judgment goes," Trilling wrote, but defined his preference for modernism as a liberal one: "I do not share his feelings about the political importance of Brooks's recent attitudes . . . and I do not share Macdonald's assumptions that socialism promises a moral and literary regeneration."[21] This separation of the novel from ideology became one of the linchpins of liberal cultural theory. Trilling argued against ideological approaches while supporting the liberal value of modernist narrative and the "disenchantment of culture by culture" it expressed.[22] Discovering modernist alienation and complexity in the novel was part of this conservative cultural shift, and the modernist emphasis meant "saving" a novelist such as Dickens from the mass culture in which he worked. "The process by which the views of former revolutionaries came into harmony with the dominant ideology of the liberal intelligentsia during the Cold War," as Alan M. Wald argues, depended on the transformation of prewar socialist radicalism into the notion of a socially critical and subversive modern culture.[23]

"Containment," as it emerged in New Historicist criticism, and the later concept of "negotiation" that replaced it, were indebted to this cold war history. George F. Kennan's historic essay of 1947, "The Sources of Soviet Conduct," defined "containment" as the centerpiece of a foreign policy opposed to communist subversion and advocated a selective and dispersed exercise of military power.[24] The origins of containment, as we have seen, preceded cold war foreign policy, and the reactions the term produced from the right and the left of the political spectrum helped to shape subsequent cultural debates. James Burnham, an ex-socialist, would popularize the term by advocating a harder line toward the Soviet Union in his *Containment or Liberation?* (1952). David Horowitz, during his New Left period, edited the collection of essays entitled *Containment and Revolution* (1967). Essays in the work conceived of containment both as a variety of warfare that "increasingly has no locality in terms of geopolitical space, no specifiable and resolvable issue," and as a paradigm of state power and its covert exercise in liberal society.[25]

This notion of dispersed power and its covert exercise became a dominating theme in New Historicist uses of Foucault as an approach to fiction. Along with the canonization of official modernism, a cold war culture of effective censorship had emerged. The collusion of American liberalism in that process was perhaps best symbolized by the participation of congressional liberals in the revival, in 1952, of the "Subversive Activities Control Board."[26] The cold war, as Geraldine McCarthy has argued, led to the development of a kind of safe modernist subversion, one that valued a literature of "fragmentation and instability," and was theorized as part of Arthur Schlesinger's "Vital Center."[27] Modernist hostility to mass culture accompanied a general acquiescence of intellectuals in cold war culture. In 1952, *Partisan Review* held a symposium entitled "Our Country and Its Culture" and asked, "Must the American intellectual and writer adapt himself to mass culture?"[28] Norman Mailer in turn found the symposium's laudatory and complacent evaluation of American society "shocking." Mailer was one of the first serious critics of containment, and doubted whether a liberal-modernist stance that believed in cultural "subversion" could produce a cultural criticism of real force. "Belief in the efficacy of attacking his society has been lost," Mailer wrote of the contemporary writer, "but nothing has replaced the need for attack."[29] In its reaction to the Progressives and to Stalinism, subversive modernism, as Mailer recognized, had turned into an endorsement of the liberal status quo. "Critical thought and cosmopolitanism," as Terry Cooney notes of *Partisan Review* and its circle, "retained their forward-moving, 'progressive' edge, even as those same values came to require, for more and more of them, giving support to the general political arrangements of established democratic societies."[30]

In this cultural setting, Dickens and Melville could be lauded as safe subversives. Van Wyck Brooks's view, comparing Melville's portrayal of working-class characters to Dickens', was left behind in the

cultural shift to containment. Instead the cultural modernism and sub-
versiveness of Dickens and Melville were declared.[31] "Proust, Joyce,
and Kafka," in Philip Rahv's view, represented an artful social "veri-
similitude" in fiction that was to be opposed to the crudity of Marxist approaches. Naturalism was rejected because its view of society's
power left the individual "wholly determined," just as Trilling had diminished Dreiser.[32] Trilling saw Dickens and Melville as mythic modernists, rather than ideologists, because of the "rare fineness and ab-
stractness of the ideas they represent."[33] The modernist qualities of
the American novel were used to link American literature with aestheticism, and to separate the concerns of the American novel from
politics. Charles Feidelson redefined Melville in terms of the European avant-garde in his *Symbolism in American Literature* (1953), and
Richard Chase argued in his influential *The American Novel and Its Tradition* (1957) for an American novel of romance rather than realistic
social commentary.[34]

This "New Liberalism" that emerged in the fifties, as Mary McAuliffe termed it, "stressed the beneficence of American political and economic institutions," while at the same time praising cultural disaffection as an aspect of the novel.[35] The aesthetic modernism that opposed
Stalinism now became a defense of the "liberal imagination," as Trilling called it. But the culturally critical force of the liberal imagination
in the novel was modernist and aesthetic and excluded mass culture
from its domain. Such liberalism saved Melville from the Progressives, in Trilling's terms, and used him as an example of a writer who
"did not serve the ends of any one ideological group or tendency."[36]
Dickens' novels, in order to be canonized, had to overcome what
Trilling called "highbrow resistance." Modernist complexity was discovered in his works, rescuing them from the taint of the consumable
commodity. "We can now see the depths and subtleties of Dickens,"
Trilling wrote, "but his contemporary readers found him as simply
available as a plate of oysters on the half shell."[37] The "free" reading of
narrative envisioned by aesthetic modernists regarded mass culture
as socially saturated, a popular form that canceled the critical force
of the modernist novel and its attack on the middle class. The "gradual absorption" of social criticism in contemporary literature, Irving
Howe remarked in 1960, was an aspect of postmodernism, not of the
subversive modernist tradition: "the middle class has discovered that
the fiercest attacks upon its values can be transposed into pleasing
entertainment."[38]

New Historicist writers implicitly defined themselves against Trilling and the liberal modernists, and the effects on American criticism were apparent where the question of mass culture was concerned. Returning the question of "ideology" to the text after consensus approaches had banished it meant finding political struggle and the exercise of power where liberals had seen pluralist agreement. Stephen Greenblatt's notion of Shakespeare's Renaissance spectacle, formative for New Historicism, defined this break from liberal cultural theory. The alienated modernism of the liberal imagination was rejected. Greenblatt instead argued that high culture produced subversion as part of a controlling mass-cultural spectacle, the "staged scene of resistance" that Alan Liu has called the characteristic trope of high cultural criticism.[39] "Subversion" in English Renaissance drama was the sign of an improvisatory mass-cultural self in the making: in the case of Shakespeare, "subversion" for Greenblatt meant a literary movement that took place within a cultural "orthodoxy," a term that also described the attitude of the American literary establishment that Greenblatt's work sought to change.[40] *Renaissance Self-Fashioning* thus revised the theme of modernist subversion as it appeared in cold war theorists and saw subversion itself as connected with the logic of mass culture. Social absorption was now a question to be asked by cultural criticism, and the "fashioned" self Greenblatt discovered in the Renaissance sketched out a kind of prehistory of modern consumer culture.

New Historicism thus accorded mass culture a prominent place and restored it from its position as the despised underside of cold war cultural theory in its liberal period. Horkheimer and Adorno, of course, had already described the production of surrogate selves in mass culture as the industrialized equivalent of such Renaissance self-formation: "mass culture . . . does not abolish the suffering of its members but records and plans it."[41] But New Historicist approaches framed cultural criticism against the aesthetic modernists, rather than against the twentieth-century Marxist thought from which the critical theory of the Frankfurt School had emerged. Jonathan Arac, writing a kind of manifesto for the postmodern position in historical studies, therefore saw postmodern criticism as a successor to "Trilling's generation," which he praised for having "eradicated from American culture the dangers of Stalinism."[42] Arac argued that "mass culture is our emphasis" and sought to think through its consequences for the modernist monuments esteemed by the generation before. Theories of "liberal" subversion had begun their transformation into New Historicist concerns with the question of power.

This "new ideology of consumption," as Gerald Graff has characterized postwar "Left" criticism in America, took over the ground that had been vacated by liberal cultural theory.[43] The powerful innovator was Stephen Greenblatt, whose version of New Historicism found in the fashions of Renaissance subversion a historical development that linked popular culture and its controls. Shakespeare, as the "fashioner of narrative selves," could now be used to describe the subversive self as a subject produced by the power interests of reigning cultural authority.[44] Shakespeare in his time, as F. R. Leavis had argued, had perhaps been the last writer to write for the masses as well as for a "high-brow" public: "it was possible for Shakespeare to write plays that were at once popular drama and poetry that could be appreciated only by an educated minority."[45] Greenblatt instead emphasized Shakespeare's connection with mass culture, and replaced Leavis' highbrow approach to his plays with arguments that exposed their collusion with early modern forms of disciplinary power. *Renaissance Self-Fashioning* explored the historical origins of a liberal culture that could use freedom in the service of social control.

Greenblatt thus helped to form the late cold war critique of liberal society. The freedom of the West, emphasized during the cold war as the antithesis of the subjection of the Soviet bloc, could now be seen as a controlling "consensus" about the critical value of liberal culture, a consensus that had in effect shielded its works from stringent cultural criticism. Christopher Lasch was among the first to see the agenda of anticommunism as an ideology aimed at the exclusion of political criticism of the "liberal tradition."[46] When Jonathan Dollimore and Alan Sinfield defined the debate over Shakespeare as a choice between "consolidation, subversion, containment" in 1985, a new set of terms was established for postwar discussion of the politics of literature.[47] Mass culture was read as a determinant of canonized works, and "cultural materialism," developing out of the tradition of British socialism, took up the "subversion" aspect of the debate. In America, the reaction to the cold war exemption of liberal cultural theory from ideological questions was to be more severe. The need to debunk a cold war theory of liberal modernism left Frankfurt School approaches, fully cognizant of the "culture industry," to the side. Raymond Williams, in a 1966 review of Trilling's *Beyond Culture*, had already argued that it represented the cultural theory of an exhausted liberal tradition.[48] The official modernism of the cold war had posited the novel as a socially critical cultural instrument, hostile to social control. But the question of narrative's complicity with mass society had been begged, and waited to return.

New Historicism: The Criticism of Containment

Michel Foucault enabled New Historicists to reconceive narrative's relation to society, and he himself noted the similarity of his notion of "discipline" and power to the work of the Frankfurt School.[49] But the critical power Adorno accorded literature was almost entirely lacking in American appropriations of Foucault. Trilling, as the evocative title of one of his late works put it, had placed the subversive power of Dickens, Melville, and Kafka "beyond culture." New Historicism promised instead a move beyond the "liberal imagination" and "the paralyzed debates" over deconstruction. Frank Lentricchia's use of Foucault to conclude his influential *After the New Criticism* was in many ways exemplary. "Literary discourse in the wake of Foucault," as Lentricchia's polemical conclusion put it, "no longer needs to be forced into contact with political and social discourses, as if these were realms outside literature which writers must be dragged into by well-meaning critics."[50] Late cold war criticism emphasized the ways in which narrative modernism had "always already," in a stock phrase of the period, been saturated by mass society and its controlling power.

Jonathan Arac's book *Commissioned Spirits: The Shaping of Social Motion in Dickens, Carlyle, Melville, and Hawthorne* (1979) was a foundational work in this new emphasis on power. Arac argued against the canonization of Dickens and Melville as novelists and liberal social critics. Edmund Wilson's Dickens, the submerged but effective cultural rebel, had been revised. The liberal interpretation of Dickens and Melville gave way to a new, more structuralist view, the notion that there was an overarching and "shaping" movement at work in the nineteenth-century historical imagination. This shaping discourse was present in narrative as well as in Carlyle's historiography, and that discourse was said to subject the social turmoil represented by these writers to the implicit dictates of social control. Repression was similarly placed at the center of Dickens' novels by John Kucich's *Repression in Victorian Fiction: Charlotte Brontë, George Eliot, and Charles Dickens* (1987). Both Arac's and Kucich's works exemplified the New Historical turn to cultural history, arguing against the "free" readings of Dickens and Melville that had gained institutional force. Modernist narrative was seen as an accomplice of social power, rather than as a subversive cultural voice. Michael Rogin connected the modernism of Melville's *Billy Budd* with that of Kafka's *In the Penal Colony*, seeing in both narratives fables of an internalized social authority that supported the oppressive power of the modern state.[51]

As I have already argued, the cold war shaped the idea of liberal "subversion," and New Historicists opposed that modernist position by a new emphasis on mass culture. The critical advances made by New Historicism were certainly substantial. Mass society suddenly emerged from modernist "subversion" as the dominant theme in the study of the novel, and the commodity once again became an issue in literary criticism for the first time since the 1930s as the naturalist novel was brought back from disrepute. But critical approaches that emphasized the commodity, because they were directed against the liberal idea of "subversion," saw novels that dealt with economics as strictly "contained." Walter Benn Michaels' *The Gold Standard and the Logic of Naturalism: American Literature at the Turn of the Century* (1987) portrayed American naturalism as exemplary of the economic logic of mass society, a society that reified modernist alienation in forms that allowed it to be consumed. Unlike the Frankfurt School, Michaels posited no possibility of critique in a narrative dominated by the process of reification. D. A. Miller's challenge to the cold war "consensus" narrative, *The Novel and the Police* (1988), was equally closed in this regard. Foucault was used to place subversion very much within culture, as a means of "containment" by which the "liberal subject," as a reader of the novel, could be seduced. Liberal freedom in Dickens' fiction was shown to be an illusion that worked in full complicity with bureaucratic power. Miller saw the social novel of Dickens as an unwitting agent of social authority, and exposed the nineteenth-century novel as a manipulator of fictional transgression that secured repressive social ends.[52] The "liberal imagination" as Trilling had defined it was opened up as cultural space, and Dickens was seen once again as an author who wrote for the mass. Miller's contribution was to politicize Trilling's "subversion" as a manipulative effect of Dickens' mass-cultural novels. But the price of moving beyond the "consensus" of liberal modernism for Miller was an almost complete denial of the novel's culturally critical force.

New Historicist writers such as Miller nonetheless faced up to the historical importance of consumer society in the development of modern culture. Naturalists such as Dreiser had already faced this problem of commodity culture directly in their fiction, but had been rejected for their socialist taint by liberals such as Trilling. "Few critics have ever been wholly blind to Dreiser's great faults," Trilling wrote, in grudging recognition of his value, "but by liberal critics James is traditionally put to the ultimate question: of what use, of what actual political use, are his gifts and their intention?"[53] Mark Selzer, in his study of Henry James, answered that aesthetic modernism was inseparable in James from the "panoptical" exercise of power in modern society, and that the claim of separation served only to cancel the critical power of his work.[54] Missing in Selzer's study, as in New Historicism, however, was any dialectical sense of commodity culture and its potentially critical dimensions. Catherine Gallagher, analyzing the politics of Dickens' *Hard Times* as "discourse," argued that the industrial novel evoked social conflict only so that its tensions could be "recontained."[55] New Historicism thus excelled in the analysis of social control. But the price of its success was a failure to develop any critical theory of mass culture or to integrate the cultural theory of the Frankfurt School.

The cold war origins of this New Historical limitation can be seen in Michael Rogin's 1967 work *The Intellectuals and McCarthy: The Radical Specter*. Rogin challenged the liberal, "consensus" interpretation of the McCarthyist uses of "subversion." His book developed what can be seen in retrospect as the first version of New Historicist containment criticism. McCarthyism, Rogin argued, was a cultural movement that raised the "specter" of subversion in order to legitimate a conservative hold on power. But the deeper claim of *The Intellectuals and McCarthy* was made against liberalism and the modernist bias of its "mass" description of anticommunist frenzy. Rogin questioned the liberal interpretation that McCarthyism could be understood as a movement of disappointed radicals who turned their frustration and "status resentment" against the eastern elite.[56] Pluralism, as Rogin declared in the concluding paragraph of his work, might best be understood as the "liberal American venture into conservative political theory."[57] Rogin's later cultural writings demonstrated this hidden conservatism of liberal culture. To confront the "liberal society" with its "Indian Question," as the title of an essay in his later book, *Ronald Reagan, "The Movie,"* put it, was to ask "how American history [and culture] would look if repression were placed at its center." But in liberating this "countersubversive tradition" from the "consensus interpretations" that "dominated the 1950s," as Rogin put it, his own approach to Melville and Kafka slighted the critical power of their novels.[58]

New Historicist cultural criticism challenged cold war liberalism and its modernist bias by examining the complicity of the novel with economic and social power. Novels such as Melville's, privileged as socially critical since the Progressives, could be judged anew against the facts and the mass-cultural traces of slavery and Western expansion and viewed as part of nineteenth-century imperialism as a whole.

At the same time Jane Tompkins and others uncovered the "Other American Renaissance" suppressed beneath the order of canonized works.[59] The debate that followed, however, lacked Frankfurt School emphasis on the liberation of repressed cultural history, and oppositional readings were rare exceptions to the dominant trend in New Historicist work. Social control as a theme predominated in arguments against the liberal consensus that modern culture and its fiction were subversive. New Historicist readings brought "containment" home from foreign policy, and read it as a political description of liberal culture that could challenge a self-satisfied vision of cold war "consensus"; challenging modernism meant emphasizing the dominating power of mass culture over art.

Fredric Jameson's criticism of the novel, however, provided cold war cultural theory with a more insistently critical source. *The Political Unconscious: Narrative as a Socially Symbolic Act* (1981) formulated a notion of narrative "strategies of containment," a term whose cold war history Jameson was in a position to recognize. But Jameson also argued for a utopian recovery of the historical suppressed in the European tradition of the novel.[60] His earlier work, *Marxism and Form* (1971), had used for its example of dialectical thought the complexities of nuclear weapons and their strategic values in the Soviet-American standoff. Containment and its conflicted history were also recognized in "Modernism and the Repressed; or, Robbe-Grillet as Anti-Colonialist." There, Jameson linked the routinization of the "subversive" quality of modern art, bemoaned by Lionel Trilling in *Beyond Culture*, to the advent of the cold war and consumer society in 1947, the year "containment" was adopted as America's cold war foreign policy.[61]

But Jameson was appropriated by New Historicists as a "containment" critic when his work argued for an oppositional cultural criticism.[62] Jameson's writing worked against the censorious effects of cold war culture, and his Marxist perspective allowed the containing effects of liberal modes of cultural criticism to be addressed. *The Political Unconscious* (1981) was a landmark that rebuked ahistorical premises in the study of the novel, and promised a return of repressed political questions that consensus history had submerged. But if the return of historicism, after its cold war suspension, made Jameson's inaugural injunction in that book—"always historicize"—quotable in New Historicist work even without attribution, that injunction also appeared without the argument for the explicitly Marxist cultural criticism it implied. Jameson's insistence at the end of *The Political Unconscious* on the "identity of the ideological and utopian," explicitly took Adorno and Horkheimer's *Dialectic of Enlightenment* as a precedent, but the critical power of literature to move dialectically beyond containment was seldom emphasized in the New Historicist reception of Jameson's work.

Appropriations of the work of Sacvan Bercovitch by New Historicist critics often followed a similar course. *The American Jeremiad* (1978) was seen as a precursor of containment criticism, but only by ignoring the oppositional frame in which its argument moved. "The American consensus," Bercovitch wrote in 1981, the same year *The Political Unconscious* was published, "has often served, rhetorically, as a fact against the facts of pluralism and conflict," an apparent invitation to allow an effectively "dissensus" view of American history, as he called it later, to emerge.[63] Bercovitch's reading of Melville in particular was less an argument for "containment" than an argument against a contained radicalism. Bercovitch later argued that the transformation of "radical potential into social integration" occurred in American culture as part of the "ideology of liberal consensus," but the classic texts of American liberalism, Bercovitch also showed, were marked with the signs of socialist discourse, an oppositional text that could be read.[64] The same teleology followed by New York Intellectuals such as Trilling was demonstrated as a pattern in America's liberal cultural history. The critical prehistory of liberalism's exclusion of socialism and its sources in America's Puritan history were available in Bercovitch's work.

New Historicists who took Bercovitch's argument as a precedent, however, pursued a "containment" rather than a "dissensus" agenda. Bercovitch's historical approach seemed to support the containment argument against textual subversion and to oppose the liberal "consensus" on the critical force of narrative as well. The debate over "indeterminacy" and "writerliness" as radical social aspects of textuality had a continental history. But in its American reception, the debate became linked to the problem of "pluralism" that Bercovitch had already addressed. Jonathan Arac, writing in the same volume in which Bercovitch articulated his version of "dissensus," used both Arthur M. Schlesinger's *The Age of Jackson* and Bercovitch's *American Jeremiad* to define the "consensus" position on political culture his essay refuted.[65] Arac argued that the regulation of social movement incorporated dissent and mastered the socially destabilizing effect of deconstructive irony. Arac's real opponent was not deconstruction, but liberalism and the "instability" that cold war liberals had theorized as a virtue of American democratic culture. Arac analyzed Hawthorne's antebellum novel to demonstrate that its modernist indeterminacy was far from democratic and was in fact in collusion with a culture of constraint.

As I have argued, Foucault and the argument for containment were often used to oppose liberal cultural theory and its cold war conceptions of a subversive novel. Arac's piece is noteworthy for the power of its exposition, but also for its containment view that American pluralism and its tradition were linked to the repressive exercise of social power. The position Arac opposed was Arthur Schlesinger's pluralist argument in *The Age of Jackson* (1945). There, Schlesinger argued that "American Democracy" had achieved a reformist and liberal social policy, a liberalism that worked through competing interest groups rather than ideology and thrived on a kind of social indeterminacy. "The struggle of competing groups for control of the state," Schlesinger wrote, was the essence of an American "liberalism" rooted in Jacksonian politics, a liberalism typified by a New Deal "movement on the part of other sections of society to restrain the business community."[66] Liberalism, figured in Arac's reading of Hawthorne in terms of the Compromise of 1850, had assented to slavery, and sustained the institution precisely through the kind of liberal "anxiety" Schlesinger described.[67] Arac turned the liberal discourse of anxiety upside down. Liberal pluralism was seen to sustain the injustice of commercial society and compromise the politics of the novel, rather than to support democracy and to motivate political change. But the strength of New Historicist attacks on liberalism, as Arac exemplified, also produced a critical blind spot where mass-culture and oppositional criticism were concerned. New Historicist critics read the prehistory of cold war containment in fiction, and opposed the modernist notion of cultural criticism in the novel, but without examining the oppositional analysis of mass culture embedded in narrative works.

Feminist critics were far more interested in the oppositional uses of containment. Ground-breaking works of revisionist feminist literary history, such as Sandra Gilbert and Susan Gubar's *Madwoman in the Attic: The Woman Writer and the Nineteenth-Century Literary Imagination* (1979), identified the alienation and disaffection from patriarchal culture expressed by women writers, a romantic feminism that had not been addressed by the Arnoldian values that composed the liberal imagination. Traditional notions of the political novel had indeed ignored the social concerns of women novelists. In Irving Howe's definition, the political novel had been limited to narratives in which characters held "some coherent political loyalty or ideological identification"; but the novels of Jane Austen were written by a "great artist" who neglected Napoleon, according to Howe, and thus were not political novels per se.[68]

At the end of the cold war, a revisionist feminism could challenge the cultural containment at work in such a notion. Nancy Armstrong saw in the domestic concerns of the novel the controlling power of culture over women and thus in the novel itself a political genre worthy of critique. For Armstrong, power was transmitted through the domestic contract that informed the rise of the novel. Containment had challenged an essentialist notion of feminine dissent: the control exercised through domesticity was shown to be at work in novels by male authors such as Dickens as well as in the fiction of Austen and the Brontë sisters, and was shown to have a constraining cultural force. The novel "gained a certain authority," Armstrong argued, "as it transformed political differences into those of gender," and thus deployed conceptions of the feminine to bring dangerous political issues under control.[69] Ultimately, feminist approaches to history were at odds with the New Historicist emphasis on control.[70] But Armstrong's contribution nonetheless bridged a gap between feminism and mass culture in the study of the novel. The rise of domesticity was linked to the novel's mass appeal, and the question of a controlling popular culture was now crucial to the question of narrative's oppositional social role.

But the cold war had made the oppositional cultural force of the novel a secondary question. Challenging liberal society meant demonstrating containment, and to show the social control of literature became the primary task of cultural criticism.[71] The cold war thus led Donald Pease to reexamine the American Renaissance. The cultural tendency of that period to "dissolve all signs of dissent into an organicist process," Pease showed, resembled the modernist culture of "consensus" that liberal theory praised during the cold war.[72] Opposing cold war modernism for Pease thus meant demonstrating containment: *Visionary Compacts* discovered censorship in American novels where cold war critics and their predecessors had found canonical evidence of cultural freedom. Pease offered a powerful late cold war debunking of the oppositional myth of the modern, but left the specific criticism of an emergent consumer society in novelists like Dickens and Melville undiscussed.

New Historicism's contribution to cold war criticism, its challenge to liberal modernism, was thus also its signal limitation. In the attack on modernist subversion as the dominant liberal interpretation of the novel, Dickens, Melville, and Kafka came to be viewed as negative images of the liberal imagination, incarcerated by culture rather than its effective critics. The socialist heritage of the 1930s was left only in traces, in the work of critics such as Bercovitch. In a situation in which, as Frank Lentricchia had put it, questions of power had to be "dragged in" to the study of literature, the determining power of history returned with a vengeance.[73] But the oppositional force of narrative had been reduced. Frankfurt School critical theory, with its emphasis on both domination and the redemptive power of culture, offered a different course.

Critical Theory: The Novel and Cultural Critique

For the Frankfurt School, the origins of modern media society were to be found in the tradition of the novel. Popular fiction was part of the culture of consumption that emerged in the eighteenth century, and flourished as the nineteenth-century novel became the popular and mainstream expression of the narrative tradition. Crucial in Adorno's "On Dickens' *The Old Curiosity Shop:* A Lecture" was a position on the novel and cultural criticism missing from New Historicist approaches. Adorno's analysis stressed the roots of realistic narrative in mass-market fiction, but insisted on narrative's oppositional cultural role. Surely Dickens was to be regarded as one of the "founders of the realistic and social novel," Adorno argued, but the narrative's rendering of economic misery was shaped by an increasingly commodified culture. The poverty and despair characteristic of the Dickensian critique, Adorno reminds his reader, had "already been recognized as the fruits of a bourgeois world."[74]

The market, Adorno recognized, determined the development of the social novel. Popular figures such as Little Nell were recognized in his analysis as sentimental and regressive representatives of a prebourgeois era shaped for middle-class consumption. Such mythical characters, however, who contributed so significantly to Dickens' popularity, were able to present the distortions of the exchange principle with critical force. Adorno argued that Dickens' novel renounced the middle-class norm of the individual: "the novel form in Dickens . . . absorbs psychological approaches into the objective meanings the novels depict." Popular fiction might satisfy the market, yet sustain a critical perspective on its controls, by demonstrating how "objectivity might dissolve itself into subjects" in mass society. While the social novel made use of the grotesque and "inimitable" characters that were its stock-in-trade, Adorno suggested, its the entertaining excesses mapped the transformation of individual experience into reified and "damaged" life.

Adorno agreed with the New Historicist linkage between alienated disaffection and the exchange principle that appears to market and neutralize its critical force. "Neuroses," as he put it in *Negative Dialectics*, "are pillars of society."[75] But in Frankfurt School terms, such "containment" of the subject as free individual, who internalizes the controls of a reified society, could be challenged by the cultural criticism made available in narrative works.[76] "Unfreedom," as Adorno put it, "always requires . . . that socially perceived phenomena be reflected upon the subject," with "psychological science" as one of its modes. But a "negative dialectic" also promised a method of reading which placed "identity against its identifications" and allowed the social and critical content of subjectivity to emerge.[77] The modern novel's decentering of the subject was thus a narrative achievement quite different from the "subversion" of the liberal imagination, and its best examples were seen to oppose the "containment" enforced by an introjected social power. "Objectively," as Adorno put it, "modernists have moved beyond the position Lukács ascribes to them," by grasping the objective historical forces at work in alienation and social withdrawal: "Proust decomposes the unity of the subject by means of the subject's introspection: the subject is eventually transformed into an arena in which objective entities manifest themselves."[78] Adorno's Kafka was not an apolitical modernist, whose novels were devoid of social context, but a radical cultural critic whose intimate writing dissected the way mass society's dictates are internalized as a force of subjective life.[79]

New Historicist and Frankfurt School approaches thus differed on the relation of narrative and history. Instead of assembling anecdotal or strictly archival evidence to ground a novel in historical situations, Adorno and Benjamin saw history as "congealed" in textual details. Peter Uwe Hohendahl distinguishes New Historicism from Adorno and Benjamin's method of historicizing literature in just these terms. The Frankfurt School tended to regard material culture as present in the "texture" of a work, not to materialize history as external and determining forces of society. For Adorno, it was the "impurity of the art work, the dependence on its own material texture [which] brings out the material aspect," as Hohendahl observes, that allows the emergence of historical critique.[80] A historical cultural criticism was implied by material traces of society that narrative bears within its form.

Modern novels, in other words, critically reflect upon the ideological pressures that shaped readership and author alike. Nor was this reflective capacity exclusively modern in Frankfurt School terms. Mass culture, to be sure, was often compared to myth, in its tendency to produce affirmative visions of society and cultural homogeneity.

Yet the "dialectic of enlightenment," while investing ideals of social progress with domination, could also turn mass-cultural justifications of power into the material of social critique. Like Benjamin, Adorno linked this critical capacity to the "Barock," whose emphasis on the fragment and ruin exemplified the importance of the textual detail in opposing false social reconciliation.[81] Both found the potential for a cultural criticism of "dialektischer Rettung" (dialectical redemption) in baroque German drama and within the marketable narrative work as well.[82] This vision of a work that could be brushed against the grain, like a "storm . . . blowing from Paradise," evoked a practice of interpreting mass-cultural artifacts subject to the domination of culture in order to recover their resistant cultural force.[83] A redemptive cultural criticism was one that could release the historical content that the conformist pressures of cultural tradition repressed.[84]

Brushing the object "against the grain" of culture was meant to describe a critical method that sustained this link between culture and domination, without giving up the work's potential to produce a redeeming cultural critique of society.[85] Benjamin's attention to the concreteness of textual detail was part of this method of *rettende* or redemptive critique. As Jürgen Habermas notes in an important essay, Benjamin's art criticism tries to redeem the critical content of a work from culture's complicity with the "barbarism" of conformity, and that criticism "behaves conservatively toward its objects," whether he is dealing with baroque tragic drama, with Goethe's *Elective Affinities*, with Baudelaire's *Les Fleurs du Mal*, or with the Soviet films of the 1920s.[86] Benjamin was intent on releasing such criticism from its cultural bondage by recasting textual details in constellation with cultural history so that their critical social value could be seen. The idea that history, congealed in cultural objects, could be dialectically redeemed through critical analysis, was a common thread in Frankfurt School practices of cultural critique.

Adorno's "negative dialectic" similarly sought to release the cultural criticism embedded in the conceptual identities that representation implied. Adorno disagreed with Benjamin, as Richard Wolin has aptly put it, that cultural objects could so easily be "emancipat[ed] from the grip of ideological falsification," but both attempted to uncover the critical force that lay congealed in the historical content of cultural works. In his unfinished Arcades Project, Benjamin sought to analyze the objects and environs of the urban shopping malls of Paris as social texts. Preference for these fragments over general social ideas, as Susan Buck-Morss observes, allowed Benjamin to show how texts might "cut through the core of truth without providing a totalizing frame."[87] These "dialectical images," which Adorno criticized as insufficiently conceptual, were "models . . . constellations in which 'the social situation' represents itself," and nonetheless became crucial to the resistance to totality that informed his thought.[88]

European fascism and the mass culture of the 1930s had called for such an analysis. The difference between the New Historicist preference for containment and Frankfurt School attempts to develop a critical theory of mass culture can be explained in part by the difference between the historical periods which shaped each group. Benjamin's messianic "Theses on the Philosophy of History" have been called his response to the Hitler-Stalin pact, and a similar point could be made about Adorno and Horkheimer's analysis of the "culture industry." The need for an oppositional analysis of mass society's relations with fascism was present and obvious for the Frankfurt School. In *The Dialectic of Enlightenment,* composed in part during World War II, the analysis of media and "mass deception," while providing an account of Western rationality from Homer forward, clearly responded to fascism and the barbarism it had unleashed. Anti-Semitism was seen to typify mass-cultural control as a classic form of "false projection." Hatred of Jews, Adorno and Horkheimer argued, served to control resentment against the social order by making the "rebellion of suppressed nature against domination directly useful to domination" itself.[89] Adorno and Benjamin examined the relation of modern media such as newspaper and film to cultural control, and argued about the critical value of popular art. Even anti-Semitism was examined for its traces of utopian opposition to power: the rise of fascism called on Frankfurt School theorists to expose the mechanisms of domination in mass culture, but also to seek out culture's resistant potential in its midst.

For Benjamin, narrative offered such a critical perspective on mass culture. "The Storyteller: Reflections on the Works of Nikolai Leskov" argued that the rise of the novel was coincident with the expansion of modern media culture. The loss of the "craftsmanship" of traditional storytelling augured a culture of modernity in which fiction offered a plethora of "newsworthy" experiences for consumption and self-identification, but failed to give meaningful shape to individual lives. "Every morning brings us the news of the globe," he wrote, "and yet we are poor in noteworthy stories."[90] In the information-saturated society of modernity, as Benjamin noted, culture lost its meaningful density, estranging the individual from everyday life. But novelistic discourse could in part free itself from the increasing homogeneity of media culture: "the narrative achieves an amplitude that information lacks." While the modern novel for Benjamin lacked the auratic glow of the traditional story, it nonetheless promised to repay, like material culture, the attention of a culturally critical eye. "The objects of daily use gently but insistently repel us," Benjamin wrote; "day by day, in overcoming the sum of secret resistances—not only the overt ones— that they put in our way, we have an immense labor to perform." Attention to literature, as well as popular artifacts from the shopping arcades of Paris, could keep culture from becoming, as he put it in a title, a "one-way street."[91]

Both Adorno and Benjamin were concerned with the fate of such an oppositional criticism in the age when novels as well as films were popular commodities. Benjamin's confidence in the critical potential of "the work of art in the age of mechanical reproduction," as the title of Benjamin's famous essay put it, was opposed by Adorno, who already suspected that alienation could be mass-produced as cultural objects to be consumed. Benjamin's Brechtian confidence in a kind of tech- nologically progressive art, Adorno insisted, missed the full force that commodification exerted over oppositional culture. Adorno therefore took Benjamin to task for placing too much confidence in the "dialec- tical image," as if literary form itself, unaided by critical concepts and history, could release the messianic potential of literary works.

Yet Adorno's own method also shared that utopian, messianic hope. Though Adorno's role in the debate, as Eugene Lunn points out, was to argue against Benjamin's overly optimistic assessment of cultural criticism, it also demonstrated the ties of his earliest public work to Benjamin's attempt to redeem the critical and historical content of the social text. Adorno shared with Benjamin an interest both in the cultural critique available in mass culture and in Jewish messianism. Both highly esteemed *The Star of Redemption,* a work by the Jewish theologian Franz Rosenzweig that played an important role in the de- velopment of the redemptive strain of Benjamin's cultural theory.[92] Both Adorno and Benjamin assumed that culture and its power were present as critical potential in the details of a literary work. As Peter Bürger puts it, "for Adorno the redemption of the individual work in its particularity was crucial. And thus he argues correctly against a determinist version of cultural history."[93] Narrative for each was sub- ject to the principle of exchange and its controlling objectification of language, yet capable of offering a dialectical response.[94]

"Autonomous" modernism, however, was not a critical panacea for commodity culture. The point cannot be made often enough that, for

Adorno, modernist narrative was thoroughly fetishized, subject to the cultural conditions established by the marketplace. Adorno's formulation in his final work, *Aesthetic Theory*, was precise: "the more works of art sought to free themselves from external purposes . . . the more . . . they reflected and internalized the domination of society." Critics who assume Adorno had no hope for critical opposition in any art but an abstract modernism also ignore his subsequent caution: "it becomes impossible to criticize the culture industry without criticizing art at the same time." This late position on modern art's dialectical implication in mass culture, moreover, is completely continuous with one of Adorno's earliest essays on exchange value and modern culture. "Complaints about the decline of musical taste," Adorno's crucial essay of 1938 declared at its start, "begin only a little after man's making the twofold discovery, on the threshold of historical time, that music represents both the immediate manifestation of impulse and the locus of its taming." [95]

The "Culture Industry" chapter of *The Dialectic of Enlightenment*, to be sure, discussed the modern audience and its appetite for consumption, but did not distinguish historically varied audiences or concentrate on differences of reception. This emphasis on the modern may have made Adorno's nascent reception theory sound ahistorical, as Hans Robert Jauss has argued. But it was also historically grounded in the Frankfurt School position that the commodity and its history were the precondition for critical examination of both high culture and popular art.[96] Critics associated with Frankfurt School critical theory, despite the school's well-earned reputation for the analysis of modern art, wrote on Goethe and Stifter, as well as Balzac. Frankfurt School critics tended to ground their approaches to realist narrative, as well as to the work of Proust, in the historical development of mass culture. Leo Lowenthal, in "Historical Perspectives on Popular Culture," pointed out that "escape, distraction, and entertainment" had been explicit concerns of literature since the sixteenth century.[97] The objection that Adorno's critical theory was biased in favor of the modern is certainly compatible with his interest in the music of Arnold Schönberg, and with the resistance of "negative" modernism to the marketplace. But this modernist view of Adorno fails to take into account the longer frame of his historical analysis. The difference between the marketable novels of Dickens and the modernist works of Kafka was for Adorno formal and historical, but their similar potential as vehicles of cultural critique was grounded in the relation of both to commodity culture.

As I have argued, the weakness of New Historicism's approach to the novel was its failure to address the critical potential of mass culture in narrative. In contrast, Frankfurt School writers made a crucial dialectical point of the critical potential of the novel as it developed into the mass-market fiction Dickens and Melville produced. Michael McKeon's important study of the tensions of the middle-class culture in which the novel was first produced has substantiated that dialectical approach to the novel.[98] Early attacks on the novel as a popular genre, McKeon points out, certainly began from the conservative point of view of Fielding, whose condemnation of the literary market was later to be matched from the aristocratic position of Alexis de Tocqueville and others. "The ever increasing crowd of readers and their continual craving for something new ensure the sale of books that nobody much esteems," Tocqueville wrote; "democratic literature is always infested with a tribe of writers who look upon letters as a mere trade."[99] Conservative writers expressed hostility toward the marketable novel, opposing this leveling effect as well as the social interests that the novel's assertion of bourgeois status served. As the middle class became the dominant reading audience, conservative antipathy toward the popular novel was transformed into a radical skepticism about bourgeois values. This aristocratic critique was then dialectically internalized as a self-critical voice in the narrative tradition: aristocratic bias was transformed into the reflexive skepticism that enabled narrative to question its own middle-class ideology. McKeon's new account of the novel's origins thus envisioned narrative as bound to the marketplace, and historically complicit with the rise of mass society, yet capable of mounting oppositional self-critique.

In Frankfurt School analysis, the dialectical potential of narrative was similarly rooted in the history of commodity culture. Unlike classical Marxism, which emphasized class contradiction in its studies of the novel, Horkheimer and Adorno centered their attention, as did the poststructuralists, on representation and on the system of social objectification fostered by the logic of exchange. For Adorno the principle of exchange—naming different objects as possessing the same abstract value, and thereby identical—was the model for conceptual thought, and promoted identitarian thinking: the privileging of abstract concepts over the historically diverse and nonidentical material of which they were composed. *The Dialectic of Enlightenment* saw myth as the primitive form of such objectification. The enlightened control of necessity depended on representing and controlling nature, but systems of representation that led to the progressive possibility of barter and its exchange of equivalents also contributed to the dominating representations of commodity culture. Logic similarly originated to name and control, or "enlighten," nature and to overcome its domination, but in the quest for identity, exclusion, and control, identitarian "reason" became more and more like the domination it placed itself above.

This dialectic linked the progress of enlightenment, as well as art, with the facts of social power. Benjamin's oft-quoted "Thesis" on the philosophy of history makes the point: "there is no document of civilization which is not at the same time a document of barbarism." [100] Liberal society's challenge to archaic authority underwent a reversal in modern society, as reason itself became mythic, assuming the character of social enslavement it had arisen to oppose. The free individual was transformed into a social subject who, through worship of the exchangeable commodity, possessed desires ever more identical and bound to the idols of value the market proposed. Art and society, however, also contained the "promesse du bonheur," a phrase Frankfurt School writers took from Stendhal. For the exchange principle, which confined the market and its culture to increasing conformity—and the false autonomy that New Historicist uses of the term "subversion" have come to suggest—was also, for Frankfurt School writers, inseparable from a qualitatively different, oppositional view of society. [101] Modern narrative for Adorno was bound up with the logic of domination, but, as for Benjamin, also retained the potential for a redemptive cultural critique.

Kafka's narrative provided for both Adorno and Benjamin a case in point. A novel like *The Trial* demonstrated the reification of experience in modern culture, the fetishized privacy that turned the individual into a manipulable social object. But it also challenged that reification from within. Kafka's "objective tendency," as Adorno calls it, reveals the marks of social construction within subjectivity, and thus "aims at historical essence." [102] From Adorno's point of view, the "subject" or individual was posited by society in a modern social order that "consolidates and reproduces itself in and through alienation." [103] But modernist works, rejecting consumption by a mass public through their difficulty, represented *in extremis* the paradoxical status of narrative's dialectical engagement with commodity culture as a whole. The idea of the self-sufficient work of art, as Adorno put it, demonstrated that "every single work of art is vulnerable to the charge of false consciousness and ideology [in that] art works are ideological because they *a priori* posit a spiritual entity as though it were independent of any conditions of material production." [104]

Similarly, attacks on society in the novels of Dickens are effective because so enmeshed in the salable form of Victorian fiction, not because his "modernity" represents some kind of exception or escape. Adorno's emphasis on modernism, so often misunderstood, is crucial for the cultural criticism of the novel because it argues for the dialectical *connection* of the realms of social opposition and commodity culture. The dialectical paths through which the pressures of the market affected the novel, of course, vary as much as the cultural contexts in which fiction is produced. Kafka's austere mode of referring to the active political culture of Prague makes him different from Melville, whose open battles with his market-centered publishers have become part of American cultural and literary history. But in a position antecedent to contemporary postmodernism, Adorno insisted that modernism and mass culture in the novel tradition were historically and dialectically linked. There could be no firm separation, Adorno argued, between the modernist novel which, according to Lukács, rejected cultural criticism, and the critical tradition of the realist social novel. The difference between a Frankfurt School reading of modernist narrative and Lukács's version bears further explication, since it explains much about the critical emphasis on mass culture these writers share. Radical skepticism and even the rejection of realistic conventions, Adorno suggested, remain critically connected to the conformist cultural market in which the modern novel developed, even if the "return" of mass culture to the text takes a sinuous and dialectical course.

Lukács, Adorno argued, had crucially erred in mistaking such an apparently subjective formalism for compliance with the material directives of society: "what makes art works socially significant is content that articulates itself in formal structures."[105] In *The Meaning of Contemporary Realism*, Lukács had denied that any such critical stance toward reification was present in modernist narrative. For Lukács Kafkan modernism symbolized only the political failure of the modernist novel: its social concerns were said to give way to a subjective quietism concerned with form, so that it entirely failed at the task of representing class division and the exercise of social power. Lukács defined Kafkan *Angst* as "the experience *par excellence* of modernism." The allegedly exclusive concern of his novels with the existential and spiritual quandaries of modernity left them "robbed of meaning" and social content, incapable of serving as cultural instruments for either criticism or social change.[106]

In unspoken accord with Lukács' political history of the novel, critics of the novel have often seen Kafka and Melville as markers on this historical road to a depoliticized or conservative narrative. Melville and Kafka are seen as modernist novelists of "despair," as Robert Alter describes them, who turned inward and away from the social. In the same vein, Robert Weisbuch appraises their "melancholy" as typically "more ontological than social," descendant of a Dickensian realism which could still—as Lukács had praised traditional realism— engage in powerful "social critique." Nina Baym's historical reading of Melville sees him similarly as a novelist who turned away from social concerns altogether when he discovered, as if anticipating a full-fledged modernism, that the novel's forms could no longer represent social reality.[107] This teleology judged the development of modernist subjectivity in fiction to augur a conservative, or at least apolitical, turn. Melville "found value in the world," as Charles Feidelson argued, "only by taking the world as symbol," treating Ahab's doubloon strictly as a figure, not as "measurable in terms of money" or crucially formed by the pressures of the market and its political terms.[108] These novelists' skepticism about representation was seen to imply rejection of cultural criticism, rather than to connect them critically to an increasingly mass-cultural world.

Adorno's important contribution to a reading of the history of the novel was to insist, against Lukács, that the development of formal self-concern and the mass-cultural criticism of narrative were far from exclusive concerns. Hans Mayer, recalling Benjamin's similar, high regard for Kafka, points out that Benjamin went public with his Kafka criticism on a radio show in 1934, the same year he published his initial Kafka essay in Robert Weltsch's *Jüdische Rundschau*.[109] Adorno's attack on Lukács therefore deplored his strict separation of realism from modernism, and opposed the resulting conservatism of his developmental scheme of the novel. The "principles of form" which Lukács had linked with the political quietism of modernism were already present in the realist novel, Adorno argued. To "anathematize" form was to turn away from history, dialectically congealed in the formal texture of a work, and thus to abandon the political effect of form. Adorno argued for the comparability of the explicit social novel of Dickens and the modernist novel of Kafka, almost devoid of historical reference, by showing how Lukács had neglected the culturally critical role of representation in both writers' works. By supposing the direct access of the nineteenth-century novel to social reality, he pointed out, Lukács had ignored the "objective" and culturally critical functions of the modernist novel's concern with form:

On the one hand, the formal principles that are anathema to Lukács as being unrealistic and idealistic prove to have an objective aesthetic function; conversely, the early nineteenth-century novels he unhesitatingly advances as paradigmatic, Dickens and Balzac, are not so realistic after all.[110]

Adorno's argument was that the "formal" or "idealistic" high art of Kafkan modernism, the mass-market novel of Dickens, and the hybrid novels written by Melville were all "formal" or aesthetic to different degrees. Modernism was not to be seen as "subjective," apolitical, or formally exclusive of politics. In Adorno's view, mass-market fiction *and* modernist novels were saturated by the pressures of the marketplace, but both were also capable of opposing the cultural pressure to conform. No priority could be given to realism as an objective narrative instrument of social criticism with access to the material practices of society. In modern society, after all, the "real" has become a fetishized, commodifiable value, as Melville was to discover when the criticism of American expansionism in his South Seas narratives made the "realistic" veracity of his account subject to debate. The "realism" of Dickens, too, would be challenged by proponents of Victorian science such as George Henry Lewes, when his violation of realist conventions in *Bleak House* broke with the cultural standards of Victorian propriety.[111] For these novelists as for Adorno, the "culture industry" and its antecedents meant facing up to the determination of realist conventions by the marketplace, but not canceling narrative's oppositional force.

Modernist works were critical for Adorno because they took commodity culture into their grain. Distance from commercialism, as Adorno recognized, ran the risk of routinization, even in difficult musical compositions such as Beethoven's. This insistence of "advanced music on its own ossification," as Adorno called it in reference to Schönberg in *The Philosophy of Modern Music*, was nonetheless part of a dialectical move.[112] The music of Schönberg that pursued form to escape the monotony of mass culture critically echoed the routinization and suffering of industrial life. Modernist narrative technique was likewise critical when it encompassed commodity culture. The disorienting effect of Kafka's *Metamorphosis*, for instance, brings into focus an alienation from menial labor that disappears in the orderly structure of the workplace: "quasi-realistic description brings what seems distant and impossible into menacingly close range."[113] Mass society and the antecedents of modernist art were therefore to be seen as linked: recalling that Beethoven on his deathbed "hurled away a

novel by Walter Scott with the cry, 'why the fellow writes for money,' "
Adorno and Horkheimer noted that Beethoven "proved a most experienced and stubborn businessman in disposing of the last quartets,
which were a most extreme renunciation of the market." [114] Beethoven's antipathy toward the market marked the integration of commodity culture and its pressures into critical art. Scott's novels similarly possessed a "consciousness" of their "own production"; Adorno
and Horkheimer suggested that the strict separation between modernist self-consciousness and the narrative realism of the historical novel
ought to be rethought. The circumstances of a work's production are
always textualized, and readable as a level of self-reflection in realist
and modernist narrative forms.

With this emphasis on representation, Frankfurt School cultural
criticism came closer to poststructural approaches to fiction than to
cultural materialism. Rainer Nägele has pointed out the similarities
between Adorno and poststructuralism: the similarity to Derrida is
apparent in Adorno's preference for the textual fragment over the
powerful totality, though the latter more often grounds his cultural
criticism in popular culture. [115] And while it is materially correct to join
Adorno with poststructuralism's critical attitude toward individual autonomy, the comparison will mislead unless the differences between
Adornian critique and current criticism are met head on. While New
Historicist criticism often starts with Michel Foucault's assertion in
"What Is an Author?" that the "function of an author is to characterize the existence, circulation, and operation of certain discourses
within a society," Adorno never "decentered the subject" to the point
of excluding the oppositional power of thought. [116]

For Adorno, individual, critical autonomy—and in particular the
ability of authors and readers to criticize the social discourses to which
they were subject—always remained a strong philosophic and literary motif. Thought is always already different, he suggested, from the
identifications that place it in the reified world of consumption and
production, retaining its utopian traces amidst even the worst self-
enforced suppression. [117] In a radio interview given in 1969, Adorno
went so far as to argue for a mass-cultural criticism of "the film industry" that would lead to critical autonomy: in many ways his practical
contributions to such efforts would fall within the confines of cultural
studies as it is now being conceived. [118] Adorno's thought was thus
placed both within and against mass society, and his cultural criticism was committed to redeeming a critical autonomy from the culture industry's mass production of false individuality. In Benjamin's

more messianic formulation, cultural criticism could be understood as that "weak messianic power," subject to cultural control, upon which the dominant culture always makes its containing claim, but which through the dialectical image could "shatter the continuum of history," the false sense of progress and liberation that mass culture might produce.[119]

In writing on realist narrative, Adorno was concerned to deflate the claims for realism as the privileged genre for cultural criticism, while at the same time establishing its connections to "modernist" narrative traits. Balzacian realism bears more than surface similarity to Dickens' similarly weighty and contemporaneous production. Though Balzac's novels were written from the perspective of the "outsider" come to the city, rather than conveyed by a Boz-like presence, his "oddness," according to Adorno, "sheds light on something that characterizes nineteenth century prose as a whole."[120] In a version of Hegel's "the owl of Minerva flies at midnight," Adorno suggests that the profuse excess inherent in realism's promise of descriptive concretion occurs at precisely the historical moment when social relations become more abstract.

Objective description in the realist novel, Adorno argued, functioned as a kind of "restitution phenomenon" for an immediacy that mass society increasingly lacked. Narrative absorption in social reality, like Balzac's almost inch-by-inch description of the pension in *Le Père Goriot*, flourished when nineteenth-century systems of industrial production were ending those "knowable communities" of a century before. "The realism with which even those who are idealistically inclined are preoccupied," Adorno wrote, "is not primary but derived: realism on the basis of a loss of reality." This false concretion is often called "reification," the transformation of human labor as well as cultural concepts into "things" or objects useful to mass culture, and the paradoxically complementary transformation of objects of exchange value into the human images individuals seek to become. The relevance of Adorno's Balzac essay to the novel is its position that realism, while compensating for reification's effects in modern culture, also sustains a kind of self-reflexive grasp of cultural production normally reserved for the modernist text.

Adorno, in other words, refused any final separation between the conventions of narrative realism and the textual self-consciousness usually considered part of the modernist novel's domain. Realist as well as modernist narrative, Adorno insisted, were subject to reification, but the critical difference between reification and the actual social

conditions in which a work was formed can be read in the details
of a text. Such an analysis requires attention to the "historical situation," as it would now be called, in which a work was formed. Thus
Benjamin, who looked for the socially critical detail, was admonished
by Adorno: "materialist determination of social traits is only possible
if it is mediated through the *total social process.*" [121] The "totality" of that
process meant close to what is now called "containment," the conformist social forces of modern society exerted upon narrative, though
for Adorno, the power of society over the novel was also broken
within the text. Just as Balzac's plot in *Lost Illusions* is set in motion by
"technical changes . . . in printing and paper that made the mass production of literature possible," so Dickens' novels, particularly *Bleak
House* and *Little Dorrit*, but also earlier works, relate realistic events
to the pressures of the Victorian system of cultural production that
stands behind his works.[122] For Adorno, the demands of writing realistic, popular fiction, in Dickens and Melville, or of Kafka's rejection
of any mass audience, left each author's novels subject to the effects of
commodity culture, but also capable in different measures of holding
its power at bay. Society's power, which was partially dependent on
the image for its mediation, was also seen as challenged by the signs
that gave it force.

Both Adorno and Benjamin, in this dialectical fashion, looked to
mass culture as the condition of narrative. Their work provides a set of
premises that resists an overarching teleological history of the novel,
like the Lukácsian model, and instead sees narrative as saturated by
the pressures of commodity culture and as offering a dialectical response. For Dickens and Melville, the use of the novel as an instrument of cultural criticism was deeply connected with the demands of
the market as they experienced the pressures of trying to sell popular
novels. In Kafka's case, the power of mass society was transmitted
through his investigation of language. Seen from the set of terms provided by critical theory, both popular realism and modernism were
affected by the pressures of the commodification of culture as well as
by the dialectical movement of culture against domination, a movement complicated by all the difficulties which the career and work of
each novelist present.

Elements of both Adorno's and Benjamin's approach can thus contribute to reading Dickens, Melville, and Kafka, and to understanding
their relevance for cultural criticism. Benjamin's emphasis on the concrete and its critical potential provides an important corrective to the
context-bound approach of New Historicism. The historical method

often pays attention to close reading, part of its formalist heritage, only to demonstrate a novel's control by society. The following chapters will be concerned with language in the novel as its texture reflects the shaping force of commodity culture on the questions with which the political novel deals. Like Adorno, Benjamin sought to rescue the critical force of the particular, not through the path of theory, but in his analysis of culture and its fragment, and it was Adorno's emphasis on the reifying force of culture through history that led him to warn against the optimism of that critique. Each may have provided, as Adorno put it, "torn halves of an integral freedom, to which however they do not add up."[123] But Adorno and Benjamin situate realist and modernist narrative amidst the concerns of mass society and provide approaches that can help us to read the effective cultural criticism in Dickens', Melville's, and Kafka's narrative work.

2

Dickens

The Radical Novel and Its Public

When Dickens concluded a speech at the Birmingham and Midland Institute in 1869, his words provoked a storm of public controversy. "I will now discharge my conscience of my political creed," he declared, and did so in a statement that was heard to attack popular enfranchisement, the "people governing," and lend its support to the repression of the popular will. "My faith in the people governing," he announced, "is on the whole, infinitesimal; my faith in The People governed, is, on the whole, illimitable."[1] The Victorian public, moreover, through accounts given by the press, heard the clear tones of an ominous conservatism in Dickens' speech. "I thought Mr. Charles Dickens was in politics a liberal," a letter to the *Birmingham Daily Post* declared, "but the last few words he uttered in the Town Hall on Monday night, would seem to indicate the reverse."[2] Such suspicions are representative of the modern reading of the politics of Dickens' popular fiction. Edmund Wilson, Myron Magnet, and recently David Musselwhite have seen his novels as cultural instruments of Victorian repression rather than as vehicles of radical social reform. Carrying a conservative cultural ethos, moreover, and appealing to the tastes of a burgeoning middle-class readership were for Dickens increasingly related concerns. His production of the novel as a mass-market commodity has been rightly emphasized by critics who have demonstrated narrative's role in enforcing Victorian social and economic norms.[3]

Yet Dickens' own explanation of his speech, when he returned to Birmingham to defend it, contradicted such a conservative reading. Dickens defined his oppositional stance by paying attention to the question of representation, both in politics and in the written form

40

of his original speech. The "people governing," whom he opposed, he explained, were people with a small *p*—those entrusted with the political *representation* of the populace, members of parliament and ministers of government. For Dickens, this was in part an easy point to make, since he began his career as a parliamentary reporter, and satirized the empty exuberance of political speech as early as *The Pickwick Papers* (1836–37). Easy wit, however, went more deeply to the question of political speech in the marketplace: the position Dickens defended linked his own production of the commodity novel with a cultural criticism of oppositional critical force. The "People governed," whom he had praised, he explained, were the democratic citizens who remained constitutively different from the forms of popular representation which mediate their political will.

Significant for Dickens' novels in this speech is his insistence that as an author in the era of the market, his "political creed" was affected by representations which mass culture had already shaped. Dickens himself was a kind of early "media figure," reading from his works in public for large profits from 1858 forward.[4] In composing his novels, moreover, he was "rarely more than one number ahead of his readers," and thus was aware of the way fictional developments had the effect of "reducing or increasing . . . the purchases" his audience might make.[5] Awareness of commodity culture filtered into the texture of his language, and became an object of explicit comment. Dickens referred to his 1870 remarks on representation later as "the little touch of Radicalism I gave them at Birmingham," and makes clear he intended to forestall the consumable reproduction of his words: "with pride I observe that it makes regular political traders, of all sorts, perfectly mad."[6] Dickens thus defined his radicalism in terms of representation and its constraints in the marketplace, cognizant at an early state of the "culture industry" that audience reactions were already shaped by books, newspapers, and "media" such as his own public lectures and the commentary they provoked. Criticizing society meant engaging "regular political traders" at a reflective remove; his radicalism was thus analogous to the modernist sensibilities of Melville and Kafka—and far from the terms "subversion," "aggression," or "desire" in which it is often described.[7] Dickensian radicalism contested the commodifiable forms, even those Dickens himself helped to create, in which the people's will could be coerced.

Dombey and Son (1846–48), a popular novel written for mass consumption, established a similar critical difference within the cultural market for which Dickens wrote. The full title of the book, sold in parts, "Dealings with the Firm of Dombey and Son, Wholesale, Retail, and for Exportation," comically marked it as a literary commodity for sale that was intended to satisfy a middle-class audience, a task at which the novel had great success.[8] Most often, the uniqueness of Dickens' social vision is remembered as his ability to evoke in striking language the alienation and disruption of social change. Raymond Williams accurately singled out *Dombey and Son* for its "power of dramatising a social and moral world in physical terms," praising the passages describing the advent of the railroad.[9] Adorno's emphasis on reification, however, corresponds to another level of Dickensian sophistication. The railroad in the novel symbolizes the "great earthquake" of industrialization, but also the social process that transforms alienation into consumable social forms. Dickens represents the "dire disorder" brought on by the railroad and its expanding market as bringing about the transformation of disorder into signs of well-being, and under those signs are palliatives to consume: "a bran-new Tavern, redolent of fresh mortar and size, and fronting nothing at all, had taken for its sign The Railway Arms."[10]

The language is critically precise: "fronting nothing," the "sign" that uses the railroad to signify human fellowship points to the emptiness of commodified satisfaction, "confronting society with its own notion of harmony," as Adorno put it, "and thereby stumbling on discord."[11] *Dombey and Son* offers a similarly critical vision of the reification of working-class life. Dickens' narrator makes the aggression of the working poor palatable with humor, calling a servant "Nippers." Such humor played no small part in Dickens' reputation as a sentimental lover of humanity, and formed a distinct part of his authorial persona. Queen Victoria would later recall after meeting with Dickens that he was troubled "by the division of classes and hoped it would get better in time."[12] While Dickens' public speeches and novels often endorsed that ethic, his language could also call into question the resolutions he preached. Adorno rightfully insists in "The Economic Crisis as Idyll" that where industrial crisis is concerned, Dickens "thoughtfully forgets all conciliatory humor and calls the horror by name."[13]

A passage deleted from the proofs of the 1848 edition of *Dombey and Son* emphasizes that Dickens' use of names also had subtler effects. Narrative onomastics evoke class friction and a critical text just beneath the comically acceptable surface his working men and women present. Mr. Dombey, the middle-class businessman, contracting with "Toodles" the stoker for the services of his wife as a nursemaid, reacts in polite shock to the family name of "Biler"—"you have called a child after a boiler?" The name points impolitely to the worker's identification with his work—he is the stoker of the steam engine—but also to the explosive bile and inner discontent his good humor fails to hide.[14] Class division emerges from the scene that makes a mockery of the Toodleses, but the conflation of a sexualized body with industrial labor in Victorian writing was complex. Even in such popular discourse, full of the good humor that made Dickens famous, the fetishizing imagination that distorts the importance of workers also complicates the notion of work. By representing Mr. Dombey's fear of the working class in his abhorrence of maternal dependence, Dickens links infant nursing to the larger economic and political domain, giving the personal a political voice.[15] Bodily fluids like Mrs. Toodles' milk, the unnamed object of the transaction, and the "bile" of her husband, metaphorically establish the fluid connection between the middle-class *labor*, both feminine and masculine, and the unspeakable dependence of the England of 1848 on its serving hands.

Dickens' public positions, moreover, do not predict the culturally critical force his novels often assert. Dickens supported Empire, for instance, and the subjection of colonial peoples, in accord with popular norms. John Stuart Mill noted during the Governor Eyre affair that opposing "abuses of power committed against negroes and mulattoes, was not a popular proceeding with the English middle-classes." Mill was attempting to bring the British governor of Jamaica to justice for murdering a black political opponent during the Jamaica rebellion of 1864, and was opposed by Dickens, who supported the governor. Later Dickens would publicly encourage the brutal suppression of the India Mutiny as well.[16] Dickens' support for the colonies as a safety valve for middle-class discontent is well represented in Micawber's fate in *David Copperfield* as well as *Household Words*, which he edited, and his racist fury was hardly masked in his famous earlier statement that "savages" should be "civilized off the face of the earth."[17] Yet in *Dombey and Son*, Major Bagstock's "Violent Assaults upon the Native" are noticed by a narrator who clearly turns against the exercise of imperial force. The Victorian representation of the native as "savage" may have justified Dickens' own exterminatory anger, but in his narrator it provokes an admiration of the native's ability to transform stereotype into an oppositional social stance.

Signs of the servant's alleged savagery, "European clothes," sit on his body "with an outlandish possibility of adjustment," but the ill-fitting garments, like the cultural stigma they represent, do not conform to the native's body. Those garments provoke admiration when

the insignia of the master's determining cultural power are turned into
the cover of its victim's defense: "[clothes] to which he imparted a new
grace, whenever the Major attacked him, by shrinking into them like a
shrivelled nut, or a cold monkey" (278–79). This "new grace" is far
from conformity to a Western ethos, whose cultural weight is impressed on the servant with physical blows. "Grace" becomes admi-
rable as the mass-cultural "fiction[s]" of home is matched by critiques
of jingoistic political propaganda, while at the same time Dickens
could confide in correspondence his own domestic troubles: "I find
that the skeleton in my domestic closet is becoming a pretty big one."[20]
Praise of domestic sanctity and criticism of family as political cliché,
produced for mass consumption, were by late career two sides of the
Dickensian fictional coin.

Little Dorrit (1855–57) typifies the self-conscious attitude toward the
mass audience for fiction running throughout Dickens' later work.
Dickens is legendary at this point in his career for his close relationship with his readers, and clearly reveled in his popular fame. Yet
his novels take an increasingly critical stance toward the mass-market
novel, often mocking the domestic values it sought to promote. Skepticism and irony are shown toward the reading public in Little Dorrit,
marking an emerging contradictory cultural attitude toward fiction.
For while Dickens was "overjoyed" at the novel's sales figures, noting
gleefully that its first number outsold even Bleak House, the novel
itself goes on to satirize the popular audience who rewarded him,
but whose imaginative limits also turned fiction into an ideological
cage.[18] Mr. Plornish, for instance, resides in "Happy Cottage," a house
painted "to represent the exterior of a thatched cottage," yet is compared to a "blind man" where society is concerned. The narrator ridi-
cules him as a naive consumer of fiction, and in mocking the Plorn-
ishes' enjoyment of the "little fiction" of home, criticizes the religion of
domesticity preached in Dickens' novels themselves.[19] Such satire of
mass-cultural "fiction[s]" of home is matched by critiques of jingoistic
political propaganda, while at the same time Dickens could confide
in correspondence his own domestic troubles: "I find that the skeleton in my domestic closet is becoming a pretty big one."[20] Praise of
domestic sanctity and criticism of family as political cliché, produced
for mass consumption, were by late career two sides of the Dickensian
fictional coin.

By the time of Great Expectations (1859–60), Wemmick's "Castle" and
its mechanism reflect the mass-produced character of Dickens' own
set pieces of domesticity. Humor works to separate the reader from the

consumable fiction of middle-class virtue on which belief in Pip's final conversion depends. The family circle, Wemmick tells Pip, must be his place of repose. The middle-class lawyer works at Newgate representing criminals, but praises domesticity as the proper alternative to the harshness of the day. "No, the office is one thing, and the private life is another," Wemmick announces, "when I go into the office, I leave the castle behind me. If it's not in any way disagreeable to you, you'll do the same."[21] Pip, like a reader of Dickens' fiction, goes on to marvel at the clerk's home life, at his "gentle heart . . . pleasant home . . . and old father" at play.

Yet the clearer this picture of the home becomes, the more it takes on a critical resemblance to the prison in which Wemmick spends his working day. Like the prison, the "castle" is surrounded by walls, and to savor the pleasures of the domestic retreat, for Wemmick, means to follow a rigid routine. Before the "Aged P." can be joined in harmonious bliss before the fire, the castle's mechanical devices must be operated in their proper order, and a set of gestures made in accurate sequence before the blessed father. "All the innocent ways" of Walworth exemplify a world of impersonality, where the most intimate gestures of family life have themselves become exchangeable. Little practical difference exists for Wemmick between home's regimen and the orderly routine Jaggers ruthlessly requires from him in "business life" (423). *Great Expectations* calls into question the mass-cultural ideology of the home as haven, promoted in Dickens' work, and matches with uncanny critical accuracy the first issue of *Household Words*, his journal, where Dickens defined its cultural function as offering the working reader a fireside sanctuary from labor, and "no iron binding of the mind to grim realities."[22] In *Little Dorrit*, considered by many critics Dickens' most satirical novel, the radical promise of his Victorian conservatism, and its critique of the limits of the popular novel, would be fulfilled.

Cultural Criticism and Mass Audience

Before *Little Dorrit*, however, commentary on *Bleak House* had already shaped Dickens' popular reputation as an inflammatory social critic. Dickens' preface to the first edition of *Bleak House* responded to the charge of George Henry Lewes that the "Spontaneous Combustion" of Krook could "not possibly be," but the undercurrent of their debate was anxiety over the mass audience for fiction, and how it would receive Dickens' text.[23] Lewes' dislike of Krook's combustion, grounded in a mid-Victorian taste for realism and scientific accuracy, was not without its political content. The Dickens he preferred in his historic essay of 1872 was the genial radical who "proved his power by a popularity almost unexampled, embracing all classes." Krook's death raised the more ominous specter of social injustice, and evoked Dickens' own stand in the "Condition of England" debate, forecasting the inflammatory consequences which might emerge for Britain's Victorian social order from social inequality and abject poverty.[24]

Yet Krook's death evokes not only the incendiary social potential of slum conditions, but also the figurative self-consumption which awaited the novelist who confronted the confines of Victorian taste too directly. Krook dies as a merchant who trades in trash—"Call the death by whatever name Your Highness will," Dickens' narrator declares—and houses "Nemo," the writer as faithful copyist who is deprived of his social prerogatives and identity, like an author who has handled his material without care: "it is the same death eternally—inborn, inbred, engendered in the corrupted humours of the vicious body itself" (512). The introduction to *Bleak House* reminds its readers of the limitations Victorian taste placed on the inflammatory potential of popular fiction, but also of the capacity of a novelist to figure his predicament as commercial writer within his novel. Dickens ends his preface with a confident belief that he can please his audience—"I believe I have never had so many readers as in this book," he concludes: "May we meet again!"—and echoes the language of a letter written in the same month, in which he rejoices at the novel's success: "It has retained its immense circulation from the first, beating dear old 'Copperfield' by a round ten thousand or more. I have never had so many readers."[25]

Dickens demonstrated this same critical awareness of social radicalism and the limits of Victorian representation in correspondence contemporaneous with his writing of the novel. As his composition of *Little Dorrit* began, Dickens wrote to a friend, the actor W. C. Macready, magnifying his novel's polemical tone as if it were a divine gift. "With God's leave I shall walk in the same all the days of my life," Dickens bragged, but in a letter which goes on to disenchant the political sanctity of polemical rage.[26] Historically, the source of Dickens' dissatisfaction in the letter was government inefficiency during the Crimean War. The deathly consequences of official bungling for British troops became the cause célèbre that helped to make Florence Nightingale famous, and produced Tennyson's most remembered public poem, "The Charge of the Light Brigade."[27] *Little Dorrit*'s tirades against the "Circumlocution Office" and British bureaucracy were understood by their contemporary audience to be radically antigovernment. But Dickens deprecated them in the letter as far from explosive, and depicted polemical fulmination as a safety valve for the controlled discharge of discontent, a release already safely built into the social machine: "In No. 3 of my new book I have been blowing off a little indignant steam which would otherwise blow me up." The popular will to political opposition—"as to the suffrage, I have lost hope even in the ballot"—is seen as voiced through a representational process that controls it, in a system of expressive containment that the image of the social engine and its safety valve suggests.

This political dissatisfaction with the mechanisms of mass politics affects *Little Dorrit*'s depiction of "the people" as well. In "Bleeding Heart Yard," home to the urban poor in the novel, imperial rhetoric serves as a mass-cultural siphon of anger that might change social conditions at home. Electoral spectacle and its media of persuasion produce a substitute popular culture, managed by ruling families as a means of control: "they were vaguely persuaded that every foreigner had a knife about him . . . they believed that foreigners had no independent spirit, as never being escorted to the poll in droves by Lord Decimus Tite Barnacle, with colors flying and the tune of Rule Britannia playing" (295–96). In such criticism of media politics, Dickens indicts the kind of prejudice his own political journalism indulged. Xenophobia is depicted as a social construction produced in a "peculiarly British way" to blunt the power of social discontent, for the working-class conviction that "foreigners were always immoral" was imposed from above: "they had long been carefully trained by the Barnacles, and Stiltstalkings." Nationalist prejudice, especially when taken up by popular rhetoric, comes in for trenchant critique. Encountering Cavaletto the Italian, the poor of Bleeding Heart yard "held it a sound constitutional national axiom that he ought to go home to his own country," while the narrator casts imperial ethnocentrism in a different light: "they never thought of enquiring how many of their countrymen would be returned upon their hands from divers parts of the world, if the principle were generally recognized" (295).

Dickens is concerned in *Little Dorrit* with just this distortion of political discontent through representation—with "Circumlocution," rather than its parliamentary office. This emphasis is apparent in the disappearance of government bureaucracy as the novel's central theme after its first numbers, as well as in Dickens' contemporary comments on political reform. His fear in a later letter on politics is of the "alienation of the people from their own public affairs," a subjection effected through a social "discontent" that is "so much the worse for smouldering, instead of blazing openly." Dickens fears that anger at social injustice will gradually neutralize its radical force in propaganda or reformist expression and will fail to act with decisive effect.[28] His letter stands against the "people" who remonstrate while accepting their social duties and subjugation—and thus against the very "blowing off" of political venom into complicity he has confessed his own novel to indulge: "I do reluctantly believe that the English people are, habitually, consenting parties to the miserable imbecility into which we have fallen, *and never will help themselves out of it.*"[29]

Little Dorrit thus makes no pretense to the objectivity of the radical reformer. Henry Mayhew's sociological work *London Labour and the London Poor*, first published in 1851, may stand in a general way behind its depiction of working-class living conditions. Though scholars have speculated on its influence on Dickens as a source of his *Our Mutual Friend* (1864–65), Mayhew's prose, despite his street savvy, sometimes seems purple, censorious, and overdrawn. Recent criticism has emphasized the reflexivity that Mayhew brought to his investigations of working-class culture, praising him for his empirical catalogues of street vendors and attention to popular voices, while Dickens is diminished for his sentimentality or ideologically derived accounts.[30] Dickens' account of working-class life, to be sure, never escaped the limiting constructs of the middle-class imagination. Yet the privileging of Mayhew over Dickens relies on a reductive view of the mainstream novel. Because fiction follows the dictates of the cultural commodity, this view holds, it is less able to exert the critical reflexivity of reformist accounts such as Mayhew's, which were less beholden to market demands. In the case of Dickens, however, the opposite argument can be made: dealing with the constraints of marketable taste made his novels necessarily more adept at negotiating his audience and their cultural constraints. Dickens's novels were, as Raymond Williams points out, the first to incorporate a "new urban popular culture": bringing working-class life to a middle-class readership required a careful negotiation of clashing and often uncertain cultural codes.[31] Adorno argued that there were critical social effects in the music of the composers who, faced with the need to appeal to "an anonymous marketplace" rather than a "prince's favor," had to bring the "organs of the market" into the inner texture of their works.[32] In a similar fashion, Dickens had to face the danger of false objectivity in depicting working-class life: the need to appeal to his audience and stay within its limitations was a constant reminder that any depiction of the urban poor was a mediated one, subject to the demands of the commodity novel. Objective sociology might pass its observations off as empirically valid, but social fiction necessarily confronted the mediating artifice involved in any construction of urban life.

Little Dorrit therefore never assumes the tone of objective, reformist representation. Instead, the author's awareness of producing images for social consumption shapes its narrative voice. Forms of audience identification, such as asides to the reader, indulge a Thackerayan taste for an intrusive author, while engaging in the modern kind of audience targeting usually associated with marketing techniques. Lionel Trilling's liberal reading of the novel downplayed the critical effect of such gestures, seeing Arthur Clennam's world-weariness as a version of Dickens' authorial boredom with the marketplace and its demands. Fiction as an entertainment commodity, however, need not imply its vacuity as cultural criticism: Trilling's distaste for stereotype and cliché serves as a reminder of the crucial role of mass culture in the social vision of the mass-market novel.[33] Liberal sympathy, to be sure, is the atmospheric substance of Clennam's love for Little Dorrit, guilt-ridden as he is about the social depredations his family's business has brought about, and weary with bureaucratic failures to help. Yet censorship marks his sympathy, as well as his will to reform: the liberal concern accompanying Clennam's gradual love for Little Dorrit is portrayed as a form of blindness. Clennam's "fictional" grasp of social reality intensifies as he becomes involved in her life.

Dickens' narrator, moreover, always represents liberal sympathy as a *product* of a market culture, establishing the link between liberal social sentiment and popular material that Trilling sought to break. Little Dorrit's paradox is also the appealing duplicity of popular mass culture: both are able to mask, but also to evoke in powerful fashion, the unpleasant realities of working-class life. Little Dorrit thus becomes attractive to Arthur Clennam because she hides her hunger, as well as her labor, as she works within the "double house" (32) that represents the middle-class home: "it was not easy to make out Little Dorrit's face; she was so retiring, plied her needle in such removed corners, and started away so scared if encountered on the stairs" (53). Yet the realities of class are never hidden in *Little Dorrit*, especially to characters within the novel. The narrator makes clear that Little Dorrit's identity was fixed by her social origin within the prison, her "birthplace and home," and that it remains an open secret to the public gaze: "she passed to and fro in it shrinkingly now, with a womanly consciousness that she was pointed out to every one" (75–76).

· Dickens' characters, in other words, often respond to the facts of social class that his readers deny. The narrator calls Little Dorrit's secrecy about her background the "genteel fiction" she sustains (72), linking her mannered duplicity with the audience expectations of the middle class. The "family fiction" (227) she maintains is named such by the narrator, who represents her as virtuous, to be sure, but also as enslaved to the expectations of proper fiction, and to the kind of social self-presentation Clennam comes to expect. In this sense Little Dorrit's *textual* desire as an observer of social experience—"innocent, in the mist through which she saw her father"—is determining for the plotted course of the novel and the family history it tells (76). Narrative suspense originates as the difference widens between the "family fiction" of middle-class virtue Little Dorrit produces and the contrary realities of urban life the narrator brings to light.

Clennam's vision of the working class is thus continually linked to mass-cultural censorship. J. Hillis Miller's influential argument in *Charles Dickens: The World of his Novels* that *Little Dorrit* represented the triumph of "imprisoning states of mind" was made from the perspective of phenomenology, yet accurately captures the 1950s sense of containing mass culture in its description of Clennam's point of social view.[34] For Mr. Meagles, the arch-middle-class figure whom Clennam meets early in the novel, reformist anger at social injustice breeds a will to the blindness of harmonious resolution. Middle-class readers who are represented in *Little Dorrit* always sympathize with working-class experience, but also sympathetically enforce the limits of proper taste. Both Clennam and Meagles befriend women of lower-class origin, yet both seek to "normalize" those women by obliterating through patronage the traces of urban life. Sympathy, of course, imagines itself as a social virtue, and not as a means of social discipline. In Marseilles where Meagles and Clennam meet, the object of their anger is travelers' quarantine: Mr. Meagles execrates the confinement which prevents his family from being able to "allong and marshong about their lawful business" like the liberated citizens of the town (15). Yet in the Meagles home, where Clennam falls in love with their daughter "Pet," confinement is the norm. "Boxed up . . . within our own home limits," as Mr. Meagles later says, they find the confinement pleasurable because it is disguised like the home itself, which is "defended by a goodly show of handsome trees" (186–87).

For these representatives of the middle-class reader, confinement and social constraint are revolting only when visible as such: both prefer the "family fiction" that Little Dorrit strives to represent. Clennam favors the conservative cultural vision of Little Dorrit as a figure of "active resignation, goodness, and noble service" (788), and Mr. Meagles likewise holds her up as paragon of "Duty" to his rebellious maid. Yet readings that emphasize the universal power of the prison in the novel require correction: the *will* to imprisoning blindness is present in the novel, but attributed to a specific audience of middle-class readers and their mass-cultural taste. Clennam's middle-class point of view, with its link to the merchandisable kind of "domestic story" such readers preferred, is therefore crucial to the novel's critical intents (374). For Clennam's limited view of working-class life has the contradictory effect of expanding the commodity novel's social frame: by focusing on Clennam's blindness, Dickens is able to bring to light the "common and coarse" (252) aspects of urban life Clennam ignores, just as the Meagleses' censorious treatment of Tattycoram brings the "History" of Miss Wade and its powerful social history into the novel's text.

Such differences in class perspective, moreover, are built into the texture of the novel's audience address. When Little Dorrit visits Clennam in his apartment, the middle-class reader's perspective is explicitly acknowledged, in an affectionate appeal to sympathize with a woman whose class experience will be foreign: "Arthur Clennam rose hastily, and saw her standing at the door. This history must sometimes see with Little Dorrit's eyes" (159). "Must," however, reads as "shall" in a different manuscript. Textual variants indicate an imperative present throughout the novel: the need to see Little Dorrit's history in terms other than those of the uplifting "domestic story." The "family fiction" Clennam prefers and the narrator's wish to view social history through "Little Dorrit's eyes" are in this way continually at odds. Clennam's construction of working-class life is identified as a specific cultural construction that must be "sometimes" differed with, and viewed through a different set of "eyes." Little Dorrit's withdrawal and modesty show up in the Clennam home as the "moral phenomena" of hiding signs of her poverty. The "scheme" that silences her working-class background, however, also represents an assertion, against the domestic mythos of middle-class culture, of working-class duress: "[she] would, of a certainty, scheme and plan—not very cunningly, it would seem, for she deceived no one—to dine alone" (53). The popular picture of Little Dorrit is similarly double, reminding the

Victorian reader that the silent surface of diminutive virtue covers a
radically different story beneath:

the remotest suspicion of the truth never dawned upon his mind. No. He saw
the devoted little creature with her worn shoes, in her common dress, in her
jail-home; a slender child in body, a strong heroine in soul, and the light of
her domestic story made all else dark to him. (374)

This pattern of reader response is modeled on the first page of *Little
Dorrit* and its famous set piece of the sun "burning" Marseilles. An
urgent and painful vision is presented which an insistent "stare" is
unable to see: "the universal stare made the eyes ache. Towards the
distant line of Italian coast, indeed, it was a little relieved by light
clouds of mist" (1). Within the confines of the novel as popular commodity, Dickens has thematized the limits of the marketable novel
and the mystification that his work goes on to resist.

Slum conditions, for instance, are sentimentalized as their popular
representation is called into question. The narrator uses Little Dorrit's
gaze to evoke her piety and the pious reader's limits as well. The
"mist" of Marseilles, city that gave its name to the anthem of revolution, is figured from the start of the novel as a blinding "glare" that
oppresses "exhausted laborers" (2) most of all. Oppression appears
universal, with narrative illumination apparently contained: "everything that lived or grew, was oppressed by the glare" of the sun.
The inaugural scene of the novel characterizes a middle-class culture
where escape from the burning vision of the "oppressed" requires
domestic self-confinement and censorship, so that the *specific* culture
of "exhausted laborers" is kept under wraps: "blinds, shutters, cur-
tains, awnings, were all closed and drawn to keep out the stare" (2).

Yet the "stare" of Marseilles can be seen by the characters who
peek through the popular novel's blinds. While the shady sanctuaries
of religion offer the safest middle-class refuge from the unacceptable vision of working-class culture—"the churches were the freest
from it" (2)—Dickensian character is less than completely sanctimo-
nious when Little Dorrit's feminine virtue is portrayed. In describing
her worshipful service to father and family, Dickens' narrator is careful
to represent his heroine as virtuously religious and deceptive at the
same time. Narrative tone makes middle-class religiosity a require-
ment of social as well as representational grace. Little Dorrit continually negotiates between working-class prison and the middle-class
world, but Dickens reminds his readers of the distinction between a
"divine" version of events and the working-class experience she actu-

ally lives: "what her pitiful look saw, at that early time, in her father, in her sister, in her brother, in the jail; how much, or how little of the wretched truth it pleased God to make visible to her; lies hidden with many mysteries" (70).

Dickens' "God" here is rendered as equivalent to a narrator of mystery—and hence, to a novelist—whose tasteful "lies" point to the very "truth" that the marketable novel must conceal. Such "fiction," Janice Carlisle points out, is portrayed in the novel as "morally debilitating," since Little Dorrit's devotion to a father who exploits her produces deceit, and contravenes the moralistic aesthetic of the Victorian novel.[35] Such "lies," to be sure, are necessary for her survival as a Victorian woman and for the protection of her reputation, but they also allude to social truths that challenge the limits of the novel as popular commodity. Dickens' narrator himself alludes to the "common and coarse things" (252) which even Arthur Clennam, with his taste for "domestic story," can notice, and which take place under the proper reader's eyes. Familiarity with audience in Little Dorrit enables Dickens to test and circumvent the restraints placed upon a novel of mass readership, and to challenge the limits of Victorian taste.

Historically, working women in the Victorian period were well aware of abusive living conditions they could speak of only at their own peril, as Martha Vicinus points out.[36] Dickens himself, in his work with Miss Coutts and actual British prostitutes at Urania Cottage, interviewed such women, taking pains to learn their stories. In letters to Miss Coutts about their education, he first emphasized the utility of the New Testament to their redemption, and later argued with her during the composition of Little Dorrit's first numbers about the seriousness of class conflict in British society.[37] The depiction of poverty and domestic violence in Little Dorrit is never separable from Dickens' awareness of the disparity between such religious language and social reality. George Bernard Shaw claimed that the novel was a "more seditious book than Das Kapital" and rightly perceived the volatility of its social vision. Yet Shaw failed to notice that it was Little Dorrit's commitment to "bourgeois security" that made the novel marketable: Dickens' work was in fact radically forceful for its self-criticism of middle-class ideology, and not for the revolutionary opposition to society that Shaw wistfully believed it to indulge.[38]

The best modern critics have nonetheless assumed the novel's complicity with the constraints of its mass readership. Dianne Sadoff has brilliantly demonstrated that the novel's entire complex plotted structure reconstitutes the shattered families of urban London it portrays.[39]

Working-class life in the prison, Sadoff shows in detail, includes representations of "metaphorical incest" between Little Dorrit and her father, when the narrator tells us she "did much more" than the "classical daughter," who nursed a starving father at her "innocent breast" (222). Victorian conventions for the discussion of slum conditions, the actual sites where such crimes of incest as well as rape occurred, were certainly censorious, and the plot's apparent emphasis on paternal and familial restoration conforms with a late-Victorian sense of audience. In 1885, the British medical journal *Lancet*, which Dickens had earlier used in his research, still felt the need to declare of its medical investigations of working-class housing: "there are things done in secret which should not so much as be named in family circles or in newspapers which have entrance into private houses." [40]

In demonstrating the complexity of the novel as popular culture, Sadoff's essay has the virtue of pointing out the cultural counterhistory of urban domestic life Dickens sketches between the novel's lines. The emphasis on "metaphor," however, argues more strongly than necessary for *Little Dorrit*'s complete collusion with middle-class propriety. Plot certainly reflects these concerns in the novel: its dissimulating effects led Viktor Shklovskij to argue that *Little Dorrit*'s masterful "manipulation of false and true solutions" made it the paradigmatic mystery novel.[41] The mystificatory movement of Dickens' plot is less than complete, and never fully cancels the less than fully metaphorical social history still powerful in the popular story he tells. The "necessary" lies of "fiction" are far from being the end of *Little Dorrit* as oppositional cultural history. In Dickens' hands, Victorian popular culture produced neither a liberal deification of feminine virtue, nor a mass-cultural fiction subject to power, but a commodity novel that tells the complex history of a working-class woman within middle-class cultural confines.

Dickens renders in powerful terms, for instance, his heroine's abuse by an abusive and poverty-stricken father. The depiction of sexual degradation, of course, is far from pornographic. Instead, Little Dorrit's relations with her father meld with the constraints of prison life, restrictions so saturated by the concerns of class and social prestige that the Marshalsea becomes a model for the officially unspoken censorship of Victorian domestic life as a whole. As in *Great Expectations*, where the long-mooted question of Estella's parentage finally links her with prisoners and crime, and *Our Mutual Friend*, where indeterminate sexual preference is connected with waterfront dives, undecided questions of parentage or sexual desire haunt Dickens' text. In *Little Dorrit*, sexual innuendo informs working-class diction, when Mrs. Chivery, wife of the prison's gatekeeper, is enraged when Little Dorrit turns down her son's offer of marriage. The code crossing of the scene is complex: Mrs. Chivery feels insulted, since her family's station as prison gatekeeper and Mr. Dorrit's as its senior inmate seem matched, and she responds by casting aspersions on Little Dorrit's character to vent her own sense of social slight.

Class insult offers the invitation to sexual allusion, breaking the constraints of proper fiction with popular speech. Little Dorrit's indeterminate marital status—appearing as child, with the duties of a woman toward her father, including sharing his bed—makes her a kind of "slave" to the family, both too much and too little a woman for her son, Mrs. Chivery suggests: "her father is all for himself in his views, and against sharing her with anyone. . . . This is the way in which she is doomed to be a constant slave, to them that are not worthy that a constant slave she unto them should be" (252). Avrom Fleischman offers a certain support to Mrs. Chivery's aspersions, noting that "a large part of the novel is given over to an excruciating record of Dorrit's degradation of his daughter."[42] Mrs. Chivery's banter, however, has its own precision: the repetition of "unto them" evokes the Christian virtue Little Dorrit holds in popular esteem, while the fact that she remains a kind of domestic "slave" to her father calls into question the character of the love to which she submits. "Degradation" remains an inescapable aspect of her virtue, and popular speech captures the contradictory status of the domestic heroine in working-class life. Like "little Mother," the name she is given by Maggy, "slave" evokes the sexual and economic abuses of working-class experience which Arthur Clennam, Mrs. Chivery's middle-class interlocutor, chooses to leave unread.

In a similar fashion, the language of Victorian religiosity in *Little Dorrit* is turned to critical social ends. The hurt Little Dorrit felt in her "gentle breast" (223), after spending the night with her father, when she was "deeply wounded by what she had seen of him," easily fits in with the religious halo the narrator gives her. The symbolic stigmata of her service to her father appear in the light of dawn on the prison wall: "the spikes upon the wall were tipped with red, then made a sullen purple pattern on the sun as it came flaming up into the heavens. The spikes had never looked so sharp and cruel" (225). But a loss of ideological innocence is also called for by the popular Christian reading. The "purple" of paternal royalty is set against paternal "spikes" in the passage, and the "red" with which those spikes are illumined

alludes to the bloody possibility of paternal rape. Such satanic illumination of the father occurs under the sign of blindness, which was
first associated with the "sun" on the novel's first page. But the "sun"
that here moves "flaming up into the heavens" points to the gaps in
the narrator's own account of daughterly affection—"for she was but
too content to see him with a lustre round his head"—and gently
reminds the reader that she has spent the previous night at his bed
(224). The phrasing calls for reflection on Little Dorrit's situation without assigning blame. The reader encounters a father who "revealed
his degenerate state to his affectionate child," with the "impurity of
his prison worn into the grain of his soul," and a daughter who is sen-
sibly reticent to describe a "life of degradation" at his hands (222, 224).
For her, as for Dickens the novelist, only social opprobrium might result. While alluding to a history of sexual abuse she is "too content"
to leave suppressed, his narrator remains unwilling to leave the dark
side of her "domestic story" out of the text.[43]

Such circumspection, however, never cancels Dickens' critical perception of urban culture. In the larger field of Victorian publishing
and popular discourse, Juliet Swindells points out, the kind of ideal-
ization of Little Dorrit's virtue was "inescapable," and was present in
even the nonfiction autobiographies of women domestic servants in
the period.[44] Whatever accolades are accorded feminine subservience
in *Little Dorrit*, however, Dickens always dramatizes the social situations in which its rhetoric becomes a necessary political gesture of
working life. When she is in a middle-class home, for instance, Little
Dorrit's reticence in identifying her prison home is entirely conventional, but her praise of her father's virtue is more complex. Flora
couches her bitter sentiments toward her late husband in defensive
prolixity. Flora, who practices a prolix and defensive femininity of her
own, becomes an ideal interlocutor: listening to Little Dorrit's praise of
her father, she "quite understood" its duplicity, and becomes a friend.
As Little Dorrit's "new patroness" (276) in gentility, Flora listens to
her praise of her father and shares "her secret" (279) without giving it
away: "she condensed the narrative of her life into a few scanty words
about herself, and a glowing eulogy about her father." Far from an
aggressive death wish, eulogistic praise here is a kind of "*narrative*" of
crucial allusion, as Dickens' narrator explicitly calls it: Little Dorrit's
eulogy *buries* the secret of prison life. This "delicate" mode of representing "where she lived" receives Clennam's blessing—"she felt sure
he would approve of her confiding her secret to Flora"—but without
his full knowledge. Flora's "natural tenderness," in which there is "no

incoherence," remains beyond grasp. By representing the "secret" of her story only to women—first Flora and later Maggy in the "Princess Story"—Little Dorrit shares her working-class history, while hiding its stigma from those who pose a social threat.

The Victorian reviews of the novel make this contradictory effect of its popularity quite apparent. Readers who were drawn to comment on *Little Dorrit*'s overt hostility toward the prison often identified the novel's attack as being on a radicalism of complicity, and pointed out the mechanisms of social control with which their own comments complied. An unsigned review in *The Leader* applauded Mr. Dorrit, the novel's long-imprisoned debtor, for his "manly detestation of servility," praising his emotional outbursts to his daughter, which are nonetheless represented in the novel as calls for domestic appeasement, rather than as a contestation of his fate.[45] The same critic was therefore put in the position of noticing "manly" radicalism, both in prison and out, as self-subjecting coercion, apparent in Mr. Dorrit's continuous appetite for genteel recognition, and thus had to attack his conformist social stance: "Mr. Dorrit is the very type of social flunkeyism, and our time needs a lesson against that sordid vice." E. B. Hamley, a conservative reader, disliked the novel's satire on bureaucracy because it showed the government's containment of "Opposition" to be all too effective: "What can be weaker in itself, to say nothing of the total want of art in connecting it with the story, than the intended satire of the Circumlocution Office? We don't in the least wish to stand up for the Circumlocution Office—curse the Circumlocution Office, say we."[46] Hamley was correct in arguing that the novel's challenge to Victorian government was weakened by its effusive voicing, and his complaint, that Dickens had merely taken up a "popular cry" against government despotism, was echoed by James Fitzjames Stephens and most reviewers. But W. H. Dixon correctly saw the distinction of the novel as lying in its linkage between Dickens' radical collusion with authority and a socially challenging will: "We see in 'Little Dorrit' no decrease of power, no closing of eyes."[47]

Little Dorrit: The Tiny Woman's Story

Secrecy and enigma are the social signs of the impoverished culture into which Little Dorrit is born. "The shadows of the Marshalsea wall," referred to in dirgelike repetition throughout the text, promise that no radically distasteful illumination of the imprisoned poor will be ventured. The sexual secret of the Clennam Home is treated similarly. For if "the sun ever touched [the house], it was but with a ray, and that was gone within half an hour" (172). In his preface to the 1857 edition, Dickens reminded his *Little Dorrit* audience of his market success with *Bleak House*, assuring them in more direct terms that no violation of middle-class taste would ensue. "Deeply sensible of the affection and confidence that have grown up between us" (lx), Dickens nonetheless promises his readers that they will "stand among the crowding ghosts of many miserable years," when the Marshalsea housed debtors and their families. Assurance of secrecy is matched with a pact of reve-lation, sealed by such audience address, that Melville will also use. So long as the *promise* of decorous concealment is made from author to reader, the rhetoric of propriety remains intact, and revelations contrary to the commodity novel's limits often proceed.

This cultural contradiction shapes Dickens' mass-cultural mode. The clichéd type of domestic servitude, whom Lionel Trilling called "the paraclete in female form," Little Dorrit at the same time retains a disturbing difference from convention.[48] The built-in difference causes problems for the liberal reading: Trilling's praise of civic virtue in such secularized Christianity authorizes a life of cruel restraints.[49] While New Historicist critics often emphasize the controlling power of such self-discipline in fiction, Little Dorrit herself remains closer to what Walter Benjamin called a "dialectical image," and retains her critical force. Such an image, as I discussed in Chapter 1, congeals the contra-diction of social ideal and material history in a livid but static symbol. For Benjamin, the source was usually mass culture, though the dia-lectical images he discovered in Baudelaire's poetry better match the paradoxical status Dickens' working seamstress attains. The size of a girl, Little Dorrit becomes a dialectical image for the infantilizing force of conventional Victorian expectations on a woman who, like the novel, retains her socially critical and imaginative power.

Biography in part explains this contradictory symbolic effect. The need to censor as well as share family history in *Little Dorrit* was famil-iar: the rhetorical circumlocutions required to explain the prison in a middle-class home match Dickens' experience as a child. Like Little Dorrit, Dickens kept the secret of a family that lived in the Marshalsea prison, while he worked outside and struggled to maintain a fiction of gentility. Dickens' father, John Dickens, was imprisoned in the Mar-shalsea for three months in 1824, and the omnipresent shadow of the Marshalsea wall in the story probably owes something to his melo-dramatic pronouncement upon entering the prison, that "the sun had set upon him forever."[50] During a portion of the sentence the Dickens family resided, like the Dorrit family, within the prison walls, while Charles, who lodged outside, worked at Warren's Blacking to support the family and made frequent trips in and out the gates.

Popular fiction does not replicate biography for Dickens as much as transpose its personal limitations into cultural ones: transit in and out of prison walls in the novel becomes socially symbolic of censored social experience, and the need to bring it to cultural light. In the 1857 preface to the novel, Dickens tells his readers of his visit to the remains of the prison and his view, with "the smallest boy I ever conversed with" from the neighborhood, of "the window of the room where Little Dorrit was born" (lx). Narrative origins are alluded to, and suppressed subjective truth is symbolically linked to the protocol of public secrecy: "I found the older and smaller wall, which used to enclose the pent-up inner prison where nobody was put, except for ceremony" (lx). Late in his fictional career, such ceremonies of taste were familiar to Dickens, confident that he would meet the "readers" he prized once again (lx).

The fictional marketplace, however, produced a critical paradox where Little Dorrit's family history was concerned. Tasteful mystification required lavish encomiums to her virtue, while description stumbles upon a sexual history whose fetishized traces are never obscured. The novel's connoisseur of "domestic story," Arthur Clennam, worships Little Dorrit as an emblem of self-sacrifice, while imagining violent penetration she heroically accepts: "he saw the quickened bosom that would have joyfully thrown itself before him to receive a mortal wound directed at his breast, with the dying cry, 'I love him!' " (374). Such fetishized subjugation, however, is revealed as partial and false—"the remotest suspicion of the truth never dawned upon his mind"—as Dickens' description points to a "mortal wound" and experience of love that is indistinguishable from pain. While it never occurs to Clennam to discover the personal source of such a "wound," his praise of Little Dorrit's virtue is exaggerated to the point of becoming lurid, encouraging readers to seek the social history that lies beneath his fetish and its social mask.

Walter Benjamin argued that such fetishized "images of women and death," moreover, were inseparable from the logic of the commodity. Urban misery, according to Benjamin, created a desire for just the kind of fetishized relation to social reality that Clennam's gaze so often can produce. Rather than perceive the actual violence of working-class life, the middle-class imagination turned images of industrial suffering into affirmative, conservative cultural representations. Clennam turns poverty into just such a comfortable package for social consumption, much like the members of the liberal "intelligentsia" Benjamin describes. His gaze retains the culturally symbolic force of the city stroller or *flaneur*, whose fetishized visions seek to cover over the disturbing power of contradictory social facts. Like Dickens, who walked the streets of London and Paris at night, Benjamin's *flaneur* sought a signifying bridge between middle-class life and the urban poor that would symbolically unify the divided culture of modern life.

But if middle-class readers of the city such as Clennam turned the city into a kind of fictional product, the resulting images, Benjamin insisted, were critically complex. "The gaze of the allegorist that falls on the city," as Benjamin notes, "is estranged."[51] The "dialectical images" he described were dialectically double: while creating the ahistorical myths of commodity culture, turning the hellish suffering of Little Dorrit into a kind of delight, the dialectical image could also deconstruct itself. Marketable fantasies of compensation for social misery such as Clennam's reveries, were marked like the dialectical image by the social history they sought to escape. The literary image could be conservative and at the same time critical, an example of "the law of dialectics seen at a standstill," embodying the flight of commodity culture from the historical and bringing its social detail to light.[52]

Clennam's fantasies of Little Dorrit illustrate this contradictory mode of commodified social vision. Fetish colors her distasteful urban history for marketable consumption: "he had come to attach to Little Dorrit an interest so peculiar—an interest that removed her from, while it grew out of, the common and coarse things surrounding her" (252). Yet Dickens' phrasing is precise: Little Dorrit's virtue is exaggerated until she is "removed from," but also clearly part of, the "peculiar" impulse of the fetishizing gaze. This imaginative investment blots out working-class culture, leaving Clennam pained by the realistic and class-bound ambitions of John the gatekeeper's son: "he found it disappointing, disagreeable, almost painful, to suppose her in love with young Mr. Chivery in the back yard, or any such person" (252). Clennam prefers to avoid such realities of class, and family guilt and hatred of commerce forge an investment in iconic domesticity. Alexander Welsh describes idealized family bonds as "the only relations in Victorian society that were not commercial," and it is precisely such domestic myth that adult sexuality can break.[53] The cultural signifier for that myth is Little Dorrit herself, whose "unselfish interest, gratitude and pity" erase the implications of her sexual abuse: "he regarded her, in that perspective, as his adopted daughter, his poor child of the Marshalsea hushed to rest" (183–84).

Such descriptions serve the function that Benjamin found in the dialectical image: fetishized visions identify their own escape from the culture of the marketplace, and point out the very urban history they evade. Dickens invests in the "hushed," fetishized childhood of his heroine in a similar fashion. The ideal "child" she represents always points to a woman's knowledge, a contradiction that becomes explicit when her virtue is most pronounced, as when Little Dorrit, missing prison lockup, is forced to sleep on the streets. The scene is both realistic and metafictional, as Dickens adverts to a kind of popular fiction that proper Victorian taste rejects: her pillow, as she sleeps in her church refuge, is a "Burial volume," given her by a " 'sexton, or the beadle, or the verger, or whatever he was' " (170). Janice Carlisle has noted the allusion to the economics of Victorian publishing: coming in "three volumes" as part of the church register, the book allows Dickens to allude to "the actual novel that the reader is holding," as well as to the form of publication"—the Victorian three-decker format—"that was the major rival of Dickens's twenty-number serials." [54] Little Dorrit lays her head on a "volume" symbolizing the conditions governing the production of Dickens's narrative, namely the moralism constraining any Victorian novelist who wished to write for the mass. The "volume" is a subtle allusion by Dickens to censorship, though the image insists that the cultural constraints of the "church" in which he publishes can be avoided with a careful hand.

The "beadle" who offers the "volume" certainly represents a narrative, and popular story, that polices a character's thoughts. But a "verger" points to a kind of discourse that "verges" on the truth without saying it, and hence avoids narrative policing or restraint. "All must die" is the safely universal wisdom passed on in the speech of the "beadle," as he describes the "burial volume" of the church, on which Little Dorrit lays her head. Yet his words also allude to the Victorian cultural politics that governed reading and writing about sex. "Buried" in Dickens' fiction is not the merely conventional wisdom the beadle passes on to Little Dorrit, a woman sleeping with Maggy, her companion, outside of the family's confines. The reference is also metafictional, and refers to a narrative restricted to ellipsis and implication when describing family violence and sex. "What makes these books interesting to most people," the Beadle tells Little Dorrit, "is —not who's in 'em, but who isn't—who's coming, you know, and when" (171). Little Dorrit's Princess Story is similar to this burial volume, contiguous with her dreams. The tale—in which a "tiny woman" who lives alone dies, along with the shadow of a secret—is similarly dying to show its audience *who isn't* there.

The Princess Story makes these shadows of sexual abuse a visible and forceful part of Dickens' novel. Little Dorrit's references to the "shadow" of the "tiny woman" carefully allude to the "life of degradation" (224) she has suffered with her father while living behind the prison walls. Care in broaching such a subject, of course, would be required in a Victorian setting. Yet the story is told to Maggy, whose mental debility produces its own breaches in censorship. Early in the novel, Maggy acts out for Arthur Clennam the abuse with "broomhandles and pokers" she suffered as a child (96–99). Little Dorrit herself encourages Maggy to tell Arthur Clennam her story: "Maggy shook her head, made a drinking vessel of her clenched left hand, drank out of it, and said, 'Gin.' Then beat an imaginary child." If the details of Maggy's account are doubtful, Little Dorrit's willingness to have her tell the history of childhood poverty is not. Both are small women, faced with a social taboo on discussing family violence, and for each, the stories of childhood provide a kind of emotional release: "'and that,' said Little Dorrit, clapping the two great hands together again, 'is Maggy's history, as Maggy knows!'" (99).

Despite this desire for narrative, it would be hard to expect anything more than silence about sexual abuse in Little Dorrit's "Princess Story," the coded "history" of a "tiny woman" like herself. Critics have emphasized this indirection, preferring to read the "shadow" hidden in silence by the tiny woman as romantic love. Establishing the bounds of the middle-class reading, Barbara Hardy sees the "shadow" as Little Dorrit's unfulfillable desire for Arthur Clennam, the secret that is "revealed but not revealed" in the tale.[55] The social and sexual situation that makes secrecy *necessary*, however, is too easily avoided, though it remains the silent center of the story's mode of address. Attempts to make its "shadow . . . bright to look at" bear more than a hint of Little Dorrit's constant efforts to exalt her father's virtue, while he is treating her, to quote Mrs. Chivery once again, as a domestic "slave." The tiny woman's isolated "cottage" evokes the Marshalsea prison, and her "shadow" a family secret: the censored domestic scene of the impoverished family, where "common and coarse things" occur.

In this coded evocation of domestic violence, the Princess Story challenges the patriarchal limits of popular Victorian fiction. Little Dorrit's "stunted deference to her father," as Garrett Stewart describes the restrictive secrecy informing the scene, shapes images that circumvent society's demand that the secret of sexual abuse be kept.[56] The shadow isolates the tiny woman, and stands for both Clennam and Little Dorrit's father, whose dominating presence rules out any hope of marriage. Clennam himself understands that Mr. Dorrit's "death" would be the "only change of circumstance . . . that might enable him to be such a friend to her as he wished to be" (183–84). Interrogated by a "Princess," the tiny woman explains why she cannot marry: the "shadow" graphically expresses shame, evoking the "mortal wound" of an abuse that Clennam can imagine in only the most idealistic terms. Fervent secrecy, to be sure, transforms the constant suffering imagined in the story into the "great treasure" of feminine devotion. Yet Little Dorrit's narrative puts out the false "light" his sympathetic vision creates. "Love" instead is depicted as a shadowed wound, and a life of constant service expiates its guilt. Social objectification and shame go together for the tiny woman, as the Princess observes: "And you keep watch over this, every day?" (285).

The "Princess" as interlocutor, of course, allows Little Dorrit to address her narrative to a world of middle-class readers. Overt suggestion of sexual trauma as the hidden secret of the story therefore remains hushed. Through its tone of audience address, the "Princess" of the fairy tale comes to resemble Flora, Little Dorrit's middle-class friend and patron: both figures remain social superiors who observe the mannered withdrawal of a working woman in "polite" society, only to comprehend part of the mortifying secret she bears. In sustaining the Victorian cultural taboo that forbids the discussion of sex in popular fiction, both Flora and the Princess take advantage of the intimacy between women, and use gender to cross the class divide. For the bond between the "Princess" and the "tiny woman" is forged between a child who "understood all her lessons before her masters taught them to her" and an equally proper yet sensitive woman, who shares her secretive "shadow" without embarrassing words (284).

Stigma and social exposure are thereby avoided: the "tiny woman" finally perishes anonymously, but not before her sharing of her "shadow" has become the story's central event. In her receptivity, the "Princess" once again resembles Flora, whose boldness, from indecorous prolixity to the hostility she bears toward Arthur Clennam, her one-time fiancé, makes her aware of truths that must be silenced as well as what needs to be shared. Retaining some of the "mortal hostility" (263) and critical attitude toward men of Mr. F.'s Aunt,[57] Flora herself speaks critically, lambasting her arranged marriage as well as her former husband in coded terms. Little wonder, then, that Little Dorrit confides in a "Princess": though living in a "Palace," she "had the power of knowing secrets," particularly those between women, and knows of the tiny woman's shameful "shadow," seeing its signs in her excessive humility without even having to ask.

This "class formation of woman in representation," as Juliet Swindells describes it, marks a Dickensian sense of audience.[58] Unlike Maggy, who speaks of her abuse directly to Arthur Clennam, Little Dorrit, strives to keep silent about the story of her domestic abuse, a sign of her social ambition that is rewarded at the novel's end. Feminine humility in Dickens differs from its male variants in this regard: class difference between men in Dickens may turn on suppressed homo-eroticism, as Eve Kosofsky Sedgwick has suggested.[59] The relations between women of "inferior" standing and men of social authority are always erotically charged, placing a special weight on female friendship. Commonly the bond shatters, as in Gaskell's *Mary Barton*, where Aunt Esther's fall into prostitution preaches aversion to sexual relations with the factory owner's son. The price of Esther's self-assertion, however, is narrative expulsion, and the attempts of women to share sexual knowledge in Victorian fiction are often equally complex. The Princess Story is Little Dorrit's attempt to sustain feminine "humility," while finding expression for the sexual and social dilemmas of a woman's inner life.

Victorian sanctions against the explicit representation of sexuality in fiction are therefore left intact. More crucial for what it suggests than for what it pronounces explicitly, the following passage and its intimate confession leave Little Dorrit's popular reputation unstained. Sexual violation is evoked as the unspeakable shadow on its heroine's devotion, forgotten except in the memory of one "gone away" but painfully present in a continuous stigma and shame that cancel the hope of married life. "Trembling head to foot lest anyone should suspect her," the tiny woman treats the shadow less like the "love she bears Arthur Clennam" than like the hidden violation that prevents it. Rape itself, or even incest, need not have occurred for its effects to be textually similar: the "degradation" Mr. Dorrit "bestow[ed]" as a "portion" on Little Dorrit, whether emotional or also physical, is spoken of openly in the text (224). Though the precise content of the "shadow" on Little Dorrit remains dark, her need to share its effects on her intimate life attains the light of narrative day. The "tiny woman" withholds the secret of the "shadow" she hides in her "very secret place"—but only so that, in a moment of supreme paradox, she can give that secret away:

The Princess was such a wonderful Princess that she had the power of knowing secrets, and she said to the tiny woman, Why do you keep it there? This showed her directly that the Princess knew why she lived all alone by herself, spinning at her wheel, and she kneeled down to the Princess, and asked her never to betray her. So, the Princess said, I never will betray you. Let me see it. So, the tiny woman closed the shutter of the cottage window and fastened the door, and, trembling from head to foot for fear that any one should suspect her, opened a very secret place, and showed the Princess a shadow. (285)

This passage represents an important moment in Dickens' popular social fiction. The window and "fastened door" promise none of the confessional redemption and punishment offered Dickens' more forthright carriers of sexual and social shame. Esther Summerson's illness, scarring her with facial marks of her illegitimate origin, would be more typical of Dickens' mode of representing the internal power of middle-class cultural codes. As Rosemarie Bodenheimer points out, the outward signs of sexual impropriety in Dickens always require a form of fictional expiation.[60] In this regard the Princess Story offers Little Dorrit a pardon from the strictures of middle-class morality his popular fiction otherwise imposed. The indefinition of her "very secret place" remains proper, while communicating the emotional state of bodily violation in all but name. Still, the censorious vision of Marseilles has given way. Maggy connects the "gaze" exchanged between the tiny woman and the Princess—"trying to stare each other out," she remarks—with the urgent, blinding "stare" of the novel's first page, where a painful, burning truth confronts a middle class that prefers not to see.

New in the Princess Story for Dickens was a means of identifying with the internalized pain of the working class—somatically evident in the tiny woman's "trembling from head to foot" as her shadow appears—without compelling the punishing external revelation that sexual frankness in Victorian fiction required. Told without the social implications of complete telling, the actions of Mr. Dorrit remain unspoken. The misery subtending the tiny woman's devotion is shared, while the "domestic story" that produced it remains, as Dickens' first title for *Little Dorrit* so precisely put it, "Nobody's Fault."[61] Emotional veracity coexists with the less than frank account of sexuality the marketplace for fiction required. The "great, great treasure" of the shadow suggests an origin dark enough that only death will conceal its terror, and the tiny woman takes its secret "quietly into her own grave."

For the critical reader, however, censorship has been broken. Feminine servility and a sense of Little Dorrit's abuse are joined in a "dialectical image," at once ideological and a source of cultural critique. The predominance of women in nineteenth-century culture, Benjamin suggests, results from this doubled culture of the market. Women provided the dream vision of a world beyond the cash nexus and a recognition of commercial exploitation as well. That tension was materialized in the prostitute, who represented a "dream image" beyond exploitation and was at the same time forced into becoming the oppressed "saleswoman" of its "wares."[62] For Benjamin, the prostitute made apparent the contradictory status of pleasure in commodity culture: images of women as utopian escape promise freedom from the marketplace, but also represent the dominating power of a commercial culture that turns the feminine into salable objects of display.[63]

Little Dorrit's meeting with a prostitute creates a similarly dialectical picture, when the latter, "from among a knot of brawling or prowling figures," mistakes Little Dorrit for a child. Confronted with an image of the exploited woman, Little Dorrit immediately takes refuge in the "family fiction," telling the prostitute about her "very dear" father at home. The encounter embodies the tension between the ideal and the exploited woman, juxtaposing the heroine's claim to popular virtue and the figure of a woman as a victim of social exploitation. Psychologically, the prostitute confronts Little Dorrit with the image of what the exposure of a woman's sexual violation means in Victorian society. Dickens reminds his audience of the contrast between Little Dorrit and the fallen woman, but Little Dorrit confesses that innocent posture to be a lie. "Let me speak to you," she tells the prostitute, "as if I really was a child" (170).

The role of subservience, however, survives to become an instrument of narrative aggression against the "lustre" Mr. Dorrit is able to hold. Paternal authority in *Little Dorrit* is subject to an unusual amount of challenge, given the paternalism of most Victorian fiction. The narrator's designation for Mr. Dorrit, the "Father of the Marshalsea," links him with the prison, so that subservience already relates his daughter to a symbol of restrictive social norms. In Bleeding Heart Yard, the working-class neighborhood, the narrator points out paternal authority as a useful economic fiction, a means to claim nonmarket relations and thereby exploit financially conservative cultural beliefs. "The Last of the Patriarchs," Christopher Casby, takes advantage of the "family sentimental feeling" of paternal reverence as a cover for extorting rent: "nobody could suppose the property screwed or jobbed under such a man [and] for similar reasons he now got more money out of his own wretched lettings, unquestioned, than anyone with a less knobby and less shining crown could possibly have done" (142). Patriarchy is revealed as an empty signifier, belied by the "last of the Patriarchs" and his rapacious greed: "Christopher Casby was a mere Inn signpost without any Inn . . . there was no place to put up at, and nothing whatever to be thankful for" (141–42). Submission to his authority bears the traces of sacrifice, whose dialectical force Adorno explained: reverence for the father in Dickens' novel also becomes a way of escaping his determining cultural power.[64]

Dickens' own running title to the 1868 edition, "She Habitually Hurts Her Father," emphasizes this oppositional effect of self-sacrifice. Blessed with sudden riches and freed from the Marshalsea, Mr. Dorrit becomes excessively guilty in the presence of his daughter, who sustains a servile devotion reminiscent of prison life. To the extent that Little Dorrit in fact can "hurt her father," as the running title suggests, the memories of prison life that disturb Mr. Dorrit to the point of distraction may recall aspects of domestic history which Dickens, unlike "The Father of the Marshalsea," may not have wished to suppress.[65] While Little Dorrit maintains a reverence toward her father "without blame to bestow upon him," he on the contrary sees his daughter as the member of the family who can "systematically reproduce what the rest of us blot out," though the specific anxiety she stirs is never brought to speech (465). A realistic substratum to his paranoia, however, is suggested when the narrator looks beneath the ethereal appearance of Little Dorrit that Arthur Clennam prefers, and questions the character of paternal love. At her father's deathbed, popular sentimentality comes into tension with critical realism, as both her devotion and the domestic pressure of submitting to her father's demands are recalled in a striking scene:

Thus for ten days Little Dorrit bent over his pillow, laying her cheek against his. Sometimes she was so worn out that for a few minutes they would slumber together. Then she would awake; to recollect with fast-flowing silent tears what it was that touched her face . . .

What "touched" Little Dorrit is bathed in sentimental tears, but in recalling the "slumber" that daughter and father shared in prison, it also represents—in an "awake" and "silent" way—a recollection of being touched. In the eyes of the narrator, Little Dorrit retains the trait of self-sacrifice that appealed to Clennam—"[she] would have laid down her own life to save his"—while the scene at the same time recalls the "shadow" (630–31) of abuse that has already been traced: "No, he loved her in his old way."

The burden of an unspeakable family history, however, does not belong to Little Dorrit alone. Frederick, her uncle, is also present: represented as a down-and-out clarinet player familiar with the music halls, he is given the "intentions of personality" in the name "Dirty

Dick" by children who scrawl the name on the walls of his garret, and lives in a house with an "unwholesome smell" (89). Frederick Dorrit is thus representative of working-class entertainment and its culture. Presented as a figure who retains his respect for popular morality, Frederick stands for the realistic environment of working-class culture when Arthur Clennam asks him for information on Little Dorrit's way of life. Fanny, her sister who works as an actress, is glimpsed as she prepares for a performance, appearing in his back room in "loose stocking and flannel" as a "young lady . . . in an undress" (89).[66] Working-class entertainment in Dickens retained its paternalistic moralism, as Joe Gargery's reaction to the raucous production of Hamlet in *Great Expectations* attests. But Frederick Dorrit's deathbed vision of "The Father of the Marshalsea" suggests an experienced vision of the misery of domestic life. With Little Dorrit present, Frederick matches her praise of the departed Victorian father—"so far superior, so distinguished, so noble" (631)—while recalling family scenes that make Little Dorrit wince: "O God, All that I have looked upon, with my half-blind and sinful eyes."

"Sin" appears in *Little Dorrit* whenever popular sentimentality is broken through, and the narrative looks through the only "half-closed lattice blinds" (632) of propriety it constructs. The demonic presence in Dickens often scourges precisely those aspects of censored social reality it thereby brings to narrative light: Dickensian moralism in this way illuminates through its use of obstructing fictional conventions. This critical duplicity of popular fiction extends to the sinful characters of the novel as well as to the archetypally virtuous: Mrs. Clennam, the novel's chief demon, is paradoxically also Little Dorrit's most committed female patron, and supports her for reasons that transcend her objectification as the evil spirit of coercion behind the plot. Charged with being the "most opinionated and obstinate of women" (759) by Rigaud, the melodramatic villain who treats the Clennam family history as a "commodity on sale" (728), Mrs. Clennam is in fact the most important countervoice Dickens supplies against the normative version of his novel, the version that certainly sells. If, as Adorno remarked, "all reification is a forgetting," Mrs. Clennam's is the perspective in the novel that looks most carefully beneath the objectified account of history produced at the end of the novel.[67] "I do NOT forget, though I do not read it as he did," she declares as the story of Arthur's family history concludes (756). The distance Dickens established from his own conservatism is apparent in Mrs. Clennam's account, as well as in the perspectives she allows Dickens to present on Victorian ideologies of the home.

Radical Reversals: Politics and the Victorian Home

"China" and Arthur Clennam's imperial "business purposes" there are largely absent from "Family Affairs," the chapter in which the plotted suspense of *Little Dorrit* begins (46–47). Dickens does not specify the nature of the commercial "consignments" the Clennam concern "completed," but British commercial involvement with China in the nineteenth century consisted largely of the forcible importation of opium from the imperial province of Bengal. This practice of "Victorian narco-terrorism," as Suvendrini Perera has called it, made contradictory demands on Victorian public discourse, as it did on Dickens' last and unfinished work, *The Mystery of Edwin Drood*.[68] *Little Dorrit* reflects those contradictory demands in its antibureaucratic discourse. Arthur Clennam's tirade against "Circumlocution" is marked by the antigovernment mood of liberals following the Crimean War: metafictionally, it reflects the social need for fictional distortion that Dickens acutely understood. Though Lord Palmerston culminated a period of public debate over the Opium Wars by subjecting Canton to bombardment in 1857, as *Little Dorrit*'s serial publication came to an end, Dickens' narrator takes care never to identify Clennam's reformist concern with British imperialism and its power.[69] Popular fiction required consumable figures for the public's antigovernment sentiment, but in Dickens also provoked critical awareness of the displacements that feminized signs of imperialism produced. Clennam turns his anger at what he calls "machinery" against his mother, never directing it forcefully at the "Barnacles" of the political establishment, a transfer that Dickens' plans for the novel already mark. "Tell the whole story," Dickens wrote in his "Working Notes" for the conclusion of the novel, "working it out as much as possible through Mrs. Clennam herself, so as to present her character strongly."[70]

This condemnation of Mrs. Clennam, to be sure, appealed to conservative taste. The novel's conclusion pulls off the trick of proving that she is not Arthur's biological mother, revealing instead that he was scandalously born of the "little beauty," out of wedlock, before the arranged marriage of his father and Mrs. Clennam could take place. Ideologically, the trick is to have it both ways as far as the family is concerned. The gloom of the Clennam "Family Affairs" takes on all the weight of an imperious empire, while at the end Arthur can be dissociated from any trace of the family's cultural and political taint. Mrs. Clennam's repressive and rebellious "ascendancy" appears to Arthur as the "cause of his [father's] going to China" (46–47), rather than the economic interests behind the Opium Wars, or the actual sexual history of Arthur's birth, which plausibly might have made China a safer haven.

Critics, however, most often accept Mrs. Clennam's condemnation in the novel, taking her demonization at face value as if this were all mass culture had to offer. Dickens's portrayal, while remaining popular, is more complex. For the Clennam family's affairs are far from cut-and-dried: the reading argued at the end of this chapter shows that Arthur's father may well have physically harmed or sexually abused the "little beauty," Arthur's mother, in a Victorian cultural situation that held the woman to blame in most sexual concerns. In one of the most powerful if underread speeches by a woman in all of Dickens' fiction, Mrs. Clennam argues against the grain of her popular representation, claiming that men, not women, are responsible for the family's economic and domestic crimes. A powerful woman, to be sure, who rises from her paralysis at the end of the novel, Mrs. Clennam speaks for the critical complexity Dickens' fiction could attain. "Mr. Popular Sentiment," as Trollope called Dickens, also produced novels that read the suppressed cultural history contained in consumable social tropes.[71]

Victorian fiction, moreover, marketed novels by powerful women in just these cultural terms. Advertising in Dickens' serially published format demonstrates the complexity involved, especially where the presentation of strong female figures was concerned. Advertisements for "Literature" in the numbers of *Dombey and Son* (1846–48), for instance, included this promotional for the work of George Sand:

In presenting a translation of George Sand's works to the English Public, it is the desire of the Translator to afford an opportunity for readers of all classes to judge for themselves, whether the productions of the greatest female genius of the day are deserving that condemnation which it is so much the fashion to attach to them, or whether the time has not come, when an unmerited stigma, having its rise in ignorance, should find no place in an enlightened nation.[72]

The explicit reference to "readers of all classes" is a reminder of the unified reading public a Victorian author might idealize, yet not in reality be able to address. "Female Genius" and its "stigma" refer to gender, but also represent signs of political differences along which a liberal audience might split.[73] While the ideally "enlightened nation" might accept powerful women and their intelligence, the demands of the marketplace force recognition of the "unmerited stigma" feminine intelligence acquires when represented as an object for sale. Targeting audiences, and hoping for a unified readership, the ad for George Sand both evokes and denies the possibility of a unified reception, and marks the doubleness in popular attitudes toward women who, like Mrs. Clennam, possessed "the strongest head, and the greatest talent" (760). Marketing the socially unacceptable woman creates a paradoxical effect: the word *stigma* both makes the "genius" of women palatable to an "enlightened" but conservative public, and reminds readers of the critical voice that demonized images of women seek to contain.

Like forms of audience in narrative fiction, the advertisement for Sand both appeases and provokes its audience, as does the similarly provocative use of "Home" in *Little Dorrit*. The use of stigmatized stereotypes of women led Dickens to a critical reading of their cultural roles. Clennam's liberalism, for instance, is defined by his rejection of the puritan strictures of his childhood as well as by his sympathy for Little Dorrit's poverty. Yet such sympathy becomes forceful through mass-cultural stereotypes, visceral and imaginative figures of woman as demon with which readers can easily cathect. Liberal concern for the poor and Clennam's antipathy for a do-nothing government work together in a psychic economy in which Mother, as the center of society's vindictive "machinery," can be held to blame. Mrs. Clennam's demonization by her servant Flintwinch at the conclusion as the "female Lucifer" (760) takes hold only because, as Elaine Showalter has pointed out, the cultural ground that reads powerful women as "emasculatory" has already been prepared.[74]

Adorno and Horkheimer analyzed this trope of mass culture in their critique of the *Los Angeles Times* astrology column, pointing out that the elevation of women to decisive roles in popular culture increases in proportion to their actual social dependence.[75] The more subject women remain socially, the more stigmatized women's social assertiveness remains, and for Dickens, the point was already valid: his treatment of demonized female power in *Little Dorrit* provides more than an anticipation of the critically self-conscious mass culture that Adorno and Horkheimer only sketched. The language representing Mrs. Clennam as powerful devil also analyzes feminine demonization as a mass-cultural trope. "No human eyes have ever seen more daring, gross and shocking images of the Divine nature," Dickens tells his audience, "than we creatures of the dust make in our own like-nesses, of our own bad passions" (754). "Shocking images" of "HOME" (26) in *Little Dorrit* are presented with an awareness that they are social symbols, and thus retain their culturally critical force.

Dickens uses the gothic, for instance, to criticize middle-class life under the sign of distortion, much as H. G. Wells's science fiction brought Western imperialism home by figuring fantastic invasions from beyond. The "wrong in the gloomy house" (182) creates gothic symbols for Clennam's critique of British capitalism, yet those images are, as the villainous Rigaud points out, a "commodity on sale" (728). Gothic distortion provides a mask for critical cultural history: Arthur's obsessive condemnations of his mother bring domesticity into the realm of commerce, precisely where the commodity novel placed it, against the grain of Victorian piety. "Even this old house in which we speak," Arthur tells his mother, "is an instance of what I say. In my father's earlier time, and in his uncle's time before him, it was a place of business—really a place of business and a business resort" (44–45). Demonic description of the fallen home defines its evil as a social con-struction, artificially sustained from without. The maternal House, it turns out, in its obsession with "business" both figures the decay of British society in the age of the market and serves as a fictional symbol that itself needs constant support: "Many years ago, it had had it in its mind to slide down sideways; it had been propped up, however, and was leaning on some half dozen gigantic crutches" (32).

Little Dorrit's popular descriptions of women, both gothic and melo-dramatic, are in this way far less imprisoned than they seem. Self-subjection remains the topic of many scenes in which the hold of its logic is broken. The "inner and permanent" states of mind that J. Hillis Miller discovered in the novel turn out to be relative rather than uni-versal, figures which are themselves subjected to critique within its Victorian cultural confines.[76] One cannot be sure, for instance, what violence, if any, has been done to Mrs. Clennam from the narrator's description that seeks to shroud her history as a woman in suspicion: "What scenes and actors the stern woman most reviewed, as she sat from season to season in her one dark room, none knew but herself" (333). The exploitive hatred of her servant, Jeremiah Flintwinch, of course, never reaches the inner history of such a "stern woman." To Little Dorrit, however, Mrs. Clennam is not only a woman who shares tenderness, but is a possible interlocutor, who might be able to share the intimate secrets of family life in the subtlest tones: "Mrs. Clennam put out her hand, and laid it on her arm. Little Dorrit, confused under the touch, stood faltering. Perhaps some momentary recollection of the story of the Princess may have been in her mind" (335).

The inference drawn by the narrator is striking: Mrs. Clennam is linked in Little Dorrit's consciousness with the "Princess," the woman who shared the secret of her most "secret place" (285). Mrs. Clennam's demonic stature, moreover, in no way frustrates this possibility. The prefiguring relationship in Dickens' fiction is the bond established between Edith Dombey and Florence, her stepdaughter in *Dombey and Son*. Narrative vilification of Edith's strength and familiarity with the marketplace coincides with a convincing portrayal of her motherly support for Florence, as both attempt to live under Mr. Dombey's authoritarian rule. Unacceptable social subtexts, moreover, were implied by such portrayals. As Steven Marcus points out, Major Bagstock, Edith Dombey, and other characters central to *Dombey and Son* bear strong resemblances to figures represented in later Victorian pornography.[77] If sexual and class relations were unrepresentable in proper terms for the fictional market, as Marcus shows, authors "found less direct means of communicating the sexual components of the situations they described." The coded social terms of Dickens' text are a powerful means of suggesting that Little Dorrit and Mrs. Clennam share intimate knowledge, and even an unspeakable feminine history: in the Dickensian variant of the popular novel, critical history and the production of cultural stereotype often go hand in hand.[78]

This potential for feminine friendship within the commodity novel, moreover, defines intimate communication as a form of resistance to patriarchal culture. Dickens' narrator distinguishes Mrs. Clennam's radical appearance to Little Dorrit as the Princess, her intimate female interlocutor, from the attitude of Jeremiah Flintwinch toward feminine history. Readers of the gothic who delight in implied violence take a superficial pleasure in the inimitably Dickensian descriptions of Flintwinch, and their linguistic play. "Screwed," as the participle of his interpretive desire, represents both his willed desire to penetrate female secrecy and the tastelessly framed ambition of a servant to rise above his class: "Mr. Flintwinch, with his wry presence . . . would perhaps have screwed it out of her, if there had been less resistance in her; but she was too strong for him" (333). Violence in Dickens, however, is rarely superficial. This "resistance" to male desire makes the point that Mrs. Clennam's story is subject to the interpretation and exploitation of men, for whom "screwed" is a term for improper narrative commerce rather than for sex. In Flintwinch Dickens defines

the figure against whom "resistance" is directed by Mrs. Clennam: the
male voice who would put the complex and conflicted social history
of Victorian women up for simplified and exploitive sale.

Lurid sexual language in *Little Dorrit*'s melodramatic scenes similarly turns popular discourse to critical social effect. Dickens presents
Affery, a maid, as suffering dutifully under a husband whose "natural acerbity and energy, always contending with a second nature of
habitual repression, gave his features a swollen and suffused look"
(37). The passage bears similarity to Victorian pornography of a later
period, a genre not foreign to Dickens' literary circle. G. A. Sala, a
writer Dickens discovered as editor of *Household Words* and appeared
with in amateur theatricals, was a contributor to late-Victorian flagel-
lant literature. As an associate of Swinburne and the Rossettis in the
1860s, Sala moved with a sexually and literarily liberated set.[79] Contemporary pornography, moreover, glossed Dickens. *Rosa Fielding, or:
A Victim of Lust,* published in 1867, turned Mr. Trabb's store in *Great
Expectations* into a hosier's and glover's shop in London where pornographic adventures begin.[80] *Little Dorrit* retains this same false front of
commercial decency. Yet in the portrayal of characters such as Flintwinch, Dickens makes use of allusively sexual language to criticize
the logic of domination that the middle-class novel and pornography
can share. His narrator cannot describe sexual abuse directly, and the
censorship required of popular fiction is duly registered when Affery
resists the clearly sexual violence of her spouse: "Mr. Flintwinch laid
his commands on her that she should hold her peace on the subject of
their conjugal relations" (334). But since "energy" in Dickens' novel,
to borrow from his description of Flintwinch, is always contending
with a popular surface of "repression," resistance on the part of its
victims always confronts the Dickensian reader with what has been
only partially obliterated from his text.

Affery's "Dreams," foregrounded in chapters such as "Mrs. Flintwinch has a Dream" and "Mrs. Flintwinch Goes on Dreaming," take
on precisely this critical dimension. Earlier chapters leave the reader
uncertain as to whether these "dreams" are to be regarded as contributions to the realistic action, or as the gothic fantasies of a servant,
whose imagination has run wild in the unhappy Clennam home. In
retrospect, however, the division between fantasy and realism for the
Victorian novel appears to be a matter more of cultural politics than
of objectivity, especially where women and their "conjugal" rights are
concerned. For thoughout *Little Dorrit*, it is Flintwinch who insists that
his wife's "dreams" of abuse be treated as fantasy, a distinction that

is given force by his physical threats. In fact, the evidence is strong in *Little Dorrit* that "dream" is the acceptable social sign for repression of marital violence: Affery is not dreaming, the conclusion shows, but suffering at her husband's hand as he struggles to acquire the "commodity" history of Mrs. Clennam's family life.

For the prospect of wife beating arises whenever Affery insists on the realism of her nightmarish domestic life. Under the insistent pressure exerted by her husband, however, Affery's "dream" finally becomes a liberated vision of domestic abuse that is shared. Late in the novel, Affery herself declares that the terror represented in her mysterious visions and Mrs. Clennam's hysterical paralysis have the same antifeminine force. Neither woman is permitted to talk about the "punishment" (340) inflicted by men upon women, yet Affery's speech defines the conditions of popular representation as a "dream" of social repression, enforced by men over women to silence the damage done. While no unmediated access to the wife's agony is possible in this mass-cultural image of marriage, "explosion" is the term Dickens' narrator uses to describe Affery's revelation of what occurred when Jeremiah "hitched my apron off my head":

"Keep off, Jeremiah! . . . You know the dream as well as I do. When you come down-stairs into the kitchen with the candle in your hand, and hitched my apron off my head. When you told me I had been dreaming. When you wouldn't believe the noises." After this explosion, Affery put her apron in her mouth again; always keeping her hand on the window-sill, and her knee on the window-seat, ready to cry out or jump out, if her lord and master approached. (751–52)

Far from pornographic, the scene evokes domestic acts which, while unspoken, make Affery appear the victim of domestic violence or worse. Fearful of her husband's approach, she remains terrified of noises whose import her auditors "wouldn't believe," were she, or Dickens' narrator, to give them fuller narrative force. The self-censorship enacted by placing her apron in her mouth may represent a kind of internalized violence, mimicking unspeakable acts of penetration: or perhaps her gestures dramatize to her audience the enforced suppression that makes further details unacceptable in a narrative of domestic life.

Dickens defines the "dream," moreover, as a cultural construct. Far from the royal road to the feminine unconscious, Affery's nightmares are foregrounded in chapter titles so as to appear as a construction of fiction. Gradually, the reader becomes aware that the fictionality signified by the "dream" is itself a construct, and that the events narrated in her visions have actually occurred. Skepticism about interpretation of the feminine unconscious is encouraged, making the feminist critique of Freud more than relevant here. Just as Freud analyzed Dora's dreams and mystified her treatment as a sexual object by her father's friend, so Flintwinch imposes a "dream" that covers what is represented as marital aggressivity and more.

Hence Affery's distant and remarkable relations with Mrs. Clennam, her unusual lady of the house. Both women face the difficulty of breaking through confining female stereotypes, and both confront the limiting paradigms of Victorian femininity that Dickens' novel produced. When Affery observes a gesture of kindness from Mrs. Clennam toward Little Dorrit, Dickens shows that readers can see beneath demonic stereotypes: "in all the dreams Mistress Affery had been piling up since she had first become devoted to the pursuit, she had dreamed nothing more astonishing than this" (336). Breaking with "dreams," described as a popular "pursuit," means perceiving the possibility of feminine solidarity that transcends the distortions of popular ideology.

Popular feminine demonology, of course, secures Mrs. Clennam's guilt, and brands her in the end as the supposed withholder of Little Dorrit's legacy. This received version of the plot deserves recounting, given its complexities. An arranged marriage between Arthur's father and Mrs. Clennam was interrupted when the father fell in love with the "little beauty," who bore Arthur out of wedlock. After being convinced to give up the child by Arthur's guardian uncle, the little beauty was banished, the original wedding was carried out, and Arthur was raised under the delusion that Mrs. Clennam was his biological mother. The uncle, however, was supposedly seized by remorse, and therefore arranged financial recompense for the little beauty. Through a complex set of conditions, the money was meant to have come into Little Dorrit's hands. This version makes Mrs. Clennam the punishing enforcer of Victorian repression, a woman who supposedly placed profit and propriety over passion, suppressing history in order to deprive Little Dorrit of her money and her son of his maternal truth.

Mrs. Clennam's own version of those events will be discussed shortly. Here it is important to note that the language of "dream" and its distortion of sexual and domestic violence is central to the plot. Affery makes the point powerfully in a scene of resistance to her husband who, besides being the author of her "dreams," is also the chief architect of our received reading of the novel's concluding events and the history they recall:

"Keep off, Jeremiah!" cried the palpitating Affery, taking her apron from her mouth again. "But it was one of my dreams that you told her, when you quarrelled with her one winter evening, at dusk—there she sits and you looking at her—that she oughtn't to have let Arthur, when he come home, suspect his father, only; that she had always had the strength and the power; and that she ought to have stood up more, to Arthur, for his father. It was in the same dream where you said to her that she was not—not something; but I don't know what, for she burst out tremendous and stopped you." (751–52)

Affery makes the strong point that her husband's reading is defensive of paternity. The "dream" enforced on Affery elides the fact that Arthur's mother was the "little beauty," but also fosters a construction of events that makes the repression at work in Victorian domesticity a strictly maternal affair. The dream of paternal exculpation requires secrecy; Affery is forbidden to tell the truth about her "conjugal relations," just as Mrs. Clennam has been forbidden to speak about the violence she has undergone: "it was in the same dream where you said to her that she was not—not something; but I don't know what, for she burst out tremendous and stopped you." Later in the same scene, as I will discuss, Mrs. Clennam powerfully resists the systematic denial of paternal agency, and provides a woman's version of the novel's central events. Here, Affery defines the suppression of paternal history Mrs. Clennam sets out to correct. Without saying any Victorian unpronounceables, Affery interprets the "dream" of fictional ending in *Little Dorrit* as ideological to the core: since Mrs. Clennam had the "strength and power"—despite her confinement to her wheelchair— unnamable crimes of the fathers in the novel must not have occurred.

Blaming Mrs. Clennam, moreover, requires a false story of social victimization, a narrative close to melodrama in the popular symbols it deploys. Mrs. Clennam plays the scorned woman turning her vengeance on Arthur's father, who plays the role of the guiltless victim and son. The emphasis on melodrama is created through Rigaud, the stock villain with a "theatrical air" (10), replete with mustache. His depiction highlights the ideological nature of the plot, and allows *Little Dorrit* to present popular theater, which Dickens enjoyed as a performer, as anything but the populist voice of the Victorian "working class."[81] On the contrary: Rigaud represents the ideology of blaming the victim that pervades mass culture, and links such ideology to the middle-class culture of the novel as a whole. What Rigaud calls his "perverted" reading of his crime, in fact, resembles Arthur's initial attack upon his mother, whom he accuses of "grasping after hard bargains throughout the world." Clennam, of course, has just returned from doing the family business in China, and there are connotations of opium dealing in this condemnation of Mrs. Clennam, paralyzed in her wheelchair, as the epitome of capitalist greed. Rigaud's speech of self-exculpation for killing his wife is quite similar, exemplary in the way it uses melodrama to outline the ideology which middle-class fiction effects. Victims are made responsible for the suffering which the desires of the powerful inflict:

Madame Rigaud grew warm; I grew warm, and provoked her. I admit it. Frankness is part of my character. At length, Madame Rigaud, in an access of fury that I must ever deplore, threw herself upon me with screams of passion (no doubt those that were overheard at some distance), tore my clothes, tore my hair, lacerated my hands, trampled and trod the dust, and finally leaped over, dashing herself to death upon the rocks below. (12)

A jeremiad against the victim frees the criminal of blame, attributing agency to the female victim of crime: the wife is represented as "desiring" her own death and violation in a fit of "passion," as if the author of her own demise. Rigaud's exculpatory account represents the woman as responsible for an act of violence and penetration that "lacerated" a helpless man's hands and clothes. Rigaud wants to claim that this "train of incidents" was "perverted into my endeavouring to force from Madame Rigaud a relinquishment of her right," but the perversion, or literal overturning, of this scene is that the violence of oppressor against victim has been upended to place its "desiring" subject on top.[82]

This transformation of exculpation into an indictment of its ideology occurs in the story of Affery as well. Jeremiah Flintwinch proposed marriage, in Affery's retelling, by asking her about his name, and her desire to take it, but in a way that produces a resistant and critical effect. " 'Affery,' he said, 'now I am going to tell you something. What do you think of the name Flintwinch?' " (39). The name's components—"Flint" and "winch"—signify more than a suspicious apparatus, and a message that works against Jeremiah's wish to "tell" Affery, in the guise of a question, what she desires. "Flint" signifies fire, of course, but more precisely the desire to make it, as do Rigaud and his victim, where it clearly does not exist, in the breast of a woman who hardly loves what she gets. Affery offers her own commentary on her suitor's attempt to impress her with a desire for subjection, in the way she pronounces her future husband's Christian name. " 'What do I think of it?' I says. 'Yes,' he said, 'because you're going to take it,' he said. 'Take it?' I says. 'Jere*mi*-ah?' " (39; Dickens' emphasis) My "ah"— the false attribution of desire to the victim in Jeremiah's dream—is precisely what creates an excuse for the "violence" he later inflicts. When it is the victim's "passions" that make her "take it," then she can indeed be "Jere[d]" at, not as the victim, but as the "perverted" perpetrator of the crime.

Perversion in *Little Dorrit* becomes an issue in such dramatic points of action, where the expectations of different reading audiences often conflict. The melodramatic trope of self-subjection often appears as a kind of perverse reaction to middle-class society, whose representatives in the novel extend a liberal bounty of freedom to women and the lower classes. Just as often, however, Dickens represents self-subjection from the lower-class point of view: as a mode of behavior required of the socially inferior but considered distasteful, marginal, or indecent if publicly exposed. The test case for audience reaction in this regard has always been Miss Wade, whose autobiographic chapter "The History of a Self-Tormentor" Dickens considered central to the novel. "In Miss Wade I had an idea, which I thought a new one," Dickens wrote to Forster, "of making the introduced story so fit into surroundings impossible of separation from the main story, as to make the blood of the book circulate through both."[83]

Typically, however, critics have marginalized Miss Wade's account of her life as a governess as a paranoid exercise in self-injury, the suspicions of class arrogance constructed by an orphan tormented by her own social insecurity. Lionel Trilling's liberal account makes the issue of class marginal, and lays its emphasis on Miss Wade's "perversion" of affection instead.[84] The word was chosen with care, and captures the inference often drawn that Miss Wade represents a lesbian woman, living alone and passionately befriending Tattycoram, the Meagleses' rebellious maid. Trilling's compassion for the alienated silences the social force of Miss Wade's story, sexualizing a story of class antagonism, and contemporary readings remain within this containing frame.[85] For Miss Wade's anger is not "perversion," but criticism of a sympathy and patronage that mask the omnipresent Victorian reality of class. Victorian social history, moreover, gives her claims support. Lilian Faderman has shown that female friendships in nineteenth-century culture were varied, differing greatly from the popular stereotype of "perversion" as a lesbian norm.[86] In addition, the social import of female friendship was a hotly debated topic in the periodical and popular literature when Miss Wade's "History" was shaped.[87] Beginning in the 1850s, as Pauline Nestor points out, concern with the "demographic imbalance" in the British population led to discussion of women's occupations, as well as of topics such as "What Shall We Do With Our Old Maids?" It may well be "impossible to read her story without sympathy," as Trilling suggests, but it is also the case that sympathy invokes patronage and cancels the very stigmatization of single women on which Miss Wade's actual torments rest.[88] For Miss Wade, a social skeptic, sympathy is a sign of social hierarchy: beneficence toward the poor idealistically meant bridging the gap between the classes, but ideologically signified social superiority through the beneficent middle-class willingness to "help."

The accuracy of Miss Wade's judgments, moreover, belies any absolute judgment of her paranoia, and Dickens puts her observations to biting effect. By befriending Tattycoram, the adopted daughter of the Meagleses, Miss Wade allows Dickens to link the perspectives of two lower-class women and give objective social ground to the torments they suffer within. Both women reject the pieties of the Dickensian home, and thus play crucial roles in the mass-cultural criticism Dickens' novel performs. Benevolent sympathy stands close to the heart of Dickens' liberal ethos, making his critique of the Meagleses' family charity all the more surprising and critically intense. Tattycoram, an orphan like Miss Wade, has been adopted to be their *daughter* and maid. The combination dissolves class differences in the myth of family and reasserts their constant presence in all the family's domestic concerns. Fiction, moreover, is the sign under which Tattycoram is brought into the Meagles house. Though promised the "Glass Slipper, or Fairy Godmother" (18), of social equality, instead she is left with the perpetual and class-bound drudgery of her work.[89]

The mass-cultural cliché that gives Tattycoram her name is nonetheless critically fractured in the powerful and extended account Dickens provides of the social construction of her identity. The Meagleses insist on renaming the child they adopt: "Harriet," which she is called at the orphanage, is first shattered into "Tatty," then merged with "Coram," Latin for "in the presence of," but also the name of "the originator of the institution for these poor foundlings" (18), as Mr. Meagles points out. The result is a painful and public contradiction: Tattycoram is nominally and audibly always *in the presence of* her lower-class status, sounded in a choice Mr. Meagles later regrets: "if I had thought twice about it, I might never have given her the jingling name" (785). Such attacks on the middle class and its benevolent patronage, in fact, were

Dickens' own assault against pious popular fiction. By 1859, a writer in *Punch* could declare that the public was already "wearied . . . with the incessant repetition of the dreary story of spirit-broken governesses." [90] By making Miss Wade's complaints border on excess, Dickens turns the mass-produced account of working-class frustration and middle-class success on its ear.

Dickens himself had contributed to these "governess novels": the normative good cheer and stifled complaints of Esther Summerson prefigure Miss Wade, whom Dianne Sadoff has aptly described as an "Esther Summerson gone cynical and paranoid." [91] But the formulation is also accurate when reversed. Miss Wade's narrative evokes the same contradictions noticed by the governess of Bleak House— the subtle disparity between her middle-class manners and the class inferiority that mark her birth and her work—but abandons her predecessor's indirection for a more direct attack. In this respect Dickens may well have intended both women narrators to represent parodies of the popular Victorian genre of the "governess novel," with its optimistic ideology of social mobility, achieved through domestic manners and work. "Esther is a master of ironic commentary," as William Axton points out: "she damns with faint praise, employs paraphrase with devastating effect, and claims to be perplexed by those whose conduct she condemns." [92] The "Trouble with Esther," as the title of his essay puts it, is that one can never be sure if her overly happy voice of self-denial can be trusted, saturated as it is with caustic and ironic remarks. Esther's gratitude, like her dream recounted in *Bleak House*, is marked by the feeling of perpetually and unhappily climbing (if not cleaning) the stairs.

In "The History of a Self-Tormentor," the suppressed content of Esther's dream finds a powerful, public voice. Miss Wade's "History" sets itself against the fiction that any social relations, no matter how well-intentioned, could be free of the signs of class. False sympathy and cheer, and the will to spurious social reconciliation, thus become Miss Wade's avowed enemies. "I tried them often," Miss Wade remarks of her middle-class patrons: "I could hardly make them quarrel with me. When I succeeded with any of them, they were sure to come, after an hour or two, and begin a reconciliation" (644). Given the primacy of goodwill and benevolence in the appeal of Dickens' fiction, this set toward exploding the fictions of middle-class amity explains Dickens' assertion of her importance to the novel, since she constitutes a strong part of its challenging voice. Cultural history rethinks the personal bases of paranoid aggression, and the "The History of a

Self Tormentor" becomes just that: an account of the *historical* experience of an English governess that grounds the psychological torments of domestic service in social facts. Ascetic discipline in Miss Wade's character is, as for Kafka, less pathology than a commitment to live without any social illusions, and a social skepticism that renders her unable to cherish the myths of the middle-class home that Dickens himself produced. "I have the misfortune," as she puts it in the first sentence of her narrative, "of not being a fool" (644).

Miss Wade's paranoia, in other words, has objective social grounds. How one reads her narrative, however, points to an ideological division in Dickens' contemporary audience that persists in current critical terms. The "happy" liberal reading must judge Miss Wade's "perversion" of affection to be regrettable, or paranoid, accepting the sympathy for the alienated accorded her as realistic and regrettably spurned. Historically, this was the view Dickens encountered in 1855, formalized in *Blackwood's Magazine*. Judging Dickens an author of "very liberal sentiments," the writer for *Blackwood's* credited his novels, "despite their descents into the lowest class," with voicing the very sensibility Miss Wade always confronts: "it is the air and breath of middle-class respectability which fill the books of Mr. Dickens."[93] It is the conservatism of such reliance on popular verities that Miss Wade's skepticism insistently rejects. Her sarcasm toward benevolence challenges the middle-class bias of Dickensian liberalism, and contributes a crucially self-critical perspective to his own mass-cultural text. Reading Miss Wade's paranoia is thus an ideological problem at best. One must decide whether to discount her indictment of happy middle-class beneficence—"Fair words and fair pretenses; but, I penetrated below those assertions of themselves and depreciations of me" (646)—or see that it is often accurate, and that her "self-torment" is grounded in the British system of class.

Walter Bagehot, the nineteenth-century historian and social critic, captured this dual quality quite well; Dickens, he wrote, was the only "contemporary English novelist whose works are read so generally throughout the house, whose works can give pleasure to the servants as well as the mistress, to the children as well as to the master."[94] In this case, however, the pleasures of the text are divided along lines of gender and class. The painful decision Miss Wade forces a reader to make about her "rack" (645) is whether to believe in the sentimental goodness of such a family, and lament her "perversion" of its "affection"—sometimes accomplished by the lesbian reading—or to see the accuracy of her claim that middle-class virtue consists in fact of "swollen patronage and selfishness, calling themselves kindness, protection, benevolence, and other fine names" (651).

Such ideological contradiction persists in texts, according to Adorno, because the social material of fiction remains double, split by the social material upon which its production depends.[95] For Dickens the popular writer, middle-class fiction was rent by two conflicting stories. One produced a controlling ideology of the home, while the dialectically different voice of self-criticism questioned those tropes from within. Sometimes the effects of the split were local, linguistic, and identifiably Dickensian: "Duty, Tattycoram," Mr. Meagles preaches in his homily at the novel's conclusion; "Begin it early, and do it well; and there is no antecedent to it, in any origin or station" (788). "No antecedent," reminds Harriet of precisely that social origin his speech claims to erase and forgive. Dickens' criticism of mass-cultural stereotypes works in a similar fashion, giving a contradictory ring to apparently submissive cultural tropes. Villains like Miss Wade and Mrs. Clennam remain the ideological antitypes to Mr. Meagles' sense of middle-class duty, but retain their contradictory force. Beneath the types of demonized females, Dickens represented the social history those types suppressed. In a plot as complex as that of *Little Dorrit*, some details first need to be examined, and factual corrections to currently accepted scholarly versions made. Underneath the condemnation of Mrs. Clennam as the archetype of Victorian repression, Dickens structured a version of events that reads domestic history in a critical fashion. Mrs. Clennam does not "suppress" the novel's prehistory, whose outer shell adds up to a potboiler—the melodramatic story of a punished father, vengeful wife, and Little Dorrit, the innocent inheritress betrayed. Instead, she identifies a different version of the past, and challenges the "commodity" that the novel's plotters seek to sell.

Mrs. Clennam: Reading against Plot

Mrs. Clennam's "opinionated" speech at the end of *Little Dorrit* challenges the popular version of events concluding the novel that most of its characters accept. Readers have likewise always assumed that the hidden crime at the center of Little Dorrit is the adultery of Arthur's father before marrying Mrs. Clennam, and the vengeance on her part it provoked. Though I have summarized these details in part already, the complexities of the Clennam family will are material, especially since the plot itself is usually understood through the summary of

the will and its provisions provided by John Holloway in the Penguin
Edition. In his version, Mrs. Clennam is accepted as the punishing
villain who suppressed her husband, and kept the money meant to
repay the harm done to "the little beauty" (757), Arthur's biological
mother, by the provision of the will meant to go to Little Dorrit herself. The problem with this version of events is not just interpretive:
Holloway makes a factual error significant to the reading I will argue
here. Holloway claims that "Arthur's father had dictated the codicil,"
when it is clear, from both Rigaud's and Mrs. Clennam's accounts, that
Gilbert Clennam, the father's uncle, was responsible.[96] Even Dianne
Sadoff's reading of the plot, by far the most sophisticated explanation of its details, encounters a difficult knot. The provisions of the
"will" that construct the ending, according to Sadoff, "make no moti-
vational, logical, or legal sense."[97] Yet the "codicil" (756, 761) that is
"dictated" (756) to Mrs. Clennam makes perfect sense if adultery—nowhere mentioned in the text—is not the only crime for which it atones.
The "will" does make sense as mystification of Arthur's father's sexual
mistreatment of Arthur's biological mother, the little beauty: this is
the "deed" (756) itself that the "codicil" is meant to hide. The will's
confusing provisions make sense as the substitution of anything but a
paternal agency for the "wrong" (47) that engendered Arthur's quest.
Sought by the son as the novel's hidden history, the will is constructed
to evade the father's guilt for the unjust commission of any literal
or figurative deed. "The manipulation of false and true solutions,"
wrote Viktor Shklovskij of Little Dorrit, "is what constitutes the method
of organizing the mystery," and such manipulation is without question what made him choose Dickens' novel as his paradigm for the
form. The "perfect mystery," as Shklovskij called Little Dorrit, would
of course be the one in which the criminal is never punished, and
Little Dorrit may well be the perfect mystery tale.[98] Suspicion of adultery substitutes female agency—the sexual desire of the little beauty,
and the rage of a wounded wife, Mrs. Clennam, that it produced—for
the possibility that male violence and its suppression are the paternal
secret of the plot.

When seen as the exculpation of engendering paternal violence,
plotted complexity appears in a new way. Arthur's repeated charges
against Mrs. Clennam, the woman he believes to be his mother, appear as the projections of a guilty son, who seeks to excuse the actions
of his father, both colonial and domestic, by using the ideology of
sex. Read in the context of the provisions of the "will," Arthur's original speech appears in harmony with its effect of displacement. "Your

stronger spirit," he charged Mrs. Clennam early on, "was infused into all my father's dealings" (47). Woman is here blamed for "infusion"— in a Victorian physiology of sex, a paternal deed—so that Arthur's own conception of his father can be tied in no way to either "business" or his presence in China. The plot reveals to us, moreover, not only the little beauty's suppression, incarcerated as she was by a "lunatic keeper" (760), but incarceration itself as the attempt to make victims culpable for their own placement under charge. In the little beauty's mind, Mrs. Clennam is responsible for her imprisonment, a belief that frees Arthur's father from his responsiblity and turns it into the woman's guilt. Jeremiah, Mrs. Clennam's accuser, tells her that the little beauty "had been always writing, incessantly writing," while in captivity, "mostly letters of confession to you" (761).

The plot thus presents in a systematic way an expiatory concealment of the agency of Arthur's father. Arthur charges Mrs. Clennam from the start of the novel, in a passage that bears repetition, with commercial power and control of the business, so that the violence and "machinery" of its commercial enterprise could be laid at her door:

"In grasping at money and in driving hard bargains . . . mother—some one may have been grievously deceived, injured, ruined. You were the moving power of all this machinery before my birth; your stronger spirit has been infused into all my father's dealings. . . ." (47)

The mother is here figured as the moving force of the "machinery" of a colonial apparatus, with sexual dominance implied as well: "As a child, I knew it as well as I know it now. I knew that your ascendancy over him was the cause of his going to China to take care of the business there" (46). In fact, an equally plausible explanation for his exile may have been his own "infusion" into Arthur's mother—the "singing girl" who was shamed into silence—a possibly criminal act, but certainly a predicament which threatened his middle-class standing, and thus for the father a willfully unspoken act. Read this way, adultery is less important to the plot than is the structure of the "will" behind it, which systematically transforms the father's role in colonial business and his suppression of a "singing girl" into what is literally an avuncular act. The "codicil" designed for reparation to the "little beauty" is written by an "Uncle," and to be carried out by another uncle, Frederick Dorrit. The paternal departure for China is explained as forced by Mrs. Clennam's rage rather than by any paternal crime. Nothing about the "will" connects any father with the "deed" that must be expiated, much less hints at his agency in a repressive or criminal act. Expiation is to be performed by the "will" precisely so that—key to the plot's complexity—the "deed" to be expiated, and its agent, never get named.

When paternal violence is seen as the plot's absent center, moreover, Mrs. Clennam ceases to be the villain whom a "rapacious" Rigaud defames (750). Instead, she appears as protectress of the "little beauty" as victim, the Nemesis of feminine justice and resistance whom Dickens, sustaining the salable frame of his narrative, necessarily must criminalize. But whatever the violence behind her own hysteria, it is not the vengeance of a wife against the woman by whom she has been betrayed. "'When I forced him,'" she says of Arthur's father, "'to give her up to me, by her name and place of abode,' she went on in a torrent of indignation and defence, 'when I accused her, and she fell hiding her face at my feet, was it my injury that I asserted?'" (754). Clearly, what Mrs. Clennam's next words assert is a wish to bring a victim beyond self-condemnation, not to punish her in selfish violence out of "jealousy" and its wound. The "injury" referred to here is neither Mrs. Clennam's—"what scenes and actors the stern woman most reviewed . . . none knew but herself" (333)—nor the fault in which Arthur, or the "machinery" of middle-class business, was conceived. Mrs. Clennam instead seeks to bring the "little beauty" to a radical rereading of her situation, a transformation of shame and guilt into righteous anger against those it serves: "Those who were appointed of old to go to wicked kings and accuse them," she asks, "were they not ministers and servants?" (754).

Scorned above all by Mrs. Clennam, even in her paralysis, is a love of the victim for her oppressor. "The Plagues of Egypt," one must recall, "much dimmer for the fly and smoky plagues of London, were framed and glazed upon the walls" of "Home" to which Arthur returns (33). Here, Mrs. Clennam very much resembles Freud's Dora, whose history of repression in the family the analyst unraveled with great skill. When Freud suggested to his patient, however, that she secretly desired the oppressive father, he tells us that Dora "would not follow me in this part of the interpretation." When Freud persisted that Dora "did fancy" a male aggressor, she brought the analysis abruptly to an end.[99] Mrs. Clennam's powerful impatience with the "shameful affections" of the "little beauty" is similar in a striking way. Though "appointed" herself, Mrs. Clennam admits, "to be the instrument of their punishment," and play the vengeful wife betrayed, what she decries instead is the self-inflicted torture of the woman who seeks to give the act of her own degradation affection's name. "My enemy," Mrs. Clennam insists, was not the woman who cowered in shame at her violation, but the male "wrath," made internal, that makes its victim shrink and quiver long after the deed is done. Self-inflicted torture, after all, is only a legacy of the vengeance of the oppressor who forces, in the act of violence, the identification of pain and love. Mrs. Clennam rises majestically from her paralysis shortly after finding herself able, through telling the little beauty's story, to make an important claim. Whatever her own "scenes and actors" (333), Mrs. Clennam tells us that neither love of oppression nor guilt for its agency—both classical roles of Satan—is hers: "Not unto me the strength be ascribed; not unto me the wringing of the expiation!" (754).

Like "Lucifer" (760), Mrs. Clennam surely voices contempt for any alliance of affection with subjection. "Love (for she said the word to me, down at my feet)" (754) is disparaged, but not without giving the little beauty every chance to escape it, "to purchase her redemption from endless misery, if she could" (755). Crucial to an end of such "sinful and shameful affections" is an honest confrontation with "injury" done to the victim, and a giving up of the illusion of "love." For this reason, Mrs. Clennam makes it impossible for the little beauty to receive the monetary expiation offered by the hidden will, since it "redeems" the crime only on the condition that it never have a testamentary say. Instead, Mrs. Clennam offers the woman another woman's sustenance: "I charge myself with your support" (755).

By suppressing the "will," in fact Mrs. Clennam brings a paternal "deed" to expression. In preventing the will's avuncular provisions from controlling popular readings of the novel, Mrs. Clennam prevents it from obliterating the traces of paternal crime. Thus it is not without "motivation," but a highly motivated detail, that the will provides for the protector of the little beauty, an uncle, to give the expiatory payment to his nearest female relative—Little Dorrit—in the little beauty's place. In either case, redemption is hush money. The legacy of an uncle would silence what is true for Little Dorrit and little beauty alike, that the "will" which speaks forgiveness makes no mention of paternal agency in the suppression of feminine freedom and voice. In fact, in either case, the woman who accepted the money would take it from an uncle who, with "all the remaining power of the honest heart" (631), confesses on his deathbed to "God" that his life has tacitly approved of unnamed crimes—"All that I have looked upon, with my half-blind and sinful eyes" (631). Fighting against the "will," Mrs. Clennam strives against an "imaginary relenting" (756), as she calls it, that would preserve the exculpatory movement of the plot.

Still, forestalling a testament of false repentance, and publicly indicting the "wicked kings" (754) who wrote it, might seem like two different things. But between a silence that "was evermore enforced upon her" (772) and the force of an absolute justice, Mrs. Clennam inserts a resistant voice into an unshakable place in the text. A society that knows "no appointment except Satan's" (754), of course, will look to use her own words against her: "Mine were days of wholesome repression, punishment, and fear" (753). The "wholesome" fruits of repression, however, can be not only the desire for justice, but a compassion for other victims born of that very same "punishment and fear." The dissenting power of Mrs. Clennam's voice is testified to by no lesser authority than the narrator, who condemns her as an antagonist who "breathed her own breath into a clay image of her Creator" (754), robbing male primacy of the last Word. Reading paternal history differently—"she took the watch-case in her hand . . . bending her eyes upon it as if she were defying it to move her" (756)—Mrs. Clennam has traced a counterhistory that challenges the novel's popular condemnation of her as a feminine demon, while protecting herself in the end from being "detected and exposed" (770).

As for Mrs. Clennam's compassion, one must trust Little Dorrit's reaction when the woman of "great energy and anger" (755) "put out her hand, and laid it on her arm" (335). Far from feeling assaulted by a woman in "appetite for power!" (760), Amy senses the grasp of a secret sharer, who might even be the friend in the narrative of a tiny woman and her "very secret" place. The passage deserves repeating ing. Perhaps some momentary recollection of the story of the Princess may have been in her mind." Of course, there can be no certainty that compassion is tendered in that "touch," given the narrator's conviction that the woman in the wheelchair is hell on wheels: "by whatever name she called her vindictive pride and rage, nothing through all eternity could change their nature" (754). If "Lucifer" is nothing more than the mass-cultural manipulation of unjust authority, however, the real "nature" of Mrs. Clennam might live otherwise, caught by Affery in a lucid moment when her husband's nightmare disappears. When Mrs. Clennam touches Little Dorrit, the "vindictive perversion of Christian values" is nowhere to be seen.[100] She "drew down the face of her little seamstress, and kissed her," the narrator tells us, "with a gentleness of which the dreaming Affery had never dreamed" (336).

3

Melville

Ironic Democracy

Melville took a more explicit and critical stance toward mass culture than did Dickens; his fiction overtly challenged the American market in which he worked. "It seems an inconsistency to assert unconditional democracy in all things," Melville wrote to Hawthorne during the composition of *Moby-Dick*, "and yet confess a dislike to all mankind—in the mass. But not so."[1] New Historicist critics have recently argued that "Manifest Destiny" and the antebellum marketplace for fiction were, as Wai-Chee Dimmock puts it, Melville's "strait-jacket," emphasizing the constraining power of the fictional marketplace: the set of political and racial attitudes "relished" by his readership produced signs in Melville's writing of a "hatred" for his audience, a spite legible in the novels as a "poetics of authorial subjection" to that audience and its ideological taste.[2] In his correspondence, Melville opposed his ambition to write critical literature to the mass market for fiction forced upon him, and execrated, in one of the best-known passages from his letter to Hawthorne, his own work as a product in between: "what I feel most moved to write, that is banned,—it will not pay. Yet, altogether, write the *other* way I cannot. So the product is a final hash, and all my books are botches."

But a strikingly modern type of cultural analysis also appears in Melville's assessment. The novel is seen as a "product" shaped for the marketplace. but remains literary ("books")—Melville refuses to rule out "altogether" the capacity of his works to remain critical and to reach a mass audience as well. Writing retains what Theodor Adorno and Max Horkheimer called in their essay on the "culture industry" that "trace of something better," its critical potential to resist ideology from within the commodified work.[3] The American reading public of

89

the 1850s, as William Charvat points out, was increasingly stratified: but the emphasis in Melville's famous statement should be on "hash" rather than "botches," so that the statement stresses his commitment to write both popular and critical mass-cultural works.[4]

Melville was surely "affected by problems of commodification and the democratic audience," as Michael Gilmore has shown.[5] But Richard Chase's warning against writing off Melville's radical vision, the Progressive Era view of his defeat by economic and political interests, bears repetition in the poststructural era of Melville criticism, when suppression is attributed to the cultural "poetic," rather than the economic interests, of the era in which he wrote: "we have inherited the partly true but finally misleading idea of Melville as a heroic failure, a baffled Titan or wounded Prometheus who could do no more than cry out with his agonized rhetoric and his mindless rage against the chains that bound him."[6] Chase's allusion to "chains" obliquely refers to the fictional marketplace, and was part of his claim for the "romance" Melville of cold war modernism. For postliberal critics of his novels, Melville often appears trapped in the same mass-cultural confines. Yet Melville was far less a writer bound by the "chains" of his audience than one able to view the novel as a commodity, ironically shaping its constraints into cultural criticism which speaks through the limits of the mass-cultural work.

Typee's popularity, for instance, did not forestall public perception of its attack on Manifest Destiny. The American missionary community was particularly outraged by the novel's implicit linkage of evangelical religion with the crass motives of imperial expansion.[7] "The book is certainly calculated for popular reading," Melville wrote to John Murray, its British publisher, "or for none at all." Melville's willingness to produce a revised edition, with its "slight purifications of style," was certainly comparable to the disposition of Dickens. Melville's willingness to revise the book was based on a desire to hold a popular readership by complying with the constraints of a genteel audience. "Passages which are calculated to offend the tastes, or offer violance [sic] to the feelings of any large class of readers," were, he wrote his publisher, "certainly objectionable."[8] Audience reaction nonetheless registered the work's culturally critical content. Discontent over the work's criticism of American imperialism in the Pacific was often masked in the furor over its status as "Romance."

To increase sales, Melville agreed to expurgate portions which to reviewers appeared contrary to fact. But Melville also valued the scandal that the mass-cultural novel could create as part of the literary value of his work: "I am persuaded that the interest of the book almost wholly consists in the intrinsick [*sic*] *merit of the narrative alone*." Evert Duyckinck's contemporaneous review of *White-Jacket* noted Melville's use of style as a way of linking the acceptably literary with political questions of labor; the similar inclusion of "daring speculation" within popular fiction in *Moby-Dick* would make him "uncomfortable": "the sharp breeze of the forecastle alternating with the mellow stillness of the library, books and work imparting to each other mutual life . . . distinguish[es] the writer of *Typee* from all other productions of their class."[9]

Melville's own reflection on books always resisted the separation between literary form and the politics of culture. In his wry "A Thought on Book-Binding" (1850), a review of the new edition of James Fenimore Cooper's *Red Rover*, Melville punningly uses the cover of Cooper's novel to observe the connection between the form of the book—its binding—and the pirate novel's sociological function of *binding* the transgressive social desires it represents.[10] Melville humorously speculates on the novel as a means of escape from the "very best society," while ironizing escape itself as a fictional product. The high-cultural pretension signified by the "dressing" of the book's "binding" is exploded, and the novel is exposed as an "entertaining volume" intent on sales. "A Thought on Book-Binding" is thus Melville's wry critique of the mass-cultural novel. The style of the genteel man of letters is mocked, but that persona is invested with the serious and "critical" consideration that "entertainment" fiction and its controls demand.

Redburn (1849) exploited the persona of an ironic yet genteel observer, by satirizing the taste of Melville's audience for the escapism of adventure and romance. Melville accounts for the origins of Redburn's desire to go to sea in personal nostalgia: Redburn recalls the ship in a bottle in his father's bookshelves that provoked the violent fantasies that led him before the mast. "La Reine, or the Queen," as the bottled ship was called, gave Redburn the "insane desire . . . to be the death of the glass ship, case, and all, in order to come at the plunder" it held.[11] But when the sunken treasure of Redburn's desire is seen as the marketable form of rebellion on the fictional market, Melville's own use of the scene appears aggressive in a different light. The bottled ship satirizes the *bottling up* of filial revolt—Melville called *Redburn* "a little nursery tale of mine"—effected by the novel as salable commodity.[12]

The ship, apparently an heirloom, is an "old-fashioned" object kept like a classic in a "case," only to be exposed as a product of "manufacture," an object whose nostalgic aura, as Walter Benjamin wrote of the traditional work, has been shattered by "the age of mechanical reproduction."[13] Rebellious desire is subsequently revealed as a mass-produced item. Redburn's longing to voyage was produced, it turns out, by a puerile and marketable form of literature: "I do not know how to account for this temporary madness of mine, unless it was, that I had been reading in a story-book about Captain Kidd's ship." Melville's criticism of the marketing of revolt in popular American fiction matches in subtler tones his send-up in the "Young America in Literature" section of *Pierre*, where "Captain Kidd Monthly" is the journal in which his satirized author-figure writes. Melville pits nostalgia against commodity culture, and the latter wins. Redburn insists that fiction, while indulging "personal" desires, is in fact the medium in which they are socially produced.

Despite this clear-sighted view of popular fiction, Melville never abandoned the critical potential of the marketable novel. "Hawthorne and His Mosses," his essay of 1850, explores the meaning of mass culture for the social novel, preparing the way for *Moby-Dick*. The "popularizing noise and show" to which Shakespeare and his theater were "forced" at first cast doubt on the critical potential of popular art.[14] Melville's high-cultural perspective is supported, moreover, by his earlier correspondence. "I would to God Shakespeare had lived later, & promenaded in Broadway," he wrote to Evert Duyckinck the previous year: "the muzzle which all men wore on their souls in the Elizabethan day, might not have intercepted Shakspers [*sic*] full articulations."[15] The optimistic sense of Shakespeare on "Broadway," however, also finds its way into the "Hawthorne" piece. Melville envisaged "popular" discourse that retained its critical perspective, a position that sets his view of mass culture apart from the New Historicist emphasis on the saturation of the marketplace by power. In Melville's own formulation, fiction could imitate Shakespeare as well as "Broadway," though the critical power of its "full articulations" might not always be perceived.

Melville's encounter with Shakespeare in this way allowed him to define his own relation to the market for fiction. "Hawthorne and His Mosses" views Shakespeare at times as a cheap propagandist, working for the sensational effects of the commodity novel. It is the popular success of such "broad farce, and blood-besmeared tragedy" that is rejected by Hawthorne, whose "rare, quiet book" is said to be "too deserving of popularity to be popular" (245, 240). Yet Hawthorne, like

Shakespeare, remains an ambivalent figure for Melville.[16] Both signify the mass-cultural artist, working for a popular audience without sacrificing critical perspective. Melville therefore takes pains to differentiate the Shakespeare who achieved "mob reknown," by manipulating the "tricky stage" (245) from the writer who provided, amidst such cheap effects, "cunning glimpses" of critical social truth (244). In recognizing fiction as an entertainment product, whose sources could be found in British culture, Melville in this way refused any hard-and-fast divide between serious cultural criticism and the problems of commercial culture.

As in the gesture of imagining Shakespeare on Broadway, Melville sought to account for the fate of traditional art in the age of the commodity, while retaining the "full articulations" of its cultural critique. "Hawthorne and His Mosses" ends in this double fashion: its conclusion stresses mass-cultural modes of surreptitiously "telling the truth" in popular fiction, while offering an exaggerated parody of literary nationalism, preparing the way for the double style of *Moby-Dick*. In his first mention of the novel in his letters, Melville explicitly makes the connection between popular representation and social criticism, refers to the difficulties of "cook[ing]" the novel, as if to taste, and declares to his correspondent: "Yet I mean to give the truth of the thing, spite of this."[17] *Moby-Dick*, as William Charvat argued, "has never been properly understood as the work of a writer who was in a state of creative tension with a reading public whose limitations he had at last defined."[18]

But *Pierre, or, the Ambiguities* (1852), recognizable as Melville's most modernist work, was also his most important investigation of the position of his novels within the antebellum American literary marketplace. Hershel Parker, in a biographical reading, has described *Pierre's* failure as part of Melville's refusal to conform to any of the social or generic expectations of a nineteenth-century audience, even those generated by his own previous works.[19] Yet *Pierre* brilliantly succeeds as an account of the politics of publishing as well as of the editorial and political restrictions Melville faced, and as such is an important guide to the effects his realistic fiction achieved in *White-Jacket* and *Moby-Dick*, his culminating realist works. In heavy melodrama, Melville's narrator discovers Pierre, torn by the unspeakable passions of "incest and parricide," as the writer of blasphemous and socially critical fiction: "Upon the pretense of writing a popular novel for us," Pierre's publishers write, "you have been receiving cash advances from us, while passing through our press the sheets of a blasphemous rhapsody, filched from the vile Atheists, Lucian and Voltaire."[20] Melvillean irony takes away Pierre's presumption to writerly rebellion, pointing out his desire to protect his father's reputation, and mocks the literary nationalist circles in which Melville himself had moved.[21]

But Melville had constructed a systematically double and contradictory book. *Pierre* transforms its protagonist into a writer who desires to inhabit the marketable world of sentimental romance—"could he now hurl his deep book out of the window, and fall to on some shallow nothing of a novel, composable in a month at the longest, then he could reasonably hope for appreciation and cash" (305)—but who also rails critically against it: "he could not now be entertainingly profitable and shallow in some pellucid and merry romance." Avoiding the concerns of his earlier works with the issues of labor and American expansion, Melville's novel is thus able to model a narrative that is genuinely ambiguous in its decisive refusal to meet the expectations of mass-cultural romance or the reflexive demands of the modern novel. Neither a mass-cultural production nor a modernist send-up, *Pierre* is resolutely both at once. Melville's "Revolt against the Reader," as Ann Douglas describes it, was expressed in this ironic response to an emerging commodity culture, through his ability to write within and simultaneously against its conventional taste.[22] But *Pierre*'s own quotation from Dante is far more effective a description of the half-traditional, half-modernist fiction, stealing from the techniques of both—the passage is from the Circle of the Thieves—which Melville's political engagement with mass culture and the novel produced: "Ah, how dost thou change, / Agnello! See! thou art not double now, / Nor only one!" (85).

The Writer and the Market: *White-Jacket*

Melville referred to *Redburn* and *White-Jacket* as "two *jobs*, which I have done for the money—being forced to it, as other men are to sawing wood," and seemed to dismiss the ability of marketable fiction to retain its socially critical edge. "So far as I am individually concerned," he wrote, "& independent of my pocket, it is my earnest desire to write those sort of books which are said to 'fail.' "[23] To dismiss popular fiction in nineteenth-century America, moreover, inescapably implied a hostility to Dickens' spectacularly successful novels, and their praise by the arbiters of American literary taste—the usual understanding of Melville's relation to Dickens. "Hawthorne and His Mosses" has been read by Perry Miller as Melville's attempt to "take

Hawthorne away" from the "genial conservatives" who had "united in adoring Dickens." Robert Weisbuch similarly argues that "Bartleby the Scrivener" was Melville's "all out attack" and acerbic satire on *Bleak House*'s transformation of opposition to commercial society into the sentimentality—"Ah, Bartleby, Ah, humanity!" Melville's story concludes—of the marketable literary work.[24]

But Melville's parody betrays a recognition of the critical content of Dickens' fiction as well. Weisbuch portrays Melville's attitude toward Dickens as one of anxiety of influence, and rightly suggests that Melville's engagement with Dickens' novels was a way of working out his own critical narrative stance. "Melville both acknowledges his agreement with aspects of Dickens's social critique," according to Weisbuch, "and asserts his own capacity to write in such a manner."[25] But the field of Melville's disagreement with Dickens was not strictly literary, but also commercial: writing for Melville, as for Dickens, meant confronting the effects of mass production on fiction as a medium of cultural critique. The fact that both *Redburn* and *White-Jacket* did sell, and that Melville immediately qualified his rejection of the mass-market novel in his letter—"Pardon this egotism"—is nonetheless rarely considered in tallying up the critical effects of the popular fiction he went on to produce.

The expanding American market for popular fiction in the 1850s, however, was dominated by sentimental fiction, making mass-cultural criticism all the more difficult.[26] Melville's famous moments of despair about his writing were accordingly intense, yet also accompanied by blinded insight into commodity fiction's critical potential—"Dollars damn me; and the malicious Devil is forever grinning in upon me, holding the door ajar"—and by the "unspeakable security" he felt in his ability to circumvent the market and its constraints of taste. "I have written a wicked book," Melville wrote Hawthorne of *Moby-Dick*, "and feel spotless as the lamb."[27] When Melville explicitly satirized in *Pierre* the Dickensian "dynasty of taste" practiced by American "editors," he also modeled the contradictory critical potential of popular fiction, within the bounds of what was his most esoteric and unpopular work. Melville figures his contempt for the sentimental novel, to be sure, in Pierre's hostility to the literary commodity "written chiefly for the merest cash," and he satirizes both the popular romance style and a reviewer who praises his work for its " 'Perfect Taste' " (249, 245).

Pierre makes fun of "popular literary enthusiasm" (246), at the same time as Melville satirizes the notion of the author as "genius" (264) who stands beyond the economy and its "slave" (260). The "Invulnerable Knight" who speaks with "his visor down" to the reader is Melville's figure of the high-cultural artist, talking openly about fiction's dependence on the market: "we are only too thankful when the gapes of the audience dismiss us with the few ducats we earn" (259). Here as elsewhere Melville constructs a genteel fiction of the novelist, and simultaneously mocks it. Monumental authorship is exposed as a fictional prop for a fading colonial aristocracy, and Pierre's own pompous literary ambitions gradually place him in the habitus of a hack. Rage at the marketplace presses its reality upon the genteel audience for fiction: resistance places Pierre in the midst of the mass-culture he rejects. When his publisher demands a "portrait" to publicize the popular novel he has promised, Pierre offers a commodified identity saturated with oppositional criticism, "submitting to his impartial inspection a determinately double fist" (254).

Melville's dismissal of *Redburn* and *White-Jacket* as "*jobs . . .* for money" was a similarly double gesture, as his denial that they were "repressed" in the same letter and his subsequent correspondence showed. Writing to Richard Henry Dana, author of the popular *Two Years before the Mast*, Melville makes clear that he regards *White-Jacket* as a similar product, asking Dana for his aid in publicity—"Your name would do a very great deal"—and discusses his prospective trip to England to sell his work. But the irony of his address to Dana as an arbiter of genteel taste who can protect him from critical attacks on the novel during his absence, "made in an unfair and ignorant way," points forward to the lapse in their friendship. Already apparent in Melville's comment is the critical edge his novel would apply to the politics of the novel as marketable commodity: "This man-of-war book, My Dear Sir, is in some parts rather man-of-*warish* in style— rather aggressive I fear." [28]

Melvillean irony, however, has been traditionally separated from his interest in the novel as a marketable commodity. In his determining description of Melville in 1856, Nathaniel Hawthorne fashioned Melville's ambivalence as a propensity for doubt, a stance which placed his irony completely outside of the marketplace, as if it were an entry into the high culture of the modernist abyss: "Melville informed me that he had 'pretty much made up his mind to be annihilated'. . . . He can neither believe, nor be comfortable in his unbelief, and he is too honest and courageous not to try to do one or the other." [29] Students of *Moby-Dick* in particular have taken its irony to be literary skepticism, or seen it as an aspect of style that deflates Melville's political commitment. "One is often uncertain," as Paul Brodtkorb puts it, "as to whether Ishmaelian judgment means what it says . . . implies its opposite, or implies both as the condition of ironical possibility."[30] The critic Carolyn Porter, deriving her terms from Mikhail Bakhtin, has attempted to reclaim Melvillean irony for politics as part of his "frustrated" relation to his audience. She defines that irony as the rhetorical principle that allows Melville's language to be "double-voiced," and sees it practiced by an Ishmael who "speaks with the full authority of the culture whose authority he is out to subvert."[31] Porter describes Melville's language as "subversive," while Melville understood such "subversion" as itself a product on the marketplace, an insight that empowered rather than frustrated the force of his cultural critique.

Moby-Dick itself is therefore playful rather than anguished or egotistical when it considers the taste of Melville's audience. The "Contrasted View" and abyssal "darkness" of the sperm whale point of view long for a readership receptive to contradiction, capable of focusing its attention on a double-voiced fictional work: "[is it possible] that he can at the same moment of time attentively examine two distinct prospects, one on one side of him, and the other in an exactly opposite direction?"[32] Ishmaelian irony asks for just such attention, often embedding the reader in a traditional cultural discourse, then criticizing its mass-cultural reduction. Father Mapple's sermon provides a powerful example toward the beginning of the novel: steeped in the tradition of the jeremiad, Melville's reader could certainly have been expected to recognize his call to "sound those unwelcome truths in the ears of a wicked Nineveh" as a call to radical social criticism (47). Melville lets Mapple's eloquence ring, only to have Ishmael satirize its plea as *theater* for consumption. It is the idea of radical religion as mass-cultural spectacle that Ishmael entertains and ironically mocks: "Father Mapple enjoyed such a wide reputation for sincerity and sanctity, that I could not suspect him of courting notoriety by any mere tricks of the stage. No, thought I" (48, 39). Critics have thus been able to produce both serious and parodic readings of Mapple's speech. Charles Foster saw in its plea for a Jonah who "destroys all sin though he pluck it out from under the robes of Senators and Judges" an attack on the Fugitive Slave Law of 1850, which Melville's father-in-law, Judge Lemuel Shaw of Massachusetts, upheld, while T. Walter Herbert and others who have focused on its religious rhetoric have seen it as a parody of popular Christianity and its "travesty of orthodox belief."[33] Melville reproduces Father Mapple as an example of antislavery rhetoric, as Foster suggests, but at the same time warns against a popular culture whose language provides only a containing release for radical ardor, replacing action with the draft of speech. "This pulpit, I see," Ishmael observes sardonically, "is a self-containing stronghold— a lofty Ehrenbreitstein, with a perennial well of water within the walls" (39).

White-Jacket begins with just this kind of alert to Melville's reader. The "Jacket" worn by the novel's narrator is used, as Melville used the "binding" of the book in his review of Cooper, to represent his awareness of the novel as a popular commodity, but also to signal his commitment to critical transformation of its constraints. "I employed myself, for several days," the narrator of *White-Jacket* announces on its first page, "in manufacturing an outlandish garment of my own devising."[34] The "outlandish" element of Melville's "manufacturing" of *White-Jacket* was less its capacity to provoke political outrage than the more subtle and "aggressive" attack by its "style," the novel's ability to allegorize and attack the conditions of its own cultural production. The jacket is likened to a "confidential writing desk," and figures a writer bound by his audience: "the living on board a man-of-war is something like living in a market," the narrator declares. "The people," as the crew is called, are yoked together with the antebellum audience for Melville's fiction: "for a ship is a bit of terra firma cut off from the main" (36, 35, 23) The popular genre of the sea adventure, to be sure, allowed the book to succeed. The "gash" made in "The Jacket," however, is a reminder that the elements of the novel Melville considered "aggressive" transformed the marketable novel into a "double" entity, both an object for sale and an instrument of serious social critique: "I folded [it] double at the bosom, and by then making a continuation of the slit there, opened it lengthwise—much as you would cut a leaf in the last new novel" (3).

White-Jacket is the proper beginning to *Moby-Dick* as a political novel because it exemplifies Melville's commitment to write effective social criticism within the constraints of the mass audience for which he wrote. "The distinct subversive spirit of American popular culture," as David Reynolds calls it, is present in both novels as the object of Melville's satire and social criticism, as both novels set themselves against the mass-cultural commodification and control of working-class rebellion and dissent.[35] Wai-Chee Dimmock, noting that the controversy over flogging in the navy, made popular in William McNally's *Evils and Abuses in the Naval and Merchant Services, Exposed* (1839), was "largely settled" by 1849, argues that it was included in *White-Jacket* as a cynical attempt to capitalize on a social scandal and sell a book without socially critical force; she notes that it was used by Melville in the novel as a mere "marketing device."[36] *White-Jacket* internalized such mass-cultural coercion, serving as an important apprenticeship for Melville's criticism of popular culture, and thus prepared the way for *Moby-Dick*'s deeper exploration of the critical potential of the novel as commodity. Melville's narrator confesses that his "jacket" is "manu-factured," and recognizes the difficulty of producing a critical product which "the people" will prefer. "But for all that," he reminds us, speaking from within "the grand democratic cookery" of the "people," and writing a literature written for mass consumption, "I can not avoid speaking my mind" (59, 61).

The Discipline of Resistance

White-Jacket places the navigation of Cape Horn as the midpoint of the journey of the *USS Neversink* it describes, "about mid-way in the homeward-bound passage" (109). Melville introduces his readers to the scene by reminding them that it is also a literary passage, already depicted with great success by Richard Henry Dana in his *Two Years before the Mast* (1840). He assumes an audience already familiar with Dana's rendition of the scene—"but you can read, so you must have read it. His chapters describing Cape Horn must have been written with an icicle" (99). Melville's recognition, however, is bestowed with more than a hint that his predecessor's work may be a brittle and cold rather than hot literary commodity. The "horrors of the cape" are described in language that evokes their mass-cultural banality. In reminding his readers of the "severe and long exposure" suffered by "crews" navigating the "passage," Melville's praise of Dana's realistic scene subtly adverts to the boredom of consumers, suffering their own overlong exposure to popular cliché.

   White-Jacket, of course, features its own version of adventurous hero-ism. Rather than compete with Dana, however, Melville used the scene to model a critical version of mass fiction. In order to save the ship from foundering, Melville's hero, "Mad Jack," seizes command of the ship from its inept captain and steers it into the wind to save it from the storm. The gesture was a paradigmatic one for Melville's sense of authorship, as his narrator would confess. "I owe this right hand," the narrator declares, "this moment flying over my sheet, and all my present being to Mad Jack" (106). To oppose the dictates of popular culture, Melville suggests, its dominating force had to be taken into the texture of fiction. Like the rule of an incompetent captain, the dominating power of the "sheet" had to be contested, if the "people," as the crew of *White-Jacket* are called, were to find critical speech.

   The passage on Dana, moreover, was a personal one for Melville, significant for the critical cultural and political stance his novel took. As members of aristocratic colonial families who distinguished themselves in the American Revolution, Melville and Dana shared similar social backgrounds, as well as a desire to turn lower-class "adventure" as sailors into a fiction that would sell. "I am specially delighted at the thought," Melville wrote to Dana in 1850, when "the Jacket," as he called it, was complete, "that those strange, congenial feelings, with which after my first voyage, I for the first time read 'Two Years Before the Mast,' and while so engaged was, as it were, tied & welded to you by a sort of Siamese link of affectionate sympathy—that these feelings should be reciprocated by you." [37] Melville and Dana's relations were cut off after *Moby Dick*'s publication, nonetheless, as Melville's "Siamese" image already predicted, and the split is consistent with the opposing attitudes held by each writer toward mass culture and ideology, particularly where the issue of slavery was concerned.

Specifically, Melville and Dana differed on the politics of race. The two authors, though they spent "convivial evenings together in the late 1840's," held opposing views on the political representations that shaped the slavery debate. [38] Dana argued a populist, Free Soil position that tolerated the continuance of Southern slavery, while Melville's fiction consistently opposed the racial bias that such false populism implied. Dana, moreover, used his literary reputation to support the principle which would become the basis of the Compromise of 1850: perpetuation of slavery in the South in return for its prohibition in the West. Authorship lent credibility to Dana's populism: *Two Years before the Mast* was a sympathetic representation of sailors as a slice of working-class life. *White-Jacket* and *Moby-Dick* criticized this version of mass-cultural populism, opposing the conformism inherent in Dana's adventure fiction. Their difference from Dana's work is doubly instructive: Melville's fiction emphasized the role of popular culture in supporting slavery, and attacked the propagandistic imagery of the Free Soil position in the slavery debate.

Dana, for instance, in his speech to Boston Free Soilers in 1848, praised General Zachary Taylor, a slaveholder and popular hero of the Mexican War. Free Soilers hoped to exchange tolerance of slavery in the South for its prohibition in the West, where white workers feared the competition of a suddenly freed black proletariat. In this brand of populist rhetoric, radical opposition to slavery was yoked together with a cultural conservatism on questions of race. The pairing worked powerfully as a mass-cultural strategy: liberatory, antislavery rhetoric could be addressed to the white working class, while appealing to latent racial antipathies. Such a position could be sold widely in the North. Before the Civil War, as Eric Foner argues, Republican party ideology often played this double game. Free Soil Democrats also used the prolabor tropes of Jacksonian rhetoric in similar fashion. *Moby Dick*'s praise of the working man often ironizes this false inclusivity of populist speech. Foner's description of Free Soil cultural politics is thus worth quoting at length. For the importance of black and Indian labor aboard the *Pequod* made central precisely the issue that populist rhetoric sought to marginalize, the question of race:

The anti-slavery Democrats were heirs of the Jacksonian political tradition, and were accustomed to couch their political arguments in terms that would appeal to labor. But there was a strong undercurrent of racial prejudice in their statements. By insisting . . . that they had "no squeamish sensitiveness upon the subject of slavery, no morbid sympathy for the slave," and that it was the influence of slavery's extension upon white labor that concerned them, the Barnburners sought both to turn anti-Negro sentiments to anti-slavery use and to answer the perennial charge that anti-slavery men were concerned solely with the fate of black men.[39]

The cultural conditions of Melville's fiction included toleration for more than code-word racism, even in extreme antislavery advocates, who did not want to appear to be overly solicitous toward blacks. Ahab's double democracy in *Moby-Dick* makes implicit use of just this racial divide. "He would be a democrat to all above," as Starbuck describes "The Quarter Deck," Ahab's first populist speech; "look, how he lords it over all below!" (169).

Melville exposed the racial duplicity of such populism, though in his dealings with the cultural market he was not above double-dealing to promote his fictional work. Friendship with Dana assisted the marketing of *White-Jacket*, while Melville's fiction and journalism subjected the racial attitudes of Dana's Free Soil politics to stringent cultural critique. The same Dana whom Melville asked to lend his "name" to the defense of *White-Jacket* for its culturally "aggressive" positions had publicly praised slave holding culture: before a Free Soil audience in 1848, Dana declared that "there is much to admire in the Southern character; in some points it is even superior to our own."[40] Two years later, Melville's *White-Jacket* would respond: flogging scenes used the popular topic of naval abuses to represent the discipline of plantation slavery in a different light. While the use of white characters to portray slaves was subtly coded, as Carolyn Karcher observes, it nonetheless set the populist rhetoric of "Free" American labor on its head.[41] *Redburn* had already spoken more directly, observing that the "social prejudice" of the "mass," from which there seemed "no escape" in America, turned to a treatment based on "humanity and normal equality" in Liverpool.[42] Melville's link in the popular imagination with Dana was thus a double blessing: in following Dana's model, *White-Jacket* satisfied America's racial conservatism, thus allowing its send-ups of racial stereotype to reach the democratic "mass." Melville's later description of Pierre as a writer adverted to the doubleness of the Melvillean persona, claiming the mantle of the democratic writer while attacking its mass-cultural confines: "you will pronounce Pierre a thorough-going Democrat in time; perhaps a little too Radical altogether to your fancy" (13).

To write such radically democratic criticism of mass culture, Melville first needed to reach its audience. Political gains, however, were to be made through a populism that strengthened racial barriers. Dana's support for the Whig candidate, Zachary Taylor, was exemplary in this regard: literary fame was used to support the latent racism of Northern workers, who feared black workers as a threat to economic opportunity in the West. "We are ready to vote for General Taylor if he owns two hundred slaves instead of twenty," Dana declared to a Free Soil meeting in Boston in 1848, "if he is with us against the extension of slave territory. The 'subject of our story' is simply this." Popular drama and social conformity are linked images in Dana's rhetoric of partial liberation. Popular culture evoked a society in which the people had "no power," magnified as they might be by the social rhetoric that offered them independent roles. The speech concluded by using the authority of literature to ratify this vision of social containment, applicable to black and white sectors of the democratic audience alike: "We have no power to assign parts in the drama of political life." [43]

The larger appeal to nationalism in the speech, of course, was not surprising, and if Melville reacted to the event itself, his response is not known. Yet this was precisely the kind of appeal to audience that *Moby-Dick* would perfect a few years later in Ahab's exhortations to the crew of the *Pequod*. The link between Dana, the popular novel, and repressive populism for Melville is in this way significant for thinking about Melville's larger relations with popular culture. For the Zachary Taylor that Dana praised in his political speech had been ridiculed by Melville in 1847 as a production of what would now be called consumer marketing. In an article entitled "Authentic Anecdotes of 'Old Zack,'" Melville ridiculed Taylor as an early form of the politician as media creation, lampooning political manipulation by advertising, using fictional headlines to parody its techniques:

PRODIGIOUS EXCITEMENT!!!

OLD ZACK'S PANTS!!!

GREAT SIGHTS AT THE AMERICAN MUSEUM!!!

Melville goes on to present Taylor's fame as a salable spectacle, and the reader is informed that the relics of the Hero of "The Battle of Buena Vista" have been sought by "Mr. BARNUM," for display in his "Museum."[44] Melville's satire takes aim at what would later be understood as the marketing of presidential candidates. The rhetoric of commodity consumption, however, also defined his sense of what the Taylor piece called the "American public" (218). The American audience, Melville suggests, was constructed through such political symbols. This sense of readership as a social construct was crucial, and its effects are apparent in the challenging demands on the reader Melville's own fictional rhetoric would make. Far from constituting an audience of passive consumers of the media image, Melville's style— replete with rapid changes of tone, sudden irony, and an almost constant metafictional distance—encouraged a critical audience response to what *Moby-Dick* calls "political superstitions," the "external arts" created to deceive the mass (148).

To this end, Melville's journalistic piece parodies the emergent racial stereotypes of mass-market political discourse. Melville's journalism used demeaning black stereotypes to signify a critical attitude toward slavery, and his fiction commented on mainstream clichés of black character as well. *Redburn* pointedly remarked the cultural relativism of racial stigma, and its peculiar American intensity, noting that an interracial couple in Liverpool was unthinkable in the North: "in New York, such a couple would have been mobbed" (202). In keeping with this critical perspective, "Authentic Anecdotes of Old Zack" uses black stereotype against Zachary Taylor, making an antiracist weapon out of the most degrading racial cliché. "The General's confidential black servant Sambo," a figure of the slaves Taylor held, drops a "hot pie"—in parody of the "shell" of battle—on Old Rough and Ready's "venerable white head" (224).

Melville had reason to know such clichés, as well as the authentic black culture that resisted dominant discourse by "signifyin(g)," a technique of refashioning its epithets into resistant speech. While no native speaker of African-American discourse, Melville likely learned its techniques from an already widespread black American culture. Henry Louis Gates, Jr., whose definition of "signifyin(g)" I use here, points out that by the 1850s *Frederick Douglass' Paper* was publishing essays entitled "What Shall We do with White People," returning fire against antiblack stereotypes in ways similar to this moment in Melville's journalism.[45] Melville and Douglass worked the New Bedford docks at the same time in the 1840s, though no direct linkage between the two figures is necessary to recall the centrality that black figures attained in American popular culture in the period when *Uncle Tom's Cabin* gained its fame. Melville's "Sambo" remains a different figure from Tom: by returning fire at a figure of presidential authority, the figure of mythical black passivity explodes the Barnum image of Zachary Taylor, and vents black resentment at the representations of popular culture.

Culture produced for the mass, as Melville understood, was based on such "mythic" images of conformity. False autonomy was frequently Melville's target in representing mass culture, and his points of attack often resembled the deceptive Enlightenment Adorno and Horkheimer scored as the essence of popular culture's false democracy. But Enlightenment always promised critical self-reflection in Frankfurt School terms, even if the terms for an immanent critique of the culture industry were never fully developed in their work.

Such analysis is developed within Melville's novels, however, providing a running self-criticism of the nineteenth-century cultural market and its effects on political positions in the slavery debate. In *Moby-Dick* Steelkilt represents both the Free Soil radicalism of Northern workers and the mass-cultural forms that shaped sentiments of popular revolt. Melville presents Steelkilt as a Free Soiler, standing up for the oppressed worker—"the common decency of human recognition which is the meanest slave's right" (245)—but also as a "fine dramatic hero" (249) who fights for his "comrades" in a drama strikingly devoid of concern for actual blacks.[46] Since the "meanest slave" stands for the lowest level of social stigma, slave status signifies the conditions white labor seeks to avoid for itself, rather than any sentiment of solidarity with a multiracial working class.

Hence the depiction of Steelkilt as a labor hero, drawn from popular art. Melville portrays his working-class hero as a stereotypic figure of music-hall entertainment. Steelkilt appears "picturesquely wicked," dressed in "brigandish guise" as if he were a hero of melodrama. Like a performer, the leader of working-class rebellion represents himself as a popular "terror," full of appeal to an audience of "smiling . . .

villages through which he floats" (249). The music hall, to be sure, had its appeal for Melville. Like the working-class habits White-Jacket observes throughout the novel, popular culture corrects the posturing of gentility, for "many sensible things banished from high life," he observes, "find an asylum among the mob" (29). This "situational autonomy" of the performance crowd, which Peter Bailey has described as an aspect of the nineteenth-century music hall, holds for Melville's account of Steelkilt as well.[47] The reader is encouraged to read fantasies of revolt as a social construction: Steelkilt's resemblance to "many thousands of our rural boys" evokes a public fed containing fantasies of revolt. Even when debased and manipulative, *White-Jacket's* shipboard theater represents "mob" frustrations, and Ishmael's ironic mode of discussing popular theater encourages a critical attitude toward its effects.

Thus when Steelkilt's revolutionaries avoid the question of Southern slavery, Ishmael pointedly follows the story's "darker thread." Popular heroism, for Melville, was to be examined for its latent ideology. Steelkilt the "picturesque" hero teaches his followers to adopt a "sort of passiveness in their conduct" (254–55), and the worker's rebellion he leads, like the Free Soilers revolt it stages, is pointedly without sympathy for actual slaves. "The Town Ho's Story" portrays rebellious Northern workers as saturated by mass culture, consumers of a glorified vision of resistance that masks the nation's racial divide. Steelkilt's revolt ends with the melodramatic eruption of Moby-Dick in a "blinding foam that blent two whitenesses together" (256). "The Town-Ho's Story" confronts this blind spot of popular rhetoric, raising the question Free Soilers refused to ask: whether radical attacks on laboring injustice could be anything more than a false confrontation of two "whitenesses," Northern and Southern, if they ignored the real plight of laboring blacks.

White-Jacket continually displays this difference between the mass-cultural rhetoric of liberation and the social conservatism it helped to entrench. The issue of slavery was a telling reminder: Dana's anti-slavery credentials were solid in the North, though largely symbolic, given his expressed admiration for the cultural institutions of the South. In 1851, Dana defended the escaped slave Frederic Wilkins from return to the South under the Fugitive Slave Law, and did so in the courtroom of Melville's father-in-law, Judge Lemuel Shaw.[48] Yet support for the popular cause in Boston was part of what Dana himself called his "conservatism" and admiration for the authority of Southern institutions. As Dana put it in a letter of 1854, "a technical abolitionist I am not," and declared himself "bound" to the "fugitive slave law."[49] Melville's distance from such conservatism is apparent: tolerance of slavery depended on the mythic figure of the happy slave, a social symbol Melville was always keen to confront. "Guineau," the "Virginia Slave" in *White-Jacket*, presents the willing servitude of blacks as emblematic of the color line: through cliché, the suffering of black workers was made acceptable, while the Jacksonian rhetoric of working-class liberation remained a staple of populist political speech. Melville breaks the color line by exaggeration. White sailors praise the ideology of black servitude, but in becoming aware of their own misery, expose the happy slave as a collective myth: "ever gay and hilarious; ever ready to laugh and joke, that African slave was actually envied by many of the seamen. There were times when I almost envied him myself" (379).

This criticism of racial stereotype carries over into *White-Jacket's* satiric stance toward symbols of the white working class. Melville's concern with the working-class uprisings in Europe of 1848 in *Moby-Dick* as well as *White-Jacket* has been noted by Larry Reynolds, though in both cases Melville is less a fearful conservative, concerned with the prospect of imminent class revolt in America, than a cultural critic, analyzing the role of culture's mass production in transforming laboring discontent into a popular commodity.[50] The "theatricals" produced at Cape Horn on "The Fourth of July" portray "*the people*" as an "audience" (92–93) that consumes a literary event: the revolutionary public and the subjects of a mass-cultural spectacle were, in Melville's staging of the scene, always to be considered in cultural analysis as the same cultural group. The obvious commercialism of the theatricals is evident in its title—"THE OLD WAGON PAID OFF"—and catches White-Jacket's attention, bringing him to scorn the popular audience and its cultural taste. In this stance of gentility, Melville's narrator takes on the tone of a critic who must "moralize" and recommends the "spectacle" as a hamless diversion for the masses, a "temporary rupture of the ship's stern discipline" (95) which, like high culture, appears exempt from political demands.

Yet as in Melville's piece "Book–Binding," the posture of genteel cultural critic soon dissolves its own apolitical mask. Theatrical "spectacle" appears political, when analyzed through a technique of juxtaposition. When White-Jacket observes the relations between popular spectacle and social discipline, the genteel and superior tone of his criticism disappears: for the "people" of the ship, he points out, the deck where sailors are whipped and where the theatricals are produced are one and the same social space. On the "next morning," after the theatricals, White-Jacket notes, "the *same old scene* [my emphasis] was enacted at the gangway," where the regular whipping of disobedient members of "the people" took place.

Theater and its representation of the working class are for the first time in Melville's work linked as forms of cultural control. White-Jacket's apparent approval of the conservative functions of mass-cultural amusement—"it is good to shake off, now and then, this iron yoke round our necks" (95)—is nonetheless replaced by an analysis of the spectacle and its social effects. Like Benjamin, Melville pays attention to the proliferation of mass culture in modern society, and the self-identifications it encourages an audience to construct. Just as any sailor can enter the "theatricals," then return to his routine, so Benjamin emphasized the multiplied opportunities for self-representation in the "Age of Mechanical Reproduction." An "increasing number of readers," Benjamin points out, "become writers" in the modern age, or "actors" in the theatrical sense White-Jacket describes.[51] Just as working sailors take part in the popular theater, so Benjamin's modern citizen is repeatedly offered a opportunities to participate in the writing of mass culture's social scripts.

White-Jacket, however, is more pessimistic than Benjamin about the liberatory potential of proliferating representation, and more critical of mass-cultural roles for the working class. *White-Jacket's* melodrama connects the "pleasurable emotions" of populist spectacle, on the one hand, and, on the other, the pain and suffering enforced on the "people" by the rigid discipline of the ship. This linkage between sadism and popular entertainment is made by conflating two cultural spaces, those of popular theater and of disciplinary punishment, in much the same way that Adorno made his famous comparison between popular jazz and the controlling mechanisms of consumer culture. Adorno's failure to perceive the resistant power of black culture did not prevent his recognition, similar to Melville's, that the industrial organization of popular culture could transform dissident cultural material into "marks of mutilation" against those without power.[52]

Melville's conflation of theater with flogging, however, emphasizes that the "sweet thing" produced by the Captain for the "cordial appreciation" of his charges, was a serious cultural affair. The pleasure of popular culture and the spectacle of punishing oppression are not only linked, but portrayed as productions carried out under the guidance of social authority, crucial to maintaining the obedience of the "people" to their shipboard state. For Melville, the affirmative character of "THE OLD WAGON PAID OFF!" and a negative evaluation of its controlling cultural authority are directly linked, as White-Jacket observes at the scene of a whipping: "uncompromising-looking officers [were] there assembled with the Captain, to witness punishment—the same officers who had been so cheerfully disposed over night" (95). The sudden transition from spectator to victim—from the empowered audience to the subjected object of social discipline—is represented by Melville as the manipulative logic of mass culture at its worst, anticipating in striking ways the idea of the "society of the spectacle" articulated by Guy Debord.[53] In fact, there were no theatricals produced aboard the USS *United States*, on whose voyage *White-Jacket* was based. Melville's actual shipmate on the voyage of the *United States* wrote in his copy of the novel, next to the theatricals, "Fiction," and came close to the topic of the scene.[54]

For Melville saw no innate desire in his audience for such a culture of suppression. The image of popular culture as staged punishment portrays subjection as an "effect" of the culture mass society encourages its citizens to construct. It was far from Melville to assume any high-cultural bias against popular culture, or to imagine the existence of any inherently depraved and self-subjecting popular taste. "Depravity in the oppressed," as *White-Jacket* describes the subjecting appeal of mass culture to the audience, "is no apology for the oppressor; but rather an additional stigma to him, as being, in a large degree, the effect, and not the cause and justification of oppression" (142). In his attention to popular vices aboard ship such as gambling and controlling spectacle, Melville shared with Benjamin a conviction that mass-cultural entertainment, while repressive, was a hold of liberating social energy distorted by the interests of governing power. "Commodities," as Susan Buck-Morss defines Benjamin's position, "(like religious symbols in an earlier era), store the fantasy energy for social transformation in reified form."[55]

Much of the explicit attention paid to popular spectacle in *White-Jacket* bases itself in this kind of critical impulse. Rather than look down on popular entertainment, Melville regarded its mechanisms as worth serious analysis. Mass culture aboard the *Neversink* offers a falsely positive picture of social conditions, and thus distorts the social dissatisfaction which might be transformed into social change. White-Jacket describes "transgression" as part of the strategy of the "governor," who can stage its expression, rather than as a form of popular subversion an ignorant people choose: "Even the most potent governor must wink at transgression, in order to preserve the laws inviolate for the future. And great care is to be taken, by timely management, to avert an incontestable act of mutiny" (359). White-Jacket himself is consistently concerned with the dangers of symbolic rebellion, even when his desire for force over the Captain and his "timely management" is least contained. Most memorably, his symbolic-fantasy of becoming a "murderer," and proving his "man's manhood" by taking Claret overboard, is rendered as a practical form of "suicide" (280–81). Such commentary is voiced by a cultural critic who recognizes the danger of rebellion's coercion by power. The subtitle of Melville's novel ironically refers to the introjection of domination by the individual as "The World in a Man-of-War."

White-Jacket is thus able to participate in rebellion with the crew, and poke fun at the manipulable symbolism of their act. "The Great Massacre of the Beards," in which the crew refuses to shave against the Captain's order, is, as Howard Vincent has recognized, "a disastrous situation set off in parody."[56] The narrator comically links his narrative with the revolt, and imagines the transformation of the crew's political resistance into a merchandisable sign. Comedy takes a serious stand against the reduction of political activity into trivialized symbols, whose cosmetic images of revolt are produced for passive consumption:

Think of it, if future historians should devote a long chapter to the great *Rebellion of the Beards* on board the United States ship *Neversink*. Why, through all time thereafter, barbers would cut down their spiralized poles, and substitute miniature main-masts for the emblems of their calling. (359)

Here Benjamin's analysis of the effect of commodity culture upon political action was anticipated by Melville, even if the latter did not share the former's optimism about breaking commodification's conservative cultural hold. Imagining political revolt as an object of aesthetic contemplation, Melville nonetheless characterized the conditions of modern politics in terms strikingly similar to those of Benjamin in his definition of the commodity's hold over politics: "the transformation of [the] political struggle from a compulsion to decide into an object of contemplative enjoyment, from a means of production into a consumer article."[57]

The difference between Benjamin and Melville regards the potential of readers to use the repressed energy of commodity symbolism to critical social ends. Melville's pessimism is defined in his striking image of rebellion in a barber's chair. In a society dominated by political symbols, a protest over beards replaces effective action. What

Benjamin called "contemplative enjoyment" never leads to political action, in Melville's view, if "consumer pleasures" and their narcissism take strong enough hold. Benjamin, however, was far more optimistic that subjects of political symbolism would take power over the images produced to control them, turning themselves from "consumers . . . into producers—that is, readers or spectators into collaborators" who turned repressive imagery into cultural criticism, and then the will to act.[58] Melville, on the contrary, was largely concerned with the political *failure* to take seriously the commodified signs of social struggle, which in American buried conflict to the point of explosion. The barber shop as symbol of the aesthetic consumption of politics evokes the later scene in *Benito Cereno*, where Captain Delano's posture as consumer while being shaved renders him unable to read the emerging signs of a slave revolt.

The Rebellion of the Beards looks forward to the more profound moment of the sinking of the *Pequod*, where the symbolism of working-class rebellion swamps any perception of the actual disaster of the ship: "at that instant, a red arm and a hammer hovered backwardly uplifted in the open air, in the act of nailing the flag faster and yet faster to the subsiding spar" (572). Larry Reynolds notes that the hammer was popular as a Union symbol, and sees in the image a "commentary on European political radicalism, namely communism and 'Red Republicanism.'" But the "new hostility toward the mass" that Reynolds discovers in *Moby-Dick* is part of that novel's criticism of cultural manipulation, already present in *White-Jacket*, rather than a sign of any antidemocratic substratum or antipathy toward radicalism in Melville's work.[59] White-jacket is parodic toward the "Massacre of the Beards" because he is hostile toward the reduction of social discontent by popular culture that the episode represents. When "Ushant," the leader of the "Rebellion," is in his prison cell, he cultivates a symbolism which mystifies his submission, and is linked to the function of literature in the act: "books were allowed him, and he spent much time in reading. But he also spent many hours braiding his beard, and interweaving with it strips of red bunting, as if he desired to dress out the thing which had triumphed over all opposition" (366). Reading is by no means a critical social activity per se in Melville's vision of resistance, since the symbolic satisfaction it offers, as his narrator points out, need not be grounded in the actual dynamic of power governing the ship. Thoreauvian disobedience appears in the scene emptied of its intellectual and political content, transformed instead into "emblems," and a subjecting form of aesthetic revolt.

Mad Jack's successful disobedience to the Captain at Cape Horn is thus symptomatic of the rite of cultural and political passage that *White-Jacket* achieved. The rebellion of the scene is lauded by the narrator, but also ironically mocked for its mass-cultural puerility: "Sailor or landsman, there is some sort of a Cape Horn for all. Boys! Beware of it; prepare for it in time" (109). Such irony toward popular fiction remained understated, allowing the action to remain convincing. Melville used elements of popular drama to create a fiction that moved beyond adventure, and engaged in a more serious commentary on the role of mass culture in manipulating social discontent. "What Melville finally rips open and sinks in *White-Jacket*," Robert Caserio observes of its narrator's casting aside of his jacket in the end, "is an endorsement of assertive will, and the idea of realizing democratic manhood through rebellious or violent enactment."[60] Melville always placed such scenes in the context of popular culture: the "jacket," symbolizing the constraints of the popular author's persona, provokes such a scene of revolt as the novel concludes. The narrator, however, having fallen overboard, extricates himself from the jacket's hold. In shedding the constraining garment of authorship, he offers instead a vision of the writer's necessarily social and oedipal formation: "a bloody film was before my eyes, through which, ghost-like, passed and repassed my father, mother, and sisters. An unutterable nausea oppressed me" (392). Far from a revolt against the "family" audience for American fiction, the passage envisions birth as entry into the family as an imprisoning cultural construction, and authorship as a critical response that removes the individual from its confining vest.

White-Jacket ends by dashing illusions of revolt, arguing instead that such self-subjecting fictions of mass culture are the first object with which a democratic public must contend. Melville projects such a critical cultural politics in his closing exhortation to the "people" and audience address: "for the rest, whatever befall us, let us never train our murderous guns inboard; let us not mutiny with bloody pikes in our hands" (400). *White-Jacket* and *Moby-Dick* were the only two of Melville's novels named after objects of manufacture, signs of their concern to examine the political limits enforced by the cultural rhetoric of revolt. The moral his narrator draws from Cape Horn—"to show how little real sway at times have the severest restrictive laws, and how spontaneous is the instinct of discretion in some minds"—looks forward to Ishmael and the *Pequod*, where it is the disaster of Ahab's manipulation of rebellious rage which the Melvillean narrator must both entertain and critically contest (111).

Moby Dick: The Novel as Critical Commodity

The fact that *Moby-Dick* is more full in its speech than perhaps any
novel in world literature should make us at least suspicious of the
repeated claim to censorship and failed speech one finds within its
bounds. Ishmael's concern with what is "well nigh ineffable" (188),
the "nameless horrors" of the Whale, its "nameless terror" (191), and
"nameless things" (195) in the "Whiteness of the Whale," like his
earlier concern with the "ungraspable phantom of life" (5), has its
precedent in *White-Jacket,* however, where its simpler form can shed
light on such rhetoric of the "nameless" and its cultural grounds. Melville developed there what might be called a marketable *rhetoric* of
the unspeakable. Presenting unpalatable social facts under the sign
of speechlessness or censorship, Melville could assure his audience
that he complied with their taste even as he violated it. White-Jacket
assures his reader, for instance, that "there are evils in men-of-war,
which, like the suppressed domestic drama of Horace Walpole, will
neither bear representing, nor reading, and will hardly bear thinking
of" (376), and refers to evils which will "hardly bear even so much
as an allusion" (375) in a popular work. But the narrator who forbids
himself "representing" or alluding to vice does so only as he clearly
alludes to the forbidden which takes place in the holds of the ship
among sailors as a recognizable sexual practice: "the sins for which
the cities of the plain were overthrown still linger in some of these
wooden-walled Gomorrahs of the deep" (375–76).

Moby-Dick is similarly far less frustrated as a novel of social criticism
than adept at using the rhetoric of frustrated speech to cover its vio-
lations of genteel taste. Critics have long recognized the importance
of despair and failure to Melville's political imagination, and nowhere
more so than in *Moby-Dick.* The novel's rhetoric of failure has been
used to characterize Melville as a failed radical, politically neutral,
or as an anguished and ineffective liberal. Sacvan Bercovitch outlines
the first position when he argues that Melville's "unsuccessful effort"
in *Moby-Dick* was an expression of radical anger: for Bercovitch Melville raged against the distortion of the "democratic ideal" in political
reality, but could only turn in paradox and pessimism "against all cultural norms, even those of rhetoric." [61] Murray Krieger similarly notes
this political indecision in *The Tragic Vision,* remarking that Ishmael's
stance as a "comprehensive narrator" appears "fundamentally without a commitment," [62] while echoes of both positions can be found in
Donald Pease's analysis of Ishmael as a liberal transcendentalist. In

Pease's activist view, *Moby-Dick* was Melville's rejection of the comfortable and socially complicit stance of "cultural despair."[63]

Melville's correspondence certainly suggests his identification with Ahab's anger as well as frustration. After being attacked for declaring in a review of Francis Parkman's *The Oregon Trail* that Indians were the intellectual equals of whites, Melville wrote to Evert Duyckinck: "what a madness & anguish it is that an author can never—under no conceivable circumstances—be at all frank with his readers . . . hereafter I shall no more stab at a book (in print, I mean) than I would stab at a man."[64] But the rhetoric of the "well-nigh unspeakable" in *Moby-Dick* is far less metaphysically frustrated or without commitment, and far more politically effective, than is credited by such conceptions. *Moby Dick's* ominous sense of foreclosure and prolific rhetoric of the unspeakable certainly can be considered the voice of Melville's political frustration. But they are less the symptoms of an "uncommitted" liberal discourse subject to coercion and tragedy, than aspects of a novel committed to examining particular *rhetorics of failure* and their mass-cultural force on different readers.

Starbuck, for instance, who represents Yankee commercialism, finds the "ineffable thing" (169) that ties him to Ahab to be popular profanity, the pessimism of the "impious" and "heaven-insulting" account Ahab gives of the whaling trade. Starbuck represents the liberal reader in *Moby-Dick*, who tries to believe in Ahab's energetic optimism, and to hold fast to the "blessed influences" governing the marketplace, while Ahab violates the repression that he himself continually announces, making visible the "wolfish gurglings" (170) of economic competition Starbuck prefers not to see. Ahab clearly represents the desire for economic domination for Starbuck, provoking loyalty by offering his middle-class auditor the assurance that these "infernal orgies" will not be brought to speech: "Will I, nill I; the ineffable thing has tied me to him, tows me with a cable I have no knife to cut" (169). Melville uses the Shakespearean theater of the scene to stage Starbuck as a reader dependent on Ahab's projections of anger, an eager consumer of the speech he finds "blasphemous" and intolerant, yet useful for the purposes of liberal disavowal: "For in his eyes I read some lurid woe would shrivel me up, had I it. Yet is there hope" (169).

Hopeful critics, however, have too easily assimilated Ahab's rhetoric with high culture. Shakespearean diction and cadences offered F. O. Matthiessen, for instance, the optimistic reading of Ahab's grandiloquence as "catharsis." Ahab's tragic grandeur allowed Starbuck to "shrink from the blackness of truth," as Matthiessen put it, and in his Popular Front terms represented an extension of the cultural tradition to the common man.⁶⁵ This emphasis on tragedy, however, obscures the basis of Ahab's mass-cultural appeal, and slights Melville's concern with the limits of popular rhetoric in the novel. For while Ahab's eloquence provides Starbuck with blindness as well as hope, that hope, as well as the "catharsis" Matthiessen describes, might be better described in the terms Adorno developed for kitsch. Starbuck's optimism, in fact, results from a rhetorical confinement he is all too happy to accept: with the "impious ends" of the whaling voyage cloaked in Ahab's Shakespearean affirmations, Starbuck feel reassured. It is the *failures* of Ahabian grandiloquence in *Moby-Dick*, however, that create its critical version of the commodity novel. When Ahabian arrogance recedes, so does Ishmael's high-cultural claim to the "ineffable," and the American realities of race and economic warfare aboard the *Pequod* begin to emerge.

According to Adorno's dialectical concept of kitsch, high-cultural discourse becomes kitsch precisely by avoiding any touch of lowering vulgarity: in resisting the ugly, art transforms itself into the kind of affirmative social vision, devoid of conflict, which adept propaganda can also produce. "True vulgarity," Adorno remarks, occurs from a posture of elitism, and exposes the claim to cultural sophistication as ideology, full of "material brutality" that is apparent despite a rhetoric of high-minded claims:

Artistic vulgarity represents, in a distorted way, the plebeian element that high art has always kept at arm's length. Whenever art succeeded in taking its bearings from the plebeian moment—and not in a tongue in cheek way, but seriously—its weight or gravity increased. . . . Now, gravity is the opposite of the vulgar. Real vulgarity comes from a posture of condescension.⁶⁶

Ahab's "gravity" does indeed define itself as the opposite of the vulgar. The "tragic dramatist," Ishmael insists, would certainly mark the pose like "Nicholas the Czar," with the "plebeian herds crouch[ed] before the tremendous centralization" (148) that Ahab assumed. It is the breaks in such "gravity" that transform "tragic" discourse in *Moby-Dick*, the vulgarity which is always the unspeakable secret behind Ahab and his "arts." Such vulgarity does not "democratize" Ahab in any sense, since his social elitism is ruthlessly and unspeakably enforced: the "hardly tolerable constraint and nameless invisible domineerings of the captain's table" maintain strict racial difference, always distinct from "the almost frantic democracy of those inferior fellows the harpooneers" (152). Ahab's "heaven-insulting" (169) inferences and "mechanical" gestures of solidarity, like nailing the doubloon to the mast, do just the opposite: high culture is revealed as vulgar, stained by "cash," and thus only a mass-cultural mask that authoritarian democracy assumes.

These breaks in the frame of high-cultural discourse prove disturbing to liberal cultural taste. It is the mass-cultural character of Ahab's high oratory that troubles Starbuck. Ahab's address to "The Candles" strikes him as mad precisely for its mixed discourse, Ahab's masterful transformation of the diction of elite culture into controlling motifs of the common man. The heavens, while still the authoritative cultural signifier of "eternity" are democratized, compared to a lonely sufferer of the lower class, a cultural order that eloquence has not yet addressed: "thou foundling fire, thou hermit immemorial, thou too hast thy incommunicable riddle, thy unparticipated grief" (508). Like Wordsworth addressing the Leech Gatherer, Ahab speaks with the promise of including the social outcast in acceptable middle-class discourse.

Unlike Wordsworth's poem, however, Ahab's revolutionary fusion of lower-class speech with the "heavens" of social acceptance becomes lurid, and breaks genteel culture's bounds. Sympathy with "creativeness mechanical" (508) produces the vulgarity of false inclusion before the crew, with its measure of elitist disdain: "Leap! leap up, and lick the sky! I leap with thee; I burn with thee; would fain be welded with thee; defyingly I worship thee!" (508). It is the promise of such social inclusion that troubles Starbuck: the "haughty agony" of working-class identification Ahab produces is distasteful because it reveals "eternity," a traditional attribute of "creativeness" in aesthetics, as a rationale for dominating power. With Ahab's boat suddenly lit up like Milton's Satan, in a "levelled flame of pale, forked fire" (508), Starbuck retreats to a humanist notion of moral high culture, begging for a high culture that remains ideal: "let me square the yards, while we may, old man . . . to go on a better voyage than this" (508).

The dark side of Northern capitalism, of course, was never invisible to readers like Starbuck. Defenders of slavery such as George Fitzhugh spoke directly about the social abuses of the unbridled economy of Northern industrial cities in works such as *Cannibals All!* and *Sociology for the South*. "The competitive system," he wrote, "is a system of antagonism and war, and ours, of peace and fraternity." [67] While the self-justification behind such an ideology is apparent in retrospect, Fitzhugh's rhetoric is a reminder of the ideological extremes which

Melville's readers might encounter in a single sentence. Fitzhugh's contrast between "peace and fraternity" and "antagonism and war" has even been located by some critics of *Moby-Dick* in Ahab's oratory. One need not make Ahab into Fitzhugh, however, to notice Melville's consistent attention toward ideological visions of the working class. Visions of laboring "fraternity" are used throughout the novel to justify the exercise of exploitive economic power. Though the "hope" of Starbuck's liberal optimism would certainly have rejected Fitzhugh's rhetoric, Northern liberals themselves used visions of laboring fraternity—not of happy slaves, but of free labor—to mask the misery of the industrial plight. Ishmael identifies himself as a Jacksonian ideologist of this sort, promising to "touch that workman's arm with some ethereal light," and rises to eloquent heights in his descriptions of the *Pequod*'s crew (117). Yet the reality beneath populist ideology remains palpable—since "men may seem detestable as joint stock-companies"—until the failure of democratic equality becomes more important in Ishmael's account than placing the socially "abased" upon "exalted mounts."

Liberal disillusion thus precedes Ishmael's production of Jacksonian mass-cultural symbols: "were the coming narrative to reveal, in any instance, the complete abasement of poor Starbuck's fortitude, scarce might I have the heart to write it; for it is a thing most sorrowful, nay shocking, to expose the fall of valor in the soul" (117). Here Melville's tongue-in-cheek address to a Northern liberal readership is palpable: "nay shocking" expresses mock alarm at revealing the "mean and meagre faces" of the common man, while at the same time serving as a promise that the "august divinity" of the working class he will describe is sure to be false. Thus Melville assures the reader of censorship at the same time he violates its strictures. Melville's central purpose in the passage is to describe the mass-cultural falsity of populist rhetoric before he indulges in its production himself:

knaves, fools, and murderers there may be; men may have mean and meagre faces; but man, in the ideal, is so noble and so sparkling, such a grand and glowing creature, that over any ignominious blemish in him all his fellows should run to throw their costliest robes. (117)

Like Starbuck, who recoiled at Ahab's suggestion of a "creativeness mechanical," Ishmael allows Melville to prick his audience on its rules for representing class. For the "ignominious blemish" marking "the arm that wields a pick or drives a spike" is the sign of labor, automatically marking the working body as fixed in station, whatever its accomplishments. Even Ahab, according to "immemorial credulities" of culture, was scarred before the white whale remarked his class injury, bearing by legend "a birth-mark on him from crown to sole" (124).

Jacksonian praise of labor in *Moby-Dick* in this way both reproduces and undercuts populist ideology, revealing democratic heroism as a social signifier of working-class compensation. The worship of Andrew Jackson, while a fundament of American expansionist ideology, was itself contradictory; while Europe might be regarded as corrupt, and the West the "area of freedom," cultural envy still marked the swaggering assertion of Manifest Destiny and its will.[68] Melville makes this recognition of ideological compensation precise: the "crown" accorded the "select[est] champions from the kingly commons" (117) is set only on the head of the working man, whom popular lore recognizes as scarred by his birth. Such heroism lays claim to cultural distinction, yet only so that it can cover the deeper wounds of class. For it is an unspeakable and unholy father, Ishmael suggests, who authored the most painful scar that a working-class crew can trace: "Ahab stood before them with a crucifixion in his face; in all the nameless regal overbearing dignity of some mighty woe" (124).

Despite such critical readings of the Captain, Ahab's authoritative use of cultural iconography coopts rebellion before it starts. Melville is conscious of this process throughout *Moby-Dick*, and uses Ishmael to consider the political force exerted over a democratic audience by the claims of high art. The pose assumed is often humility, confronting the social inferiority of the working class of sailors head-on: "if a stranger were introduced into any miscellaneous metropolitan society, it would but slightly advance the general opinion of his merits, were he presented to the company as a harpooneer" (108). Humility, however, soon gives way to an exaggerated effort to persuade, as the title of the chapter "The Advocate" suggests.

In response to a mock interrogation by his imaginary reading public, Ishmael assures his audience that whalemen possess all the signifiers of cultural authority. Soon, all the "aesthetically noble associations connected" (111) with the "heathenish sharked waters" of "colonial" commerce have invested the working sailor with cultural capital. Questions of whether working whalers have included a *"famous author,"* possessed *"dignity,"* been *"respectable,"* or possessed *"good blood in their veins"* are posed and answered. The list, printed in italics, reads like an advertising broadside: yet the "anxiety" (108) Ishmael refers to at the start, whether readers can be convinced that an "unpoetical and disreputable pursuit" (108) meets the test of high culture, has been laid to rest. The "glory" of whaling is finally to be taken as a sign of "real repute in that high hushed world" which Ishmael, for whom a "whaleship was my Yale College and my Harvard," might not "be unreasonably ambitious of" (112). The reversal serves here as a form of class mapping: the apparently compensatory force of over-blown rhetoric allows the conflicting codes of literary value applied by a democratic audience to be sketched.

Melville often uses the apparent failure of decorum in *Moby-Dick* to trace the contradictory demands of his American reading public, and to teach it a kind of self-critique. Melville imagines a reader-ship that is skeptical of popular representations. The "good blood" of whalers, of course, is as much an authorial fiction as the opposing "popular conceit" (109) that whaling's "terrors" are individualistic and democratic. Together, both testaments figure Melville's ideal audience. Neither genteel nor a fictional denizen of the working class, the reader addressed by Ishmael is a citizen encouraged to remain skeptical of symbols of social identity. Melville adverts to "anxiety" about meet-ing the expectations of high culture as well as populist democracy: the hidden object of Ishmael's address is often the rhetorical codings of social class. While Ishmael "spread[s] a rainbow" over the work-ing man's "disastrous set of sun" (117), he also instructs his reader to look beneath the elevating discourse of "tragic graces," and to doubt mass-cultural transformations of high culture into propagandistic rep-resentations of democratic truth.

"Piety itself," he points out, is a means of censorship. Sympathy is perfectly able to "stifle her upbraidings" (117) at what Ishmael clearly recognizes as Starbuck's subjection to the mass. In America, where the reading audience demands independent virtue, Starbuck's en-slavement must be masked. Grand apology assures the audience of compliance with democratic style: just as Dickens' shadows in *Little Dorrit* signified a narrative in compliance with middle-class fictional standards, assuring readers he would not illuminate more than was acceptable about working-class life, Melville assures his reader that "divine equality" (117) will remain his norm. Narrative eloquence thus inflates Starbuck's grandeur, while critical observation deflates his pretensions and depicts him as a member of the mass.

Once "piety" is pointed out as censorious, its constraints are soon undercut. Starbuck's "fall of valor" makes him a character more exter-nally symbolic than individually substantial: "a staid, steadfast man, whose life for the most part was a telling pantomime of action" (115). Praise of the democratic hero allows Ishmael to emphasize dissolution of his political substance. Starbuck eventually becomes the empty signifier of equality, unable to sustain its front. Democratic heroism, fulsomely praised, is finally exposed by Ishmael as a privatizing image of mass culture. Starbuck's power is available only in withdrawal. Like the culture offered the modern consumer, fictions of action often substitute for the role of active political agent. It is this kind of mass-cultural heroism Starbuck enjoys, which Ishmael calls the "immaculate manliness we feel within ourselves, so far within us, that it remains intact though all the outer character seem gone"(117).

This notion of outer character as an empty cipher represents the passivity of the cultural consumer. What Ishmael calls "outer character" is political action, and Starbuck fails to act, all the while enjoying a sense of his independence "within." In this respect Starbuck's claim against Ahab's rage is key: "it will not fetch thee much in our Nantucket market" (163). Starbuck's mistake is the realistic assumption that rhetoric itself does not *already constitute a product*. Stressing practical insight into the marketplace, Starbuck ignores the crucial role of symbols in commercially shaping the working man's "rage." *Moby-Dick* conveys a sense of this omnipotence of representation in consumer culture, where the signifiers of products and even authorial identity become objects which the customers in Nantucket wish to "fetch." *Pierre* would fully represent publishing as a business. There, the author's reputation and "future popularity" (263) are already considered a product for sale before Pierre's novel itself has been produced.

In *Pierre*, the ideal of high art and consumerist symbolism meet head-on. "Speculators" seek to trade in Pierre's celebrity before it is dashed, offering to "start a paper-mill expressly for the great author, and so monopolize his stationary dealings." Such skepticism about the power of the "great author," the kind of figure whom Balzac, Adorno notes, linked with printing press and material production, pervades *Moby-Dick* in subtler form.[69] The most powerful readings of American politics in the novel account for mass-cultural symbolism, decoding the "emblems" that signify political positions or examining the mass-cultural quietism that is certainly part of Ishmael's fate.[70] Melville, however, resembles Kafka in often representing subjection in order to analyze the language that gives it force. Scenes of submission to Ahab offer some of *Moby-Dick*'s most strikingly critical observations, and many are offered by obedient members of the crew. The fictions of democratic inclusion Ahab offers a multiracial audience in "The Quarter-Deck" scene are remarked, and its members remain conscious of the techniques of democratic coercion. When Ahab interrogates the crew's "clubbed voices," they question the power which the symbolic consensus of such false pluralism exerts: "the mariners began to gaze curiously at each other, as if marvelling how it was that they themselves became so excited at such seemingly purposeless questions" (161).

This vision of an audience questioning its own response is crucial, anticipating as it does the more radical speculations on rhetoric in the novel Melville produced in *Pierre*. Lack of address to any uniform set of readers in that novel, as Larzer Ziff notes, "destroyed the contemporary audience for the novel," but does illuminate the more popularly critical stance toward mass culture included in *Moby Dick*.[71] Melville's novelist protagonist is hostile toward popular fiction, spurning "the countless tribes of common novels," and scorning their "atmosphere of light and mirth" (141). Pierre's literary failure to produce any "profounder emanations of the human mind," however, works much like the political failures of Ishmael and the *Pequod*'s crew. Paralysis of action activates criticism, making the novel a brilliant success at figuring what Eric Sundquist calls "authority at an impotent crossroads."[72] The "paralysis" of action in Melville's novels and the "subtile acid" of ideological critique often go side by side.

This corrosive of skepticism in *Moby-Dick* accompanies its most fervent expression of cultural solidarity. "I myself am a savage, owning no allegiance but to the King of Cannibals," Ishmael declares, "and ready, at any moment, to rebel against him" (270). The declaration carries metacritical weight, part of Melville's rebellion against his public's demand for a commodified exoticism from the author of *Typee* and *Omoo*. In a letter to Hawthorne written close to the end of *Moby-Dick*'s composition, Melville expressed his resistance to his already marketed literary fame in just these terms. "To go down to posterity is bad enough, anyway," he wrote, "but to go down as a man who 'lived among the cannibals!' "[73] Primitivism is by no means Melville's version of neutral, socially critical ground. *Moby-Dick* depicts commodity production to break the illusion of cultural marginality, in a novel in which acts of rhetorical and material production crowd every scene. "Lively sketches of whales and whaling-scenes" are available as touristic representations "throughout the Pacific, and also in Nantucket, and in New Bedford," Ishmael announces, just as "ladies' busks" are "wrought out of the Right Whale-bone" (269). In *Moby-Dick*, commodity production and the proliferation of cultural images are linked: narrative styles, like fashion, have their "natural" authority called into question by Ishmael's constant reminder that both are socially produced.

"A Squeeze of the Hand" satirizes the rhetoric of classless affection in this manner, turning the material of commodity production into a critical trope. The well-known scene is often cited as the paradigmatic example of Melville's support for laboring solidarity: in squeezing the whale sperm with his comrades, Ishmael waxes eloquent about brotherhood while touching their hands in the liquid. The material worked on speaks differently: while "bathing in that bath" (416), an "abounding, affectionate, friendly, loving feeling," the scene becomes a self-describing metaphor for rhetorical bathos, centered on a recognition of perceptual error: "I squeezed that sperm till a strange sort of insanity came over me; and I found myself unwittingly squeezing my co-laborers' hands in it, mistaking their hands for the gentle globules" (416). Critics have sensed both the social quietism and irony of the episode: Paul Royster observes that Ishmael's "universalizing ritual of labor is . . . in no sense an indictment of the system of economic relations," while Wilson Cary McWilliams' liberal reading manages to catch the obscene irony of the scene that mocks rhetorical solidarity from within.[74] Both fail to emphasize the centrality of the American consumer to Melville's critical vision: consumer preference in both ideology and literary consumption is the subject of Melville's mockery throughout the scene.

When the consumer's role in culture becomes a concern, the relation between kitsch and catharsis is brought to the fore. The more falsely affirmative Ishmael's release from class antagonism becomes—"why should we longer cherish any social acerbities"—the more Melville describes the kitsch atmosphere in which such stereotypic images are consumed. Domestic life and its "attainable felicity" are described as a sacrifice of intellect, an intellectual mediocrity Ishmael praises in high eloquence, while his tone is further undercut by the sperm covering his hands. Ishmael recommends classless social solidarity while ironically depicting it as stereotype, the American replica of Dickensian mass culture molded to consumer taste:

I have perceived that in all cases man must eventually lower, or at least shift, his conceit of attainable felicity; not placing it anywhere in the intellect or the fancy; but in the wife, the heart, the bed, the table, the saddle, the fire-side, the country; now that I have perceived all this, I am ready to squeeze case eternally. (416)

The wish to "squeeze case" eternally, of course, offends precisely that middle-class taste to which the rhetoric of domestic sanctity appeals. Adorno warned that the banality of such style was not restricted to mass culture, arguing that the false affirmation of catharsis infects high-cultural rhetoric as well as works of mass culture. Ishmael's construction of kitsch lends support to Adorno's point that "it is useless . . . to try and draw a fine line between what constitutes aesthetic fiction (art) and what is merely sentimental rubbish (kitsch)."[75] Grandiloquence and scholarly reference combine with the sentimental in Ishmael's Dickensian reverie: both classical learning and popular bathos are shown to contribute to the false rhetoric of social harmony. "I almost began to credit the old Paracelsan superstition that sperm is of rare virtue in allaying the heat of anger," Ishmael declares; "while bathing in that bath, I felt divinely free from all ill-will, or petulance, or malice, of any sort whatsoever" (416). Sentiment pours like "globules" of sperm to authorize his feeling that "Constantine's bath" (415), and homespun domesticity, though separated by hierarchy, are cultural twins.

For violence lurks beneath all forms of social affirmation in *Moby-Dick,* a novel providing better evidence than any other for Benjamin's adage that "there is no document of civilization which is not at the same time a document of barbarism."[76] Cultural icons are constantly juxtaposed with the horrors practiced by the powerful against the weak in civilization's name. Ishmael begins with anthropological references: "The Whiteness of the Whale" compares "the barbaric, grand old kings of Pegu, who placed the title 'Lord of the White Elephants' above all their other magniloquent ascriptions of dominion," with the dialectic of culture and barbarism in the West; the "ermine of the Judge" similarly serves as a cultural justification for domination, giving the "white man ideal mastership over every dusky tribe" (189). The barbarism mystified in consumer culture is foregrounded, however, in the many chapters detailing the transformation of whales into marketable products. In "Stubb's Supper," the cultural pretense to morality of Northern consumers is mocked. Eating for Stubb signifies middle-class gentility, Ishmael notes in an earlier chapter, a social ritual of consumption that covers the brutality of labor: "good-humored, easy, and careless, he presided over his whale-boat as if the most deadly encounter were but a dinner, and his crew all invited guests" (118).

Before describing Stubb's actual meal, Ishmael compares the barbarism of warfare to the civilizing pretense of table manners: "while the valiant butchers . . . are thus cannibally carving each other's live meat with carving-knives all gilded and tasselled, the sharks, also, with their jewel-hilted mouths, are quarrelsomely carving away under the table at the dead meat" (293). Dinner is parodied by figuring its consumers as sharks—those "outriders of all slave ships crossing the Atlantic" (293)—while the liberal claim to social civility is tweaked by the barbarism always present beneath the surface of culture: "sleepers below . . . were often startled by the sharp slapping of their tails against the hull, within a few inches of the sleepers' hearts" (293). Both production and consumption of commodities in *Moby-Dick* produce false rhetorics of social affirmation, while Ishmael reveals the concrete conditions—the slave trade, and the lack of "intellect" in domestic culture—that require the production of social myths.

For "Fleece" the black cook, kitsch becomes part of a dialect that releases social anger, parodying dominant constructions of both commerce and race. Submissive posture is deceptive in the scene, as the name "Fleece" already suggests. The stance of "seeming innocence" Melville would later use in *Pierre*, Henry Louis Gates, Jr., points out, was similar to the structuring irony that governed slave narratives written at the same time.[77] Fleece is ordered to produce both a "steak," as consumable commodity from a whale, and a religious rhetoric that will cover the voracious world of consumption sharks embody as they feed on the whale outside the ship. "They are welcome to help themselves civilly, and in moderation, but they must keep quiet," Stubb declares. The order of middle-class propriety is in this way defined as censorship, before Stubb commands Fleece to silence the violence of commodity consumption: "go and preach to 'em!" (294).

Fleece responds with a doctrine of liberal cooperation which allows his employer to continue his dinner in peace: "Your woraciousness, fellow–critters, I don't blame ye so much for; dat is natur, and can't be helped; but to gobern dat wicked natur, dat is de pint . . . don't be tearin' de blubber out your neighbour's mout, I say" (295). But as "Fleece" is praised by Stubb for his doctrine—"Well done, old Fleece, that's Christianity; go on" (295)—his sheepish subjection to the kitsch version of Christian doctrine requested by his master is transformed. "Wish, by gor!" he concludes in a prayer for the future of Stubb, "whale eat him, 'stead of him eat whale"—an act that "fleeces" Stubb with the very ideology of "gobern[ing] de shark in you" he was commanded to produce (297). "Old Ebony," as Fleece is also called, uses a white doctrine in a resistant figure of his own exploitation—"I'm bressed if he ain't more of shark dan Massa Shark himself"—turning kitsch around to contest the master's containing command of his laborer's speech.

Ishmael is able to achieve a similar effect with the rhetoric of Manifest Destiny. In discussing "Fast-Fish and Loose-Fish," the doctrine which gives a ship "property" in the whales it hunts, Ishmael extends the concept of the "Loose-Fish"—"fair game for anyone who can soonest catch it"—to the process of imperial expansion. Ishmael exults jingoistically and performs an imperial extension of his trope:

What was America in 1492 but a Loose-Fish, in which Columbus struck the Spanish standard. . . . What was Poland to the Czar? What Greece to the Turk? What at last will Mexico be to the United States? All Loose-Fish. (398)

Such parody of Manifest Destiny is present even in *Moby-Dick*'s most serious scenes, such as Ahab's Shakespearean soliloquy in "Sunset." There, Ahab's serious commitment to expansionism is coupled with subtle mockery of the "Young America" literary movement and its quest to found a national literature through praise of the West as the American Sublime. That nationalism was turned into propaganda by John O'Sullivan, the Young American who founded the *Democratic Review* and also coined the phrase "Manifest Destiny" itself.[78] Melville was accustomed to "toy with the reader," John Gerlach notes, and thus would appear to give strong endorsement to the expansionist positions he mocked.[79] But here, Ahab invokes the majesty of the Hudson River School, only to reveal the "rifl[ing]" of a plundered West that praise of its natural grandeur concealed: "Over unsounded gorges, through the rifled hearts of mountains, under torrents' beds, unerringly I rush!" (168).

The doctrine which regards countries as properties to be speared, or "rifled," once recognized as "internationally and universally applicable" (398), is quickly transformed into a satire on Melville's audience. Ishmael had already satirized, in "Knights and Squires," the class differences that subtended popular praise of democratic principles. In his kitsch version of Jacksonian rhetoric, eloquence in exaggeration had produced a satire indistinguishable from endorsement of popular democracy: "The great God absolute! The centre and circumference of all democracy! His omnipresence, our divine equality!" (117). Later the pointed wit of "Fast-Fish and Loose-Fish" spears those ideals more directly. Democratic principles are shown to be sacrificed to the idolatry of property, and social agents are envisioned as products: "What are the Rights of Man and the Liberties of the World but Loose-Fish? What are all men's minds and opinions but Loose-Fish?" (398). Ishmael entertains popular rhetoric until the point of his own rhetoric can be sharpened—"what to the ostentatious smuggling verbalists are the thoughts of thinkers but Loose-Fish?" (398)—and his own reader identified as the subject of his attack: "And what are you, reader, but a Loose-Fish and Fast-Fish, too?" (398).

Ahab's high-cultural rhetoric, by contrast, steps back from the effects of mass production. The "equatorial coin" (431) offered by Ahab in reward for Moby-Dick is defined as the mirror of a "mysterious self" rather than a medium of exchange, and Ishmael rightly defines his Captain's attitude as "disdain [for] all base considerations" (212). Ahab prefers to see the self in the "magician's glass" (432), rather than as subject to the "common, daily appetites" of "manufactured man" (212). Melville would portray his satirized author figure in *Pierre* in similar terms, as a writer who fears a loss of "true distinction" (254), and abhors the commodification of his image as "public property" (254) on the marketplace, just as Ahab despises "hopes of cash—aye, cash" (212).

To Ishmael, however, the rhetoric of the "mysterious self" and its "mystic sign" in the whale is quite close to the process Marx would later describe as "The Fetishism of Commodities." In Marx's analysis, as in "The Doubloon," the "mystery" of the commodity results from the fact that the use of money as a medium of exchange necessarily implies that commodities are of equal value despite the unequal amounts of labor, and its history, which have gone into their production. Fetishism and commodity worship mask the painful reality of social inequality. "There is a definite social relation between men," as Marx puts it, "that assumes, in their eyes, the fantastic form of a relation between things."[80] For Melville, to fetishize the commodity "superstitiously," by "immemorial credulities, popularly invested" (124), is also to look at the unpleasant realities beneath its exchange, unrepresented in monetary transactions, but involved, like Ahab's injury, in the production of the commodity for "cash." The "nameless horror[s]" Ishmael sees in the whale thus bring "panic to the soul" (188). Like the "spiritual throes" (202) of Ahab, the rhetoric of fetish covers but fails to cancel the painful inner truth behind economic production, what Ishmael defines with precision as the "charnel-house within" (195).

This contradiction in the commodity is foregrounded when Ishmael reflects on working for money in chapter 1. Comic despair at "commerce" brings Ishmael—"having little or no money in my purse"— to reflect on the exchange principle as an explicit principle of culture. Labor is no immediate fact at the beginning of *Moby-Dick,* but a social fact represented by a series of different signifiers. High-cultural symbols take precedence, as work is first examined from a "metaphysical point of view," and thus distanced from the painful site of commodity production. With Ishmael's need for work explained philosophically as part of "the grand programme of Providence," the abuses suffered by workers "pent up in lath and plaster . . . tied to counters, nailed to benches, clinched to desks" (4) disappear. Labor's grievance becomes a "universal thump" suffered equally, "passed around" (6), yet enforced by the mysteriously "invisible police officer of the Fates" (7). In the humbler discourse of mass-cultural common sense, Ishmael dismisses the need to go "before the mast" as "wholesome exercise" (6). Work remains an "ungraspable phantom," as exchange value renders the concretion of labor abstract. Ishmael's hatred of laboring servitude is certain—"I abominate all honorable respectable toils, trials, and tribulations of every kind"—while his view of work at sea, like Narcissus' gaze, is fetish, deceptively pleasant and therefore dangerous: "he could not grasp the tormenting, mild image he saw in the fountain, plunged into it, and was drowned" (5).

For products are not intrinsic in worth, but valuable because desired by others, as Ishmael points out of the literary world: "why did the poor poet of Tennessee, upon suddenly receiving two handfuls of silver, deliberate whether to buy him a coat, which he sadly needed, or invest his money in a pedestrian trip to Rockaway Beach?" (5). The coat, while tangible in its use value, pales in value next to the "meditation" of water. In a society ruled by exchange value, the fetish value of being "seen" at the proper resort exceeds the use value of clothes as a means to keep warm. Commodity fetishes foster the worship of the "image," as goods are produced for exchange and satisfy the need for what consumers regard as valuable, thereby distorting the perception of actual social needs. Ishmael therefore dwells on the phenomenon of money, and the double concept of value it promotes. The meaning of the commodity centers for Ishmael on what he calls the act of *"being paid"*:

The act of paying is perhaps the most uncomfortable infliction that the two orchard thieves entailed upon us. But *being paid*,—what will compare with it? The urbane activity with which a man receives money is really marvelous, considering that we so earnestly believe money to be the root of all earthly ills, and that on no account can a monied man enter heaven. Ah! How cheerfully we consign ourselves to perdition! (6)

The "urbane activity" of receiving wealth, Ishmael observes, is at radical odds with the "perdition" of social struggle in which commodities and wealth are produced. The "affliction" of "being paid" is thus a contradictory one, yet the commodifiable wisdom of popular culture obscures its oppositional force. The commonsense religious explanation of "labor" as punishment ("two orchard thieves") transforms its "infliction" of pain into an acceptable mass-cultural banality ("on no account can a monied man enter heaven") thus imagining the "perdition" of work and canceling the serious recognition of its "infliction" at the same time.

Ishmael always stands ready to use irony against the religious wisdom of a falsely affirmative culture. The "New Testament" (6) is far less at issue in Melville's criticism than the repressive force of its mass-cultural reduction. Common sense, *Moby-Dick* suggests, retains an ideological force, and Melville's wit takes it seriously. In justifying his demeaning servitude, Ishmael refers to his service under an "old hunks" of a captain. While the reference is trivial, the conformism it refers to was not: in 1850, a "hunker" was a Northern merchant who profited from slavery and refused to oppose its continuance in the South. In this context, Ishmael's justification of his obedience as a sailor—"who aint a slave?" (6)—is not only an acceptance of working-class slavery, but also a parody of the banalized Christianity that tolerated the enslavement of blacks. This ability to "cheerfully . . . consign [oneself] to perdition" is connected to the immense power of Ahab's magnificent satanism, in that both are attempts to find a language for the "horror" of the production of the commodity—the realistic substance of *Moby-Dick*'s journey—a horror that can represent the consequences of a human and economic process, in Ahab's grandiose or Ishmael's mass-cultural terms.

Moby-Dick itself, as critics have always noted, is both a metaphysical and a realistic novel, and its concern with "perdition" is hardly a trivial affair.[81] The two cultural registers reflect Melville's critical concern with commodity production, and with both mass and high-cultural rhetorics which attempt to account for its workers' despair. Throughout Ishmael's narration, popular legends that represent working misery and the high Miltonic and Shakespearean rhetoric Ahab uses to account for the loss of his leg are paired. The "agonizing bodily laceration" (184) suffered by Ahab is used by Melville to yoke together the physical and psychic "calamities" (180)—"not restricted to sprained wrists, and ancles, broken limbs, or devouring amputations"—with what twentieth-century sociology would aptly call the hidden injuries of class.[82]

Ahab's grand posture achieves power by using the economic origins of his injury mystically. "Men may seem detestable as joint stock-companies and nations," Ishmael observes (117). But obedience to the social order can be fostered through evoking a notion of virtue beyond social class, by provoking the sense of symbolic injury. Emotional and spiritual anguish are thus for Ahab a way of achieving cultural authority, turning the injury that "bleeds" into a powerful social sign. "Tragic graces" (117) give him power over the "most abased," who defer to the status signified by formal rhetoric. Members of the middle class like Starbuck despise such intellect in practice—"I am here in this critical ocean to kill whales for my living" (116)—yet remain spellbound by the veneer of culture eloquence provides. Ishmael himself mocks eloquence, praising cultural authorities with a suspect reverence. But like the "Late Consumptive Usher to a Grammar School," who begins the novel with "Etymology," *Moby Dick*'s narrator recognizes the dominating power of transmitted culture: "he loved to dust his old grammars; it somehow mildly reminded him of his mortality" (xv). The aura of narrative authority, as Benjamin recognized in "The Storyteller," has the power of mystifying death.[83] Ahab's "shrewdness" similarly recognizes that the hunt needed to be "stripped of that strange imaginative impiousness which naturally invested it," and his "magnet" hold on Starbuck would be complete (212).

For while religion's cultural hold is shaky in *Moby-Dick*, the claims of high culture represent a powerful, controlling social force. The power of Father Mapple's oratory does not speak to Starbuck in the novel, but the spiritualization of working misery produced by Ahab's personalized political rhetoric has compelling force. Ishmael treats his subjection to high culture with humor. As part of Melville's need to justify "impiousness" to a genteel readership, however, his claims for the "Honor and Glory of Whaling" constitute what Wai-Chee Dimmock accurately calls Melville's authorial subjugation by culture: "I am transported with the reflection that I myself belong, though but subordinately, to so emblazoned a fraternity" (361).[84] Such underlying bitterness, however, spurred Melville's critical sense. Spiritualized projections of authority in *Moby-Dick* are always recognized as powerful, but also regarded as suspect legitimations of social class. Starbuck serves Ahab because he "cannot withstand those more terrific, because more spiritual terrors, which sometimes menace you from the concentrating brow of an enraged and mighty man" (117). "Spiritual throes" (202), as Ishmael calls them, are in *Moby-Dick* a means of generating high-cultural authority, a kind of spiritual exaltation that promises to place the speaker who can evoke them above "the dead level of the mass" (148).

Ahab's cultural power is thus depicted as offering him a sense of interior elevation: "these spiritual throes heaved his being up from its base." Ahab's most painful and literal nightmare, accordingly, imagines demons beckoning him to enter what is recognizable as the painful caldron of labor. The actual laboring conditions of the ship are voiced in elevated Miltonic language, but figure the panic of *déclassement* and social descent: "a chasm seemed opening in him, from which forked flames and lightnings shot up, and accursed fiends beckoned him to leap down among them" (202). Henry Nash Smith, the most acute critic of Ahab's insanity, argues that Ahabian madness results from the intensity of Melville's own rejection of mass society, and from his hostility toward "the mediocrity of a culture which lacks all distinction."[85] The point is correct, though if anything Nash understates the contradictory cultural divide that Ahab and his actions represent. Despising the "hell in himself" (202) of working-class culture, Ahab allies himself with Milton's Satan and his willful pretensions to enter the culture on high. In hating a "somnambulistic" mass culture, however, Ahab's "tormented spirit" despises the very sources of "common vitality" (202) that might heal his cultural wound.

Despite this tortured rejection of the common, Ahab's language is saturated by labor and its culture, fully conscious that the high-cultural rhetoric of agony has been motivated by working-class wounds. The "Iron Crown of Lombardy" he covets thus grates him with pain. " 'Tis iron—that I know—not gold,' " Ahab confesses as he recalls the separation of physical from mental labor which the division of labor requires: " 'Tis split, too—that I feel; the jagged edge galls me so, my brain seems to beat against the solid metal' " (167). In confronting the ship's workers, Ahab recognizes "madness" itself as a form of displaced *anger*, an excess of emotion produced at the site where commodities are formed: "Thou shoud'st go mad, blacksmith; say, why dost thou not go mad? How can'st thou endure without being mad?" (487). Ahab is most insane when he seeks a cure from working-class life and its painful injury, and Melville most powerfully critical when Ahab's grandiloquence must face labor as the central "scar" (507) of *Moby-Dick*, whose divisions cannot be healed: " 'if thou coud'st, blacksmith, glad enough would I lay my head upon thy anvil, and feel thy heaviest hammer between my eyes. Answer! Can'st thou smoothe this seam?' " (488).

Ahab's relation to the working class centers on this common "scar" (487). Enlightenment and high-cultural rhetoric serve instead as a replacement for empathy, as the commitment to technology and progress gives anger an outlet: "the path to my fixed purpose is laid with iron rails, whereon my soul is grooved to run" (168). Such passages reflect the continual disparity that Adorno and Horkheimer analyzed in *The Dialectic of Enlightenment*, between the liberated promise of industrial society and the suppression that accompanied its rewards. Technocratic society could master nature, they argued, but its instrumental culture would offer only substitute satisfactions: "men pay for the increase of their power with alienation from that over which they exercise their power."[86] Ahab suffers from this deferred *promesse de bonheur* in the "sunset soothed" (167) he imagines and his inability to enjoy it due to the self-subjection required by his laboring task: "Gifted with the high perception, I lack the low, enjoying power; damned, most subtly and most malignantly! Damned in the midst of Paradise!" (167).

But commodity culture leads to cultural criticism rather than just alienation in *Moby-Dick*. Antiquity, shaped into a palliative for cultural consumption in Ahab's speeches, retains the traces of something better, a vision of the world as it would look redeemed. Dense cadences of Homeric speech give the "solid metal" (167) of Ahab's industrial commitment an antique cast, and mystify his subjection— "the warm waves blush like wine. The gold brow plumbs the blue" (167)—as imagery like "the goblet's rim" (167) renders the culture of consumption poetic. Such language offers a utopian prospect of happiness that is imagined within the bounds of "gold" and the culture of exchange but looks beyond its substitute satisfactions. Hence the intimate and genuinely liberatory force of Ahabian speech when the working commitment to the "doubloon" it promotes leaves the crew debased and socially enslaved. The substitute satisfactions of commodity culture, as Adorno recognized, were dialectically tied to an oppositional cultural vision, in the deferred promise of liberation they produced: "There is no happiness which does not promise to fulfill a socially constituted desire, but there is also none which does not promise something quantitatively different in this fulfillment."[87]

Bridging the gap between utopian visions of whaling and the "nameless invisible domineerings" (152) it requires is the Ahabian anger that gives a paranoid account of his pain. Ahab's famous accusation against the White Whale—"he tasks me; he heaps me; I see in him outrageous strength" (164)—blames the Whale for a laboring "task" that is self-imposed, while the outer origins of internalized social dictates remain unseen. As Ishmael observes: "with little external to constrain us, the innermost necessities in our being, these still drive us on" (165). Ahab's relation to the lower class is similarly split between attraction and paranoid resentment. The "Quarter Deck" scene orchestrated by Ahab pretends to elevate the ship's lowest racial castes to social dignity, but actually manipulates lurking resentment against them instead. The crew's Western officers are first commanded to act as "cup-bearers," a command that exacerbates racial tension. Ahab knows the gesture will provoke resentment, and in "Forecastle—Midnight," two chapters later, members of the crew will engage in the race baiting of Daggoo. "The Quarter Deck" manages such tension by offering the promise of an upended hierarchy. Its social symbolism thus mobilizes envy of "pagan" pleasure, turning racist imagery into a theatrical scene. As the Captain drinks with his crew, Melville dramatizes libidinal release as a controlling cultural demand: "I do not order ye; ye will it," Ahab declares; "cut your seizings and draw the poles, ye harpooneers!' " (166).

The upended spear, an instrument of aggression, then becomes a ritual instrument for the symbolic consumption of social discontent. "Stab me not with that keen steel! Cant them; cant them over!" he tells the harpooneers; "know ye not the goblet end?"(166). To "cant" the harpoon is to tip it, but also to *disable* it as a means of mutiny pointed at the Captain. The weapon's menace is transformed into a means of intoxication instead. Elevating the harpooneers has also served to disguise their social subjection. In the Pequod's division of labor, it is the "pagan" harpooneers of its lowest racial castes who are in fact the most technically proficient and economically useful members of the crew. Their temporary elevation to the status of "gentlemen and noblemen" by Ahab occurs only while their tools are branded as "murderous chalices," marking them falsely as lowly cannibals who devour the symbolic blood they are served. Exposed in the scene is a kind of false or managed *communitas*, as Victor Turner calls it, a fracture of hierarchy and release from social obligation that serves to manage fractious social energy.[88]

Ahab's control over the crew takes the form of camaraderie rather than overt domination: "in Ahab, there seemed not to lurk the smallest social arrogance" (150). As a result, Tashteego, Queequeg, and Daggoo become participants in Ahab's racist symbolism in "The Forge," without envisioning him as a threat:

"Will ye give me as much blood as will cover this barb?" holding it high up. A cluster of dark nods replied, Yes. Three punctures were made in the heathen flesh, and the White Whale's barbs were then tempered. (489)

Fetishizing the injury of labor is here effected through a symbolic use of its "barb," and its threat to Ahab's masculinity. Magical repetition of the scar transfers its mark of injury to the body of the "heathen," and the baptism which follows is crucially represented as an act that *renames* the emasculating social force represented in the painful "barbs" of work. "Ego non baptizo te in nomine patris, sed in nomine diaboli," the omen Ahab pronounces over the spear, transfers a symbolic injury of the workplace to the skin of the inferior "devil" of another race, offering escape from paternity: "Our age builds sepulchers to the father," the first sentence of Emerson's "Nature" had declared. The limits of class identity are transcended in the scene only when rebellion has been demonized, and primitive fantasies of racial superiority are activated instead. Mythic repetition of the act of sacrifice symbolically replaces the "insufferable anguish" (202) and class division that commitment to the actual "spear" of labor will produce.

Sacrifice, symbolized in the baptismal rite, is in this sense a form of mass-cultural regression. The whaling voyage as industrial venture depends on this prehistoric ritual to cloak in the myth of communal brotherhood the modern reality of renunciation and self-inflicted pain. Cloaked in the name of "defiance" (507), Ahab's "scar" (507) ties him to the "doubloon" (506) of finance, turning his enslavement into the false euphoria of fictitious solidarity. "Good!" he declares of the spear and cable that will bind him in isolation to the whale and his labor; "and now for the seizings" (489). Ahab's speeches are full of a subjection announced as freedom, and a suffering his eloquence fails to reconcile. The elaborate rituals of sacrificial commitment he undertakes with the crew mask an inner misery, but the excess of his rhetoric also points to a system of labor he can never accept. The "belief in sacrifice," as Adorno and Horkheimer suggest, "is probably already an impressed pattern according to which the subjected repeat upon themselves the injustice that was done to them." [89]

Pip, the Alabama slave, thus chooses to revere Ahab as "master, master, master!" Historically, Pip would have faced a similar choice. The Fugitive Slave Law of 1850 had just been passed, an act that assured the continuance of the liberal marketplace based itself on the assumption of a servile slave population. Pip represents the insistence of the voice of suffering within the most commodifiable version of slavery, the myth of the happy slave. Earlier, before his madness, Pip rejected levity and foresaw disaster: "Jollies? Lord help such jollies! Crish, crash! there goes the jib-stay!" (178). The excessive glee with which Pip finally commits himself to Ahab and accepts subjection points to his suffering in disguise: "Do ye but use poor me for your one lost leg; only tread upon me, sir; I ask no more" (534). As Adorno wrote in his tentative conclusion to *Aesthetic Theory*, "it would be difficult to imagine what would become of art if it wiped out the memory of accumulated suffering." [90] For Melville, the disaster of the *Pequod* is assured when the critical voice of its slave and his sorrow goes unheard: "Oh, Pip! thy wretched laugh . . . all thy strange mummeries not unmeaningly blended with the black tragedy of the melancholy ship, and mocked it!" (490).

Epilogue: Queequeg's Coffin

A contemporary review of *Moby-Dick* saw that such suffering aimed at shock value, and judged it to be part of a novel whose author, craving popular success, was motivated by "a most unbounded love of notoriety."[91] The scene of disaster in fiction, Melville himself recognized in "Hawthorne and His Mosses," was a fundamentally sentimental one. Writing in the persona of a "Virginian Spending July in Vermont," Melville invoked the tones of a Southerner, promising a harmony that would issue from the apocalyptic tones of the debate then raging over the Compromise of 1850: "at length, nothing is left but the all-engendering heart of man; which remaining still unconsumed, the great conflagration is naught." The voices of Daniel Webster and John Calhoun clashed in the debate, and both have been seen as sources for Ahab's speech. Rhetorical disaster in the America of 1850 could immediately turn into sentimental and political jubilation, like the false resolutions of popular fiction. Washington hailed Webster and Calhoun as forgers of the compromise that extended slavery in scenes of "conviviality and jubilation," though their speeches had evoked national apocalypse not long before.[92] Melville's prelude to *Moby-Dick* imagined the scorching edge narrative could give to such celebrations of national redemption. The popular novel might represent conflagration, he suggested of Hawthorne's work, yet produce an attack on such cultural clichés. "All vanities and empty theories and forms," he wrote of Hawthorne's work, "are, one after another, and by an admirably graduated, growing comprehensiveness, thrown into the allegorical fire."[93]

The ending of *Moby-Dick* militates against such populist conformism. Melville's notion of allegory, like Benjamin's, saw "melancholy" as the writerly mood that could remain critical within a falsely affirmative culture, a view he projected in his reading of Hawthorne's work: "Hawthorne's melancholy rests like an Indian Summer, which though bathing a whole country in one softness, still reveals the distinctive hue of every towering hill, each far-winding vale."[94] The allegorical vessel of Ishmael's salvation is empty, a reminder of the falsely cheerful tone of popular speech. Exhausted tropes of American redemption conclude *Moby-Dick*, perhaps, as Michael Gilmore has suggested, merely to make the novel more commercially viable. English readers had complained of the British version, which ended with the *Pequod*'s wreck, and thus could not account for the survival of the novel's narrator. Salvation as a tone, whatever its psychological grounding in the novel, for Melville may have meant a more marketable text.[95] Kitsch, which flaunts its commercial purpose, is a significant aspect of *Moby-Dick*'s concluding scene.[96] Yet melancholy accompanies Ishmael's magical return on the "coffin life-buoy" as a critical and double reminder: narratorial life rests on unnarrated deaths, and silenced stories. The salable conclusion is sustained with full recognition of the marginalized suffering mass culture contains.

For while the Epilogue of *Moby-Dick* satisfies the popular taste for a happy ending, Melville expressed his fear in a letter to Hawthorne that his authorial celebrity would link his novel to popular taste as demanded by the market, and miss its socially critical and ironic force.[97] Melville had exposed the reality of Native American suffering in the clichéd exoticism of his early work, and set himself against the power of popular culture from within. In a review of Francis Parkman's *The California and Oregon Trail*, Melville abandoned allegory and opposed the normalized destruction that kitsch concepts of Indian life made possible. "When in the body of the book we are informed that it is difficult for any white man, after domestication among the Indians, to hold them much better than brutes," Melville had announced; "when we are told too, that to such a person, the slaughter of an Indian is indifferent as the slaughter of a Buffalo; with all deference, we beg leave to dissent." [98]

The wreck of the *Pequod* in *Moby-Dick* preserves that dissent by recovering melancholy and the resistant "powers of horror," as Julia Kristeva has called them, from the normalizing force of cultural cliché.[99] Queequeg's suffering is allegorized as absence, in accord with the popular historical imagination. Ahab's final order, to "sink all coffins and all hearses to one common pool!" (572), envisions a similar evacuation of collective memory. But Ishmael, as he clings to the coffin inscribed with the "hieroglyphic marks" (480) of exterminated races, disobeys. The noble Indian, loyally subject, appears amidst his narrative of disaster, when "the last whelmings intermixingly poured themselves over the sunken head of the Indian," and Tashtego nails Ahab's flag to the mast. Yet "the submerged savage," in the clichéd tableau of his "death grasp," manages to catch a "sky–hawk," a "bird of heaven" with an "imperial beak" that taunts him, and hold him in the arc of his swing. Death comes to the Indian as the melodramatic act that precedes Ishmael's survival, but only as Tashtego nails the "captive form" of an American eagle to the mast, symbol of the American empire, and fights his cultural absorption by the wreck.

4

Kafka

Criticism and Social Change

Theodor Adorno remarked that Kafka's long works were rather "like detective novels in which the criminal fails to be exposed."[1] The Kafkan protagonist, in his unsuccessful attempt to unravel the criminal secret of powerful authority, has seemed to other critics to resemble those of Dickens, and in particular Arthur Clennam's quest. "The Castle," as Mark Spilka notes, "recalls the bureaucracy of *Little Dorrit*," a connection drawn by other readers as well.[2] Like Melville, Kafka is concerned to confront his readers, and to examine the traditional language for the political novel.[3] Kafka's diary notes his own avoidance of realism, particularly the "Barbarentum" of Dickens' mass-market fiction, yet saw a kindred spirit in Dickens for his capacity for self-critique: "Herzlosigkeit hinter der von Gefühl überströmenden Manier" (there is a heartlessness behind his sentimental, overflowing style).[4]

"Demolition," Adorno's word for Kafka's style, is said to be a "popular word" from the year of Kafka's death, 1924, linking Kafka's technique to the popular culture in which he worked. "Kafka seeks salvation in the incorporation of the powers of the adversary," as Adorno puts it, defining Kafka as a modernist for whom the prospect of Lionel Trilling's openly adversarial culture was already foreclosed. Instead, Kafka recognized the containment of cultural resistance in commodity culture, making use of a difficult style to challenge a society whose differences were becoming identical. "The crucial moment . . . towards which everything in Kafka is directed," Adorno observes, "is that in which men become aware that they are not themselves."[5]

Critics of Adorno's essay have argued against its reading of Kafka's politics.[6] But they at the same time separate Kafka from concerns with a mass audience and popular culture which, for all his modernist abstraction and epistemological complexity, were central to his own reflections on his work. In his diary, Kafka emphasized the importance of fiction's mass audience, expressing envy of the connection with its public that popular music enjoyed. Performance reminded Kafka of his own writerly confinement: "die gehörte Musik zieht natürlich eine Mauer um mich . . . daß ich so eingesperrt, anders bin als frei" (The performance of music has the natural effect of enclosing me with a wall . . . and confined in this way, I am different from what I am when I am free). The literature to which he was committed, on the contrary, lacked just such an audience: "Solche Ehrerbietung wie vor der Musik gibt es im Publikum vor der Litteratur nicht" (There is, among the public, no such reverence for literature as there is for music).[7]

But Kafka's commitment to the politics of both music and literature, and to examining their critical value to a modern audience, is apparent in his fiction, as well as in his extended comments on literature and society. His late story, *Josephine the Singer, or the Mouse Folk,* centers on the conflict between a performer and her public. This story of an artist with a vexed relation to her "fans," who misunderstand her complex productions, provides an analysis of the significance of audience to the modern novel. The narrative dramatized the split between Kafka's politics and his narrative style: Josephine's singing, while promising ethnic solidarity for the "mouse folk," remains distant from the sounds of communal life. Its paradoxically silent sound, like Kafka's contributions to Prague's pro-Zionist movement, forces readers to reflect critically on attempts to promote a boisterously political popular art.[8]

Yet while Kafka's writing may appear at times to be the work of a formalist, distanced from politics by his craft, Kafka himself regularly engaged the question of Jewish identity and its relation to the complex cultural politics of Prague. Crucial to Kafka's engagement with the Yiddish theater was his work as a publicist for its Prague productions in 1912. Kafka organized the printing of tickets, arranged publicity, and even submitted an advance copy of the program to the police for censorship. Audience address became more than a narrative affair, as Kafka took it on himself to introduce the Eastern European troupe to the assimilated Jewish public of Prague. Kafka confronted head-on their prejudice against Yiddish as a distasteful form of popular culture; middle-class "arrogance" that scorned Yiddish was scored, as Kafka insisted that the populist expression of Jewish culture was a serious form of art:

Ich habe nicht eigentlich Sorge um die Wirkung, die für jeden von Ihnen in dem heutigen Abend vorbereitet ist, aber ich will, daß sie gleich frei werde, wenn sie es verdient. Dies kann aber nicht geschehen, solange manche unter Ihnen eine solche Angst vor dem Jargon haben, daß man es fast auf ihren Gesichtern sieht. (I am not really worried about the experience this evening holds in store for each of you, but I should like it to be universally comprehensible, if it merits it. Yet this cannot be the case so long as many of you are so frightened of Yiddish that one can almost see it in your faces.)[9]

Kafka here refuses any hard-and-fast division between popular and highbrow culture. "Dread" of "Jargon," he insists, is intolerable: "von denen, welche gegen den Jargon hochmütig sind, rede ich gar nicht" ("of those who take an arrogant attitude to Yiddish I do not even speak"). In the place of cultural snobbery, Kafka imagines a reflective audience, capable of subjecting its cultural prejudice to self-critique: "Angst vor dem Jargon, Angst mit einem gewissen Widerwillen auf dem Grunde ist schließlich verständlich wenn man will" (dread of Yiddish, dread mingled with a certain fundamental distaste, is, after all, understandable, if one has the good will to understand it). To understand a "distaste" for "Jargon," in Kafka's terms, is to engage in an act of cultural criticism. Resistance to popular culture, he suggests to his Prague audience, could itself become an object for analysis, often with startling effects: "dann werden Sie die wahre Einheit des Jargon zu spüren bekommen, so stark, daß Sie sich fürchten werden, aber nicht mehr vor dem Jargon, sondern vor sich" (you will come to feel the true unity of Yiddish, and so strongly that it will frighten you, yet it will no longer be fear of Yiddish but of yourselves).[10]

Yiddish, however, could be a threat to middle-class standing, with its connotations of the poverty of the East. Its danger was therefore cultural as well as economic. Popular culture threatened a Jewish audience, Kafka insists, not because of its marginality but because of the central anxieties it provoked about Jewish assimilation to mainstream society. Kafka's novels are far from popular "Jargon," yet literature produced by Prague's German-speaking Jews was never far from the dilemmas of Yiddish that Kafka's speech adduced. His own relatively neutral German, in fact, was a marker of Prague German, whose Jewish speakers faced a divide. While largely cut off from Czech nationalists agitating for independence, their minority status in Prague also removed their German from regional intonations and their roots. One aspect of the situation encouraged cultural criticism: as Klaus Wagenbach points out, German's status in Prague as a "dry and papery . . . foreign implant" fostered an "objective apprehension" of individual words.[11] For it was not language alone but its cultural context that made it political, as Kafka pointed out to Max Brod in a letter. Staying at a pension in Meran with German-speaking guests, Kafka described the peculiarity of his Prague German, and the cultural inquiry on the part of an Austrian general it produced:

Nach den ersten Worten kam hervor, daß ich aus Prag bin; beide, der General (dem ich gegenüber saß) und der Oberst kannten Prag. Ein Tscheche? Nein. Erkläre nun in diese treuen deutschen militären Augen, was du eigentlich bist . . . fängt er wieder den Klang meines Deutsch zu bezweifeln an, vielleicht zweifelt mehr das Auge als das Ohr. Nun kann ich das mit meinem Judentum zu erklären versuchen." (After the first few words it came out that I was from Prague. Both of them—the general, who sat opposite me, and the colonel—were acquainted with Prague. Was I a Czech? No. So now explain to those true German military eyes what you really are . . . he once more began to wonder about the sound of my German, perhaps more bothered by what he saw than by what he heard. At this point I tried to explain that by my being Jewish.)[12]

The anecdote makes evident Kafka's strong sense of the politics of language. "Military eyes" use language to question identity, and the effect, while polite, is described as if it were an ideological interrogation. Linguistic enigma called for political examination, especially in an atmosphere charged with nationalist fervor, and the relatively blank German Kafka spoke had to be marked: unaccented speech could be identified as a sign of Jewish assimilation, even though Kafka's German was the official language that long enforced Austrian dominion over Prague. The general's confusion over Kafka's enigmatic accent, moreover, was likely feigned, itself a social mask for prejudice based on more than words. For "perhaps," as Kafka observes of the general, he was "more bothered by what he saw than by what he heard."

Such linguistic enigmas, like the general's curiosity, had an ethnic and political force, recalling the similar inquisitions that constitute much of the action of *Das Schloß*. Hence the usefulness of Kafka's reflections on obviously minority writing, such as Yiddish, for the mainstream literature he produced. Both German as spoken by the Prague Jews and Yiddish transmute the signs of cultural domination into critical, differing cultural gestures. As Kafka emphasized in his "Schema zur Charakteristik Kleiner Literaturen" (A Character Sketch of the Literature of Small Peoples), the writing of a "small people" emphasizes the political gestures that emerge through indirection, as minorities cope with the everyday necessities of living amidst the dominant group. While Kafka meant to differentiate his own German writing from popular Yiddish culture with the term "small literature"—as he himself wrote in the German mainstream—the model of "popular" culture provided by Yiddish defines the internally critical power of popular sources in his work. The compensations of writing for a "small nation" were thus similar to those intended for his own German narrative: gestures produced under cultural pressure could indicate what was hidden from normative perceptions. Traits listed under the heading "Popularität" in Kafka's Diary "Sketch" of 25 December 1911 define culture as a sphere of activist engagement:

A) Zusammenhang mit Politik (Connection with Politics)
B) Litteraturgeschichte (Literary History)
C) Glaube an die Litteratur, ihre Gesetzgebung wird ihr überlassen (Faith in Literature, can make up their own laws)

Each trait serves as a reminder that literature is a form of social intervention. Canonical literary history, Kafka points out, excludes "Jargon," and thus makes palpable the political values embedded in literary categories. The response of "small" literatures is to improvise—literature "can make up its own laws"—and construct genres which, while subject to the kind of "distaste" Kafka addressed in 1912, speak to the emergent cultural voices in modern society. Beyond the Czech and Jewish literature to which Kafka refers, literature as a whole is seen as an "Angelegenheit des Volkes" (affair of the people): the "Popularität" of "Jargon" is seen as a challenge to fixed literary categories and their boundaries, modeling a breach of the barriers between traditionally separate literary and cultural realms.

During the composition of *Das Schloß*, Kafka described in similar terms his cultural isolation in writing for a mainstream German audience. Kafka's famous formulation refers to his "literature" as an assault on "the boundary," or "border," but an assault that was to be distinguished from an overt or ideological interest in Zionism, or Jewish politics: "diese ganze Litteratur ist Ansturm gegen die Grenze und sie hätte sich, wenn nicht der Zionismus dazwischengekommen wäre, leicht zu einer neuen Geheimlehre, einer Kabbala entwickeln können" (All such writing is an assault on the boundary and it might easily have developed, had not Zionism intervened, into a new secret teaching, a Kabbalah).[13] The passage has often been understood as spiritual or mystical rather than political, an indication of the private language for redemption Kafka pursued. Gershom Scholem explains the Kabbalah's central tenet in relation to the Jewish messianic idea, the notion that "all being has been a being in exile," and that in such a world, where "everything has a flaw, everything is unfinished," everything is therefore open to messianic redemption. And in the Hebrew Kafka studied while composing *Das Schloß,* Evelyn Torton Beck notes, the word for land surveyor, *Moshoakh,* one who determines legal bounds, and the word for Messiah, *Moshiakh,* one who transforms the law, are only one letter apart.[14] Reading the political Kafka, present in his relations with popular Jewish culture as well as with modernism, requires a rethinking of his placement as an aesthete, and obliges us to follow the lines where modernity, mass culture, and politics in his fiction met.

Kafka and Politics: Antipathy and Antithesis

Direct political expression, even figurative opposition, seems ruled out by the religious tone of one of Kafka's late aphorisms: "eines der wirksamsten Verführungsmittel des Bösen ist die Aufforderung zum Kampf" (one of evil's most effectual means of seduction is the challenge to fight).[15] Max Brod, Kafka's friend and literary executor, and the architect of the existential reading of his work, pointed out the debt of *The Castle* to Božena Němcová's *The Grandmother,* a nationalist Czech novel, with its sources in the revolutionary literature of the "Young Germany" movement of 1848. Kafka's novel, by contrast, ascetically refuses to represent the contemporary political situation in Prague with any specificity, enabling one to see why Brod, like the many interpreters who followed his lead, construed the novel as a "religious allegory."[16]

On the surface, Theodor Adorno agreed, Kafka's novels took a "hermetic stance toward history," never naming the dissolution of the Hapsburg Empire through which he lived, or the anarchism, Czech nationalism, and Zionism which were of critical interest to him throughout his life.[17] A direct stance of opposition, Kafka suggests in his diary, might take up radical politics which seem original, yet lends itself to incorporation by the governing rituals of social experience. The aphorism I quoted in the Introduction, as a general warning to populist enthusiasm for mass culture, also applies to the political passions Kafka himself followed: "Leoparden brechen in den Tempel ein und saufen die Opferkrüge leer; das widerholt sich immer wieder; schließlich kann man es vorausrechnen, und es wird ein Teil der Zeremonie" (Leopards break into the temple and drink the sacrificial chalices dry; this occurs repeatedly, again and again: finally it can be reckoned upon beforehand and becomes a part of the ceremony).[18] But the critical wrangle over Kafka's real or alleged political affiliations

is not as revealing about his novels and his politics as the postcard
he sent while vacationing in Berlin to an anarchist acquaintance in
Prague, which while extending a friendly greeting bore a picture of
the seat of government on the other side.[19]

Adorno's essay on Kafka redefined the political content of Kafka's
novels by calling attention to their attack on such self-canceling representations of alienation—taken in large part from the method of German expressionism—through what he called Kafkan "demolition," a
technique which allowed the social content of his apparently subjective novels to emerge.[20] Rather than conclude, with Lukács, that the
severe abstraction of Kafka's modernism is complicit with political
power, Adorno saw that its "alleged solipsism" implied not "a denial of the object," and history, but a systematic attack on "disguised
domination" (260), hidden in the "eternalized gestures" (252) of his
characters. In Adorno's social theory, the modern subject of political
power is envisioned as one who "swallows the object" and internalizes social control, "forgetting how much it is an object itself," but his
critical practice finds in Kafka's formalism a method that brings the
hidden social determination of apparently individual and subjective
experience into critical view.[21]

Neurosis, apparently privative and subjective in his fiction, is for
Adorno, as for the Kafka who famously declared, "Zum letzten Mal
Psychologie!" (For the last time psychology), curable not by psychoanalysis but by the political and social knowledge that personal anguish has a historical cause: "instead of curing neurosis, he seeks in
it itself the healing force, that of knowledge: the wounds with which
society brands the individual."[22] In *The Metamorphosis*, the wound
Gregor's father heaves into the back of his son is caused by an "apple,"
but it also critically represents the social process of the *metamorphosis*
or transformation of a social demand—the refusal of alienating labor,
which produces its plot, and Gregor's backbone—into a controlling
oedipal neurosis, one that is crucially depicted by the fantastic modernism of Kafka's story as *imposed* on the rebellious "reptile" from
without, in keeping with a long literary tradition, rather than as a
diseased emanation of his psyche. "He does not stop at the subject
as does psychology," Adorno wrote, "but drives through to the bare
material existence that emerges in the subjective sphere."[23]

Kafka's diary saw as the task of the writer to uncover the hidden
politics of experience. "Kleine Litteraturen" (minor literatures), he
wrote in the same extended reflection on Czech and Jewish writing, had to be "etwas ganz anderes . . . als Geschichtsschreibung"

(something entirely different from historiography), or from an objective social chronicle, filled with "politische Schlagworte" (political slogans), though this is what the "judgment," or "Erwägung," that its inner focus was somehow separate from "äußere Verbindung mit der Politik" (external connection with politics) often produced.[24] Kafka's self-reference in this section is clear—he refers to such a literature as "dieses Tagebuchführen einer Nation" (diary keeping of a nation)— and his definition of his own literary project argued for the engagement of his writing with larger political concerns. From a position of constant threat, the writer of a small people could obtain a vantage point on the power which permeated everyday life as well as the larger society: "was innerhalb großer Litteraturen unten sich abspielt und einen nicht unentbehrlichen Keller des Gebäudes bildet, geschieht hier im vollen Licht" (what in great literature goes on down below, constituting a not indispensable cellar of the structure, here takes place in the full light of day). Writing for Kafka could reproduce the "Einschränkung" (limitation) which held a people in check, as well as "ennobling" literary themes, like "Besprechungsmöglichkeit des Gegensatzes zwischen Vätern und Söhnen (discussing the battles between fathers and sons). Such a literature was "weniger eine Angelegenheit der Litteraturgeschichte als Angelegenheit des Volkes" (less a concern of literary history than of the people), and thus defied its ethnic boundaries, enabling it to engage in the "Darbietung der nationalen Fehler in einer zwar besonders schmerzlichen, aber verzeihungswürdigen und befreiender Weise" (portrayal of national mistakes in, as it were, a particularly painful but forgiving and liberating way).[25]

This political aspect of Kafkan modernism is apparent in his most Freudian text, "Letter to His Father" (1919). Oedipal anxiety over paternal "abusiveness," and the desire to escape it, are irrepressible in the work's biographical detail, even if one does conclude, with Charles Bernheimer, that the issue for Kafka in the work is his status as a writer in his father's "representational domain."[26] But representation and politics were not separate domains for Kafka. What he calls the "rednerische Mittel" (rhetorical methods) used to deliver his father's "Schimpfwörte" (words of abuse), "besonders im Geschäft" (particularly in business), directed at his Czech workers—"Schimpfen, Drohen, Ironie, böses Lächen, und—merkwürdigerweise—Selbstbeklagung" (swearing, irony, spiteful laughter, and oddly enough, self-pity)—are examined as part of his own political genealogy: "[ich war] als kleiner Junge manchmal davon fast betäubt . . . und keinen Grund hatte, sie nicht auf mich zu beziehen" (as a little boy, I was sometimes almost stunned, and had no reason not to apply them to myself too).[27]

In such scenes in the "Letter," the original shaping status and determining power of oedipal conflict are opposed—" 'Immer alles contra' ist wirklich nicht mein Lebensgrundsatz" ("Always agin you" was never my basic principle)—and the issue of individual identity, and its origins in sexuality, is instead shifted to history: "hier entscheiden die allgemeinen geschlechtlichen Standes-, Volks-, und Zeitsitten" (what is decisive here are the general sexual customs of class, nation, and time) (128, 153). Ritchie Robertson has concluded, from Kafka's attempts to construct a "sociology of literature," that his conflict with his father was not oedipal rebellion as much as an attempt at "escape."[28] But Kafka's own description of his flight in the "Letter" envisions a positive critical confrontation with the social content of family relations, portraying his life's work as a writer as the attempt to clear oedipal distortions from real political ground. He writes: "Manchmal stelle ich mir die Erdkarte ausgespannt und Dich quer über sie hin ausgestreckt vor. Und es ist mir dann, als kämen für mein Leben nur die Gegenden in Betracht, die Du entweder nicht bedeckst oder die nicht in Deiner Reichweite liegen" (Sometimes I imagine a map of the world, and you stretched out across it, and I feel that the only possible regions in which I might live are those which you don't cover, or which are beyond your reach) (158).

Kafka criticism has begun to recover this political dimension of his fiction, but often from a linguistic point of view. "The radicality of Kafka's methods," as Judith Ryan has put it in a review essay of recent theoretical approaches to his work, has been supported in the work of Margaret Walter-Schneider, Sabina Kienlechner, and others. This school of Kafka interpretation accepts "indeterminacy as a functional part of the text," and argues for the critical capacity of Kafka's text to attack representation and the self's certainty about the world it perceives.[29] Ryan sees the Kafkan novel's instability as critical and productive, unlike early criticism of his work, such as Wilhelm Emrich's, which tended to see it as a sweeping register of Western culture in contradiction, or Friedrich Beissner's, which argued for a Kafkan protagonist universally trapped in subjectivity.[30] Other critics, however, argued that the narrative point of view in Kafka's novels is unstable, based on a subjectivity one would now call "decentered," neither subjectively enclosed nor with access to reliable objective perspective.[31] But such philosophically and linguistically skeptical approaches have remained separate from the historical and biographical work that could help to situate their political force.

Historical and biographical studies, such as Hartmut Binder's, have valuably placed Kafka's work against the background of anti-Semitism and nationalist fervor surrounding the First World War. Today, the significance of Kafka's writing as a register of the crisis of the individual in Western culture has been recognized by traditional and deconstructive critics alike.[32] Yet this linkage of his novels to specific events or historical trends too often assumes either that they support specific political positions, or that his philosophic skepticism or psychological anguish precluded his novels' committed social concern. "The same Kafka who has been presented as a prophet of alienation and hopelessness declares," as Russell Berman reminds us, "that 'literature is an affair of the people.'" "It would be possible," Berman suggests, "to construct a new Kafka, inimical to the established image, as a radical in search of a collective."[33]

Kafka's "secret doctrine" and his reference to Jewish mysticism were similarly understood by Walter Benjamin, his most subtle critic, as a form of engaging modernist narrative in politics. "This most recent world of events," Benjamin wrote in the 1930s, and later referred to the world of "modern warfare" and mass extinction, "was conveyed to him by precisely this mystical tradition."[34] Benjamin praised the parabolic character of Kafka's works, even his long novels, for their ability to give up "truth"—the claim of realism and popular fiction—while at the same time committing themselves to social commentary. Like Adorno, Benjamin saw Kafka's fiction as turning against the acceptance of domination, which threatened the "masses," and as doing so under the guise of accepting an apparent subservience to power. "Though apparently reduced to submission," he wrote of Kafka's parables, "they unexpectedly raise a mighty paw against it."[35]

Kafka's remark on literature as an "assault on the boundary" suggests that his own work is a kind of raid on the border between privacy and politics. The messianic or Kabbalistic content of such a doctrine for Kafka is, as he puts it, a "new" one; more than a messianic hope for redemption from exile, it is an examination of realistic cultural boundaries and an "assault" on the mystifications of political struggle that keep a people in check. In 1922, as he began *Das Schloß*, Kafka suggested that such an assault could be waged only by giving himself over to the power that trampled him, an "incorporation of the power of the adversary" that Adorno saw as the political method of his work: "Das Pferd des Angreifers zum eigenen Ritt benützen. Einzige Möglichkeit. Aber was für Kräfte und Geschicklichkeiten verlangt das? Und wie spät ist es schon!" (Take the horse from your attacker and ride it yourself. The only possibility. But what strength and skill

that requires! And how late it is already!).[36] Politics and its specificity
are left out in such parabolic formulations, as Benjamin suggests, precisely because its force on Kafka's work was so present. The "doctrine"
which his parables "interpret," as he put it, was present only by "allusion," but "in every case it is a question of how life and work are
organized."[37] The sense that it was "late," as in Kafka's parable, but
also the "strength and skill" to capture the "power" of his adversary,
were present in the words with which *Das Schloß* was to begin: "Es
war spät abend als K. ankam. Das Dorf lag in tiefem Schnee" (It was
late evening, as K. arrived. The village lay in deep snow).[38]

A Conservative Ideology: Anxiety, Interpretation, Subjection

"Sicher ist mein Widerwille gegen Antithesen" (My antipathy for antitheses is certain), writes Kafka in a diary entry of 1911. This antipathy, he explains, results from the close connection between antithesis
and oppressive illusion. The antithetical offers the promise of a truth
near at hand immanent in the experience of the everyday: "sie kom-
men zwar unerwartet, aber überraschen nicht, denn sie sind immer
ganz nah vorhanden gewesen" (They are unexpected, but do not sur-
prise, for they have always been right there).[39] Antitheses repel him,
he explains, because of the false sense of grounding they inspire, and
the feeling they offer that the mastery of a full interpretation of experience is at hand: "Sie erzeugen zwar Gründlichkeit, Fülle, Lückenlosigkeit aber nur so wie eine Figur im Lebensrad; unsern kleinen
Einfall haben wir im Kreis herumgejagt" (They make for a sense of
thoroughness, fullness, a completeness without gaps, but only like a
figure on the "wheel of life": we have chased our little idea around in
a circle). The "wheel of life" was a toy of Kafka's time which contained
a series of printed figures in slightly different positions. When rotated,
the "wheel" produced the illusion of a figure in movement. The secure
grounding, and consequent progress toward understanding, promised by antithesis, Kafka suggests, produces the same illusion. The
individual who presumes to have located the "Fülle" (fullness) and
"Gründlichkeit" (reason, grounding) of his experience moves, as the
image suggests, not toward such solid ground, but in a circle which
presumably leaves him in the childlike, circular position in which
he began.

The formal closure of Kafka's sense of opposition is deceptive,
however, unless its cultural ground in Kafka's politics is perceived.

False opposition defined the difference between Prague Jews and their Czech and German neighbors: every attempt to posit the Jews as nationality equal yet "opposite" to the Czechs or Germans always failed. Anti-Semitism persuaded Kafka, as Gary Cohen puts it, "to abandon the Jewish-German symbiosis," and Czech nationalism could also manifest itself in anti-Semitism, making Zionism a practical political expression for Max Brod and the other members of the Prague Circle who were Kafka's close friends.[40] Yet this means of establishing a cultural identity antithetical to the Czech majority was also prone to the kind of false certainty that Kafka's meditation on antitheses feared.

Jewish culture, moreover, led to anything but the "Gründlichkeit" of stable identity. Jewish writers of his generation lived, Kafka wrote to Max Brod in 1921, while *Das Schloß* was being conceived, "mit den Hinterbeinchen klebten [sie] . . . noch am Judentum des Vaters, und mit den Vorderbeinchen fanden sie keinen neuen Boden" (with their posterior legs glued to their fathers' Jewishness, while with their waving anterior legs they found no new ground).[41] In 1921, of course, the Jewish nation was literally without titled "Grund" or property, at least as far as statehood was concerned. Kafka's critique of "Gründlichkeit," moreover, suspects any concept of Jewish identity that could be firmly *grounded* as a political ideology with firm geographic or demographic bounds. The regulations Kafka followed when registering at the university allowed him to define national allegiance as only a "German" or a "Czech," granting Jewishness no status as an ethnic or national term. His diary entries and letters make clear that no categorically simple definition of the Jewish individual would suffice where matters of ethnic and political identity were concerned.[42]

The land surveyor in Kafka's *Schloß* makes the delineation of such antitheses his central concern, seeking "Gründlichkeit" in a survey of the Castle's "Grund" or "ground." In the modern society Kafka depicts, however, tangible political positions are notoriously difficult to fix. The Castle's bureaucratic system, moreover, thrives on such uncertainty. Adjudicating confusion makes its officials powerful, regardless of the grounds its antagonists use to confront its power. The solid "Grund" or ground K. seeks bespeaks a governing ideology or political program that governs by the rule of law. Yet the most dominating ideology, Kafka suggests, is not on the right or left, but an ideology that controls by encouraging perpetual questioning of the individual's proper relation to the state. The fact that "Grund" suggest both "ground" in the sense of property, and "grounds," in the sense of a principle or rationale—while the Castle itself in Kafka's novel remains unsurveyable—connects K.'s desire for grounded social identity with the modern logic that meld's the autonomous individual with the power of the state. The "wheel of life," in Kafka's image—whether Zionist Jew or cultural German—remains like K., a cipher to be filled in with the dictates of authority. Refusing to name his protagonist's ideological choices, Kafka instead surveys the psychological ground that turns ideological choice into a mechanism that subjects. The "wheel" that operates the individual has different scenes from which to choose, while Kafka challenges his reader to fill in the concretion of politics and history that his characters' personal obsessions continually erase.

For surveying the Castle in Kafka's novel homogenizes subjects still marked by cultural difference. In K.'s initial view, the Castle turns to emptiness, then into a visual indefinition that bridges social authority and the individual by turning into a "seeming" unity of one: "Lange stand K. auf der Holzbrücke die von der Landstraße zum Dorf führt und blickte in die scheinbare Leere empor" (On the wooden bridge leading from the main road to the village, K. stood for a long while, gazing out into the seeming emptiness) (7). The surveyor, whose job might be to delimit the ground of both castle and village, is emptied of concretion by an antithetical authority that drains specificity out of the cultural gaze. As a center of authority at once above the village and in a "Nebel," or fog, an image not just of "Finsternis," or darkness, the Castle deprives the subject who gazes at it of the crucial ground that is history, the past that K. can never name. Dramatized at the beginning of Kafka's novel is thus the process of liberal citizenship: K.'s willed desire to enter the Castle does not alienate him as much as describe cultural amnesia as a kind of social norm. The "seeming emptiness" of the Castle urges on the project of defining public authority, while it is the evacuation of K.'s history and culture—all the "history" that precedes the events of the novel—that defines K.'s relation to public space.

Radical opposition to the Castle for K. therefore consists in his attempt to mark his "official" status—to know whether he has actually been hired—and the realm "outside the official," of privacy, so that he can measure the extent of the Castle's power. Though these are never identifiably ideological or historical positions in the text, critics have perceived K.'s portrayal as linked to the temptations of modern political radicalism, even to a desire to seize the state. "Im Wesen der Landvermessung liegt ein revolutionäres Element" (in its essence, land surveying has a revolutionary element), Wilhelm Emrich observes, but is of importance beyond the all too realistic "Opposition" he finds in the village, since K.'s intention is first to define the boundary between the Castle's power and the private self, to preserve himself from what all the villagers perceive as its omnipresent threat:

> Nur glaube ich daß hier zweierlei unterschieden werden müsse, nämlich erstens das was innerhalb der Ämter vorgeht und was dann wieder amtlich so oder so aufgefaßt werden kann, und zweitens meine wirkliche Person, ich, der ich außerhalb der Ämter stehe und dem von den Ämtern eine Beeinträchtigung droht. (I believe only that two things must be distinguished here: first, what goes on in the office, and in one way or another can be construed as official, and secondly, my real self, me, the self outside the offices, and threatened with harm by them.) (105)[43]

Mass society, K. recognizes, draws no hard-and-fast line between political power and private life, whose fantasies and anxieties "can be construed as official." As Michel Foucault has demonstrated in detail, discourses of the self such as sexuality turn private affairs into large-scale replications of official ideology, and a similar ruptured boundary between public and cultural politics runs throughout the Castle's domain.[44] That which draws the land surveyor toward the Castle is the enticement of such an irregular division for one whose business it is to draw straight lines, and to define the division between clearly separate realms. Every instance of the "brüchig" (crumbling) and "unregelmäßig" (irregular) boundary between political power and private life provokes K. on to questioning and analysis, in the hope that the definite limit of Castle power might be drawn.[45] K. is Kafka's unrepentant activist, seeking public redress and institutional power, while attempting to sustain a traditional politics: for him, a clear border between the private sphere and his status as a political agent must be drawn.

Kafka's liberal citizen, however, always stumbles on the shifting forms of power of mass society. No general rules hold for relations with the Castle in Kafka's novel, except that bureaucratic authority continually slides from the public realm where K. seeks to fix its boundaries into the traditionally private sphere. Literal intercourse between village women and Castle officials is plentiful in the novel; many scenes portray Castle officials making use of their position to make sexual demands. This exploitation of women in Kafka's novel, Marjanne Goozé notes, has been "raised to the level of religious allegory" in traditional readings, an interpretive mode that has masked the political content of these scenes.[46] For despite the willful obscurity of the Castle, such "knowledge" of its representatives is readily available: sex is depicted as a private exercise of social authority.

Obsessed with the Castle as a public entity, however, K. largely ignores such coercion and its effects. Yet Kafka does not, and his awareness of feminine subjugation takes on a self-critical dimension. Late in the novel, the Castle's "Herren" or gentlemen meet in the "Herrenhof," a locale named after the Vienna café where Kafka's friends met. Among them was Oskar Polak, the husband of Milena Jesenská whom Kafka later romanced.[47] It is the gentlemen of the "Herrenhof" in *Das Schloß* who exploit women most blatantly. While K.'s public position remains indeterminate throughout the novel, he retains authority over women through much of Kafka's text. The more K. seeks a public accounting of Castle power, the more he comes to treat Frieda as an object, thus sharing in an indeterminate but nonetheless specifically male exercise of its power.

The indeterminacy of power in *Das Schloß*, in other words, promotes determinate social effects. While sexual relations remain crucial to Kafka's analysis of private power, the narrative's public symbolism makes uncertainty a concrete part of its ethnic subtext as well. Reaching the Castle suggests a desire to obtain a fixed national identity: K.'s efforts to achieve self-determination at times resembles the political ideology of contemporary Zionists, who described the precarious civil status of Jewish Prague. Much as K. despises uncertain status as a sign of the "Untergeordnetsein" (subjection) (58) that characterizes village life, Zionist ideology sought to end the politically indeterminate status of Jewish Europe once and for all. Theodor Herzl saw Jewish Prague as a symbol of such uncertainty and its pernicious social effects. In "Die Juden Prags zwischen den Nationen" (The Jews of Prague: Between the Nations), Herzl loathed the lack of political recognition accorded Jews, who remained a "Sündenbock" (scapegoat) for recognized nationalities: "in Prag warf man ihnen vor, daß sie keine Tschechen, in Saaz und Eger, daß sie keine Deutsche seien" (In Prague Jews are criticized for not being Czech, in Saaz and Eger, for not really being Germans).[48]

Herzl's piece, it should be noted, was printed in 1917 in a special edition of the Prague Jewish journal *Selbstwehr* entitled *Das Jüdische Prag*, along with Kafka's short piece "Ein Traum," an introduction by Martin Buber, and an essay in political theory by Max Brod. Another section was entitled "Über Prager Künstler" (On Prague Artists), in which Otto Pick described Kafka's work as resistant to the mainstream ideological or religious positions his contemporary readers held: "Kafka verrät nicht, zu welchem Glauben er sich bekennt" (Kafka does not betray the belief he embraces). For a Prague Jewish audience, however, Pick argues that Kafka's writing was "so heftig ins irdische Dasein verpflanzt" (so powerfully rooted in earthly existence) that its "sachkundigen Darstellung" (detailed portrayal), while evoking social reality, might seem ghostly and surreal.[49] In such abstractions of his ethnic dilemma, Pick suggested, Kafka was not a "Schriftsteller" (writer) or a "Literat" (man of letters), not "aktiv" or political in the usual sense— as Herzl once was in Vienna—but an author rooted in Jewish culture who was, at the same time, critical of ethnic bounds.

In *Das Schloß*, K.'s ambitions as land surveyor evoke something of Herzl's quest to end the uncertainties of indeterminate cultural identity. Herzl's response to the Jewish predicament, of course, was unambiguously nationalistic and ideological. For Kafka, however, Zionist ideology was no cure-all for the ills of modern political culture, and K.'s story is in part an expression of Kafka's skepticism of popular ideologies *tout court*. K. often rejects "official" explanations, despite his relentless commitment to define his role in public life. In this consistent failure to achieve political identification or even recognition, K.'s portrayal speaks against uncritical absorption in any populist cause. For Kafka's own historical context, K.'s position of tortured engagement would have argued against devotion to nationalist or ethnic enthusiasm of the sort Martin Buber preached in Prague, to the Jewish cultural circle of Bar Kochba in which Kafka moved.

Speaking in Prague in 1910, Buber recommended Zionism as a fusion of the private Jewish self with public identity. The kind of centered public identity sought by K. was for Buber to be found in a cataclysmic religious turn to Zionism. While discussing "den Sinn des Begriffs 'Blut' " (the meaning of the concept of "blood"), as well as "spezifisch jüdische Eigenschaften" (specifically Jewish characteristics), Buber urged a solution to the Jewish question through the creation of a new Jewish subject under political sovereignty.[50] The attraction of a move beyond reformism was powerful: Buber asked Jews to reject the politically self-subjecting negotiations with civil power, precisely the kind of bureaucratic negotiations that K.'s dealings with the Castle depict. Kafka's letters, nonetheless, criticize this romanticized vision of Jewish political culture, despite its appeal to his contemporaries. "Persönlich [ist Buber] frisch und einfach und bedeutend," Kafka wrote to Felice, "und nichts mit den lauwarmen Sachen zu tun zu haben scheint, die er geschrieben hat" (as a person [Buber] is lively and simple and remarkable, and seems to have no connection with the tepid things he has written).[51] The irreducible and powerful split in *Das Schloß* between private life and "official" status reflects Kafka's sense that Zionism, while a necessary corrective to the anxieties of assimilation, in no way abolished the dominating power of mass society. "Er macht auf mich einen öden Eindruck," Kafka wrote Felice, complaining of the writing time he would lose by going to hear Buber lecture in 1913: "allem, was er sagt, fehlt etwas" (I find him dreary . . . no matter what he says, something is missing).[52]

For Kafka, Buber's certainty that the boundaries of modern Jewish selfhood and nationality could be redrawn was sophistic. K.'s endless attempts to define his status focus attention instead on the impossibility of finding adequate public recognition for the ethnic or minority self. In *Das Schloß*, this quest is never defined as "Jewish" in explicit terms: the modern struggles for ethnic liberation in Central Europe Kafka knew firsthand were a general rather than particularly Jewish affair. No specific ideology is scorned in the novel, but the problem of Jewish identity produced a perspective generally critical of the ideological demands that ethnic nationalism might make. Cultural criticism in *Das Schloß* for this reason moves beyond the ethnic question that so preoccupied Kafka, as it did Buber's questioner in 1913, who asked him how Jewish "Selbstbefreiung" (self-liberation) could be sought.[53] While the proper relation of ethnic background to public identity in modern society for Kafka was finally indeterminate, the story of the land surveyor insisted that the political *effects* of trying to solve the question could be mapped.

The Castle, for instance, resembles an image of assimilationist desire. The wish for full recognition by the bureaucracy leads K. to idealize its shabby environs, and to imagine escape from village life and the transcendence of humble origins. Hence the Castle's ennobled appearance, despite its apparent corruption: its edifice rises for K. under the sign of an immigrant's will to identification "mit höherem Ziel als das niedrige Häusergemenge und klarerem Ausdruck als ihn der trübe Werktag hat" (With loftier purpose and clearer expression than the lowly mass of houses and the sullen, workaday world can have) (18). Here Kafka's style marks its modernist difference from the realist tradition, breaking with the external emphasis of Dickens or of Balzac in *Illusions Perdues*. For Kafka, the overarching perspective implied by realistic description was false, implicated in the conservative logic of the story of social integration. Balzac's style, Kafka suggested to Willy Haas, falsely privileged culture's hold over the individual, making its power seem absolute.[54] Kafka's modernist abstraction, far from apolitical, challenged this false immediacy. By refusing to specify an objective location for the Castle, Kafka recognized the role of subjectivity, particularly the desires of the worshipful outsider, in giving objective power to political authority.[55] Neither K.'s family history nor the precise historical referent of the Castle bureaucracy is as important to Kafka as sketching the modern process whereby authority becomes powerful through the representations it encourages its subjects to construct.

Hence the peculiar external appearance of the Castle to K.'s view. The roof is described as a set of signs, whose partial signifiers suggest the process of acculturation, rather than any substantial or determinate set of political ends: "unsicher, unregelmäßig, brüchig wie von ängstlicher oder nachlässiger Kinderhand gezeichnet" (uncertain, irregular, fragmentary, as if drawn by the anxious or careless hand of a child) (18). The differing self's wish to assimilate is depicted as requiring an infantilizing reconstruction of subjective feelings: legitimating authority is substantively absent but *imaginatively* constituted by the assimilationist gaze. Objective social facts, or the actual legitimacy of such authority, is irrelevant: K. sees the Castle buildings as representing the "Kirchturm der Heimat" (the church tower of his childhood) (18), constructing a cathexis of order and moral authority from "brüchig" (fragmentary) surroundings in decay. The wish for assimilation grounds itself in an image of dissolution—"Das Schloß, dessen Umrisse sich schon aufzulösen begannen, lag still wie immer" (The castle, whose outlines were already beginning to dissolve, lay silent as ever) (156)—while the mysteries of authority to which the outsider is beholden are shown to exercise determinate political effects:

Wenn K. das Schloß ansah, so war es ihm manchmal, als beobachte er jemanden, der ruhig dasitze und vor sich hinsehe, nicht etwa in Gedanken verloren und dadurch gegen alles abgeschlossen, sondern frei und unbekümmert; so als sei er allein und niemand beobachte ihn; und doch mußte er merken, daß er beobachtet wurde . . . (when K. looked at the castle, often it seemed to him as if he were observing someone who sat quietly there gazing in front of him, not lost in thought and so oblivious to everything, but free and untroubled, as if he were alone and no one observed him, and yet must notice that he was observed . . .) (156)

The effect of indeterminate power is to enforce a sense of surveillance from which the signs of social authority appear exempt: the Castle observer appears to K. as able to gaze in untroubled fashion, without feeling subject to the examining gaze. In such a quasi-divine position, freedom is defined as the subject who is not subject to surveillance—

"no one observed him"—and thus transcendent, like the church tower
of his home, which rose beyond the world of labor, "with clearer
expression than the sullen, workaday world can have." But the transcendent freedom of such a determining gaze immediately gives way
to its opposite. The gaze beyond, if he can observe it, K. concludes,
must indeed be subject to another—"he . . . yet must notice that he
was observed"—and is thus fixable, connected to the subject territory
of the village below and thus never completely free. The moment of
vision breaks off at the moment when K. is unsure whether the Castle
viewer is free and powerful, or subject to his own vision. Transcendent
authority's status remains moot, establishing a kind of boundary zone
of acceptance whose lines an observer, even a surveyor, can never precisely fix. Castle authority consists of just this uncertainty it produces,
always preserving the doubt—"man wußte nicht war es Ursache oder
Folge (one didn't know if it was cause or effect)—of the assimilationist
subject wishing to know the meaning of authority's gaze: "die Blicke
des Beobachters konnten sich nicht festhalten und glitten ab" (the gaze
of the observer could not concentrate itself and slid away) (156). For
all the vagueness of the scene, its definition of modern political power
is precise: without indicating whether subjection by anxiety is indeed
its "cause or effect," bureaucracy becomes authoritarian through the
anxiety its indefinition encourages its subjects to produce.

The history behind such scenes certainly suggests a conservative
reading of their force. Critics have identified the border ground occu-
pied by Kafka as the in-between space of his Jewishness, and what
is sometimes described as his paralytic inability to identify either
with the "Kirchturm" of German- and Czech-speaking Prague, or
with the Yiddish culture and Zionism he also pursued. Marthe Robert
has argued that Kafka saw himself "as the product of a cross between two species, neither of which recognized itself in him, a condition which condemned him not to die, but to wander eternally, in a
zone intermediate between life and death."[56] Such self-alienation affected the German word for "mother," from which the Jewish speaker,
Kafka observed, felt estranged: "wir geben einer jüdischen Frau den
Namen deutsche Mutter, vergessen aber den Widerspruch, der desto
schwerer sich ins Gefühl einsenkt . . . auch das Wort Vater meint
bei weitem den jüdischen Vater nicht" (We give a Jewish woman the
German name "Mutter," and as we do, forget the contradiction that
anchors itself in our feelings . . . the word "Vater," too, doesn't by
a long shot express what the Jewish father is).[57] But Kafka's description of what he called "die schreckliche innere Lage dieser Genera-

tionen" (the awful inner predicament of these generations), and the "Verhältnis der jungen Juden zu ihrem Judentum (relation of young Jews to their Jewishness), relied less on language than on class. Kafka referred to German-Jewish speech as "Mauscheln," a dialect form that mixed Yiddish and German, but gave assimilated Jews only an uncertain position in the "sprachliche Mittelstand" or linguistic middle class.[58] The space he called "dieses Grenzland zwischen Einsamkeit und Gemeinschaft" (this boundary zone between loneliness and community), when he figured his predicament in his diary, lacked any mention of Judaism or the politics it engaged. Kafka's political comprehension of modern society as a boundary zone extended beyond his ethnic background, as his use of the term "linguistic middle class" can attest.[59]

Kafka's discussion of the "Grenze" (boundary) in the literature of "small peoples," moreover, was critical of precisely this tendency to use ethnicity to mark off a separate and psychologically handicapped cultural realm. "Weil die zusammenhängenden Menschen fehlen, entfallen zusammenhängende literarische Aktionen" (Since people lack a sense of context, their literary activities are out of context too), he wrote of minority culture and its writing, but what is usually translated as "context" comes from *Zusammenhang*, literally "hanging together," precisely the solidarity based on ethnic and nationalist separatism from which he stood apart. The "Grenze" or boundary that could link individuals with their community Kafka saw as a creation, rather than viable substratum for culture, and understanding the individual predicament meant being suspicious of boundaries as a source of ethnic or cultural solidarity:

Wenn auch die einzelne Angelegenheit oft mit Ruhe durchdacht wird, so kommt man doch nicht bis an ihre Grenzen, an denen sie mit gleichartigen Angelegenheiten zusammenhängt, am ehesten erreicht man die Grenze gegenüber der Politik, ja man strebt sogar danach, diese Grenze früher zu sehen als sie da ist und oft diese sich zusammenziehende Grenze überall zu finden. (Even though the predicament of the individual is often thought through quite calmly, one still does not reach the boundary where that predicament connects one with those in a similar situation; one reaches this boundary soonest in politics, indeed, one even strives to see it sooner than it is really there, and often to find this cohesive boundary everywhere.)[60]

Ethnic boundaries as a means to define the self or the political content of writing are here the object of Kafka's critique. A literature of explicit ethnic and political concern, convinced of its "innere Selbständig-

keit" (inner independence), is imagined as degenerating into "poli-
tischen Schlagworte" (political slogans), and what Kafka soon calls
its more critical "Zusammenhang mit der Politik" (connection with
politics) is seen to depend on the questioning of boundaries and the
false sense of solidarity they inspire. The difficulty of setting borders
to one's identity is seen as a social rather than psychological issue,
and the false resolution of a nationalist literature of propaganda is
used to make anxiety over identity—"die einzelne Angelegenheit"—a
political rather than ethnic question, with significance beyond narrow
religious or national bounds.

The project of self-definition in *Das Schloß* is therefore devoid of
ethnic identification, and far more than a Jewish question, though the
political sources of Kafka's personal anxiety were not. One can see,
for instance, in K.'s anxiety over access to the Castle the double standard of ethnic inclusion and exclusion, the predicament of minorities
guaranteed a form of political equality and denied access when real
power is up for grabs:

Zwar heißt es, daß wir alle zum Schloß gehören und gar kein Abstand besteht
und nichts zu überbrücken ist und das stimmt auch vielleicht für gewöhnlich,
aber wir haben leider Gelegenheit gehabt, zu sehn, daß es gerade wenn es
darauf ankommt, gar nicht stimmt. (Of course we're all supposed to belong
to the Castle, and there's supposed to be no gulf between us, and nothing to
be bridged over, and that may be true enough on ordinary occasions, but as
we've unfortunately had opportunity to observe, it's not true when anything
really important is at stake.) (309)

Kafkan abstinence from historical specificity in such a passage moves
the focus from specific groups to the exercise of domination in society.
The recognizably modern world of *Das Schloß* is one in which signs
of social inclusion are always in flux, placing the rights of ethnic minorities in particular doubt.[61] Yet bureaucracy makes access to political
power a general problem in mass society, and collecting symbols of
such entrée to authority becomes the villagers' chief concern. Such
neurosis about identity and social status was for Kafka a general problem of modern politics, not the angst of any minority per se: subjective
uncertainty is revealed as crucial to the disciplinary system by which
the modern state works. By placing all signs of entitlement in question, the Castle encourages its subjects to enter a process of protracted
investigation and interpretation, while the deferral of finality commits
them to the subjection of endlessly pursuing the self-definitional task.

Barnabas' jacket, for instance, resembles the uniform of the Castle

officials, which defines them as wielders of power absolutely different from the villagers: "das Auffallendste an den Kleidern ist," Olga
explains to K., "daß sie meistens eng anliegen, ein Bauer oder ein
Handwerker könnte ein solches Kleid nicht brauchen" (The most remarkable thing about these clothes . . . is their tight fit, a farmer or
laborer could not use such a garment) (274). Barnabas' jacket is "eng"
like those of the powerful Castle officials. Yet it is also a construction
of his sister's: "die hat ihm Amalia gemacht, noch ehe er Bote war"
(Amalia made it for him, before he was a messenger) (272). The jacket
thus neither confirms the power of the messages Barnabas transmits,
nor denies it, placing him clearly neither within the Castle's official
sphere nor firmly outside it. Out of the anxiety to secure this difference, however, there arises the "unzählige Abstufungen der Hoff-
nung oder Verzweiflung" (the infinite gradations of hope and despair)
(278) Olga describes as the result of trying to make such a determination. The anxiety to decide Barnabas' official status, and to define the
political force of the words he brings, produces not decision, but the
fearful wish to obey anything that appears decisive. Since Barnabas
"niemals weiß, was diese Langsamkeit bedeutet" (never knows what
this delay might mean) (272) in the determination of his official status,
he obediently accepts any task at all which might give final proof.
Though he can never be sure whether any directive is an official one
or not, each task he accepts promises the possibility of such a conclusion to interpretation. Any duty is acceptable in the hope that the
question of his "official" duty might be decided once and for all.

This anxiety to distinguish between the official and unofficial produces a servility which makes the distinction, in the end, of little difference. Whether Barnabas serves the Castle officially or not, he serves
it without question, and involves the villagers in scrutinizing their
own behavior in relation to the standard of the "official" which his
own ambiguous political position asks them to construe. The unstable
political meaning of Barnabas' jacket, as it flickers in between affirming and denying his participation in public power, finally resolves into
the sign of one who obeys and serves:

[Er] hatte sich bezaubern lassen von des Barnabas enger seiden glänzender
Jacke, die dieser jetzt aufknöpfte und unter der ein grobes, grauschmut-
ziges, viel geflicktes Hemd erschien über der mächtigen kantigen Brust eines
Knechtes. ([K.] had been bewitched by Barnabas' close-fitting, silken-
gleaming jacket, which, now that it was unbuttoned, displayed a coarse, dirty
gray shirt patched all over, and beneath that the huge muscular chest of a
servant.) (52)

K. intends, through interpretation of the Castle, to avoid just this servile status. He recognizes in the Castle official Klamm's first letter to him the same indecision that plagued Barnabas' relation to political power. Like Barnabas' jacket, the letter is a sign which indicates both K.'s subjection to the Castle's authority, and his status as a private individual outside the sway of its commands:

Er war nicht einheitlich, es gab Stellen wo mit ihm wie mit einem Freien gesprochen wurde, dessen eigenen Willen man anerkennt. . . . Es gab aber wieder Stellen, wo er offen oder versteckt als ein kleiner vom Sitz jenes Vorstandes kaum bemerkbarer Arbeiter behandelt wurde. . . . (It was not a consistent letter, there were parts which dealt with him as a free man whose own will was recognized . . . but there were also places where, explicitly or secretly, he was treated as a minor employee, hardly visible to the heads of departments.) (41)

K. makes it clear that he is aware of the dangerous consequences of anxiety over such a question: "dabei aber bedrückte es ihn schwer zu sehn, daß sich in solcher Bedenklichkeit offenbar schon die gefürchteten Folgen des Untergeordnetseins, des Arbeiterseins zeigten" (he was oppressed heavily to recognize already in these qualms that feared result, subjection, and the working life) (58). In order to avoid such subjection, K. resolves not to obey, but rather to distinguish carefully the official realm of authority, where power has its place, from the unofficial one, where his status as a free man can be enjoyed with assurance. The consequence of anxious indecision—obedience—is to be avoided by a careful process of separation of the "wirkliche Person . . . der ich außerhalb der Ämter stehe" (the real person . . . the me outside the office) (105) from the individual tied up in political and collective life.

The attempt to draw such a distinction, however, draws the "wirkliche Person," the "real person," in all his privacy, ever farther into the restrictions of official procedures. What K. conceives of as mistakes or "Fehler" of administration in the Castle's decision to call for a land surveyor are in fact central to the regular principle through which the administration of the Castle maintains its vitality. The "mistake" of K.'s case produces exactly that inquiry and interpretation which are not the exception in village life but the rule: "Aber selbst wenn es auf den Umfang der Arbeit ankäme, wäre Ihr Fall einer der geringsten, die gewöhnlichen Fälle, also jene ohne sogenannte Fehler geben noch viel mehr und freilich auch viel ergiebigere Arbeit" (Even if we judged only by the amount of work, your case would be one of the smallest, in fact those without so-called mistakes cause much more red tape)

(107). What K. judges to be the confusion of his case allows the administration of the Castle to swing into gear, and multiply both his inquiries and the ambiguity of its replies: to retain, in other words, its usual practice. To be confused about the boundary between the official and the unofficial, just as K. wonders about his status in relation to the Castle, is perpetually to implicate oneself in bureaucratic procedures set up to adjudicate the question endlessly.

Castle bureaucracy exerts its control over the village subjects by preventing such questions from ever reaching resolution. When K. asks the mayor if there exists a control authority to prevent the ambiguity of such cases as his own, he is told that "nur ein völlig Fremder kann Ihre Frage Stellen. Ob es Kontrollbehörden gibt? Es gibt nur Kontrollbehörden" (Only a complete stranger could even pose such a question. Is there such a control authority? There are only control authorities) (104). Every office becomes an office that exerts control not by resolving the ambiguity of the official, but by producing borderline "mistakes," such as K.'s, which create and prolong the need for official investigation. The more such a question requires clarification, the more the individual becomes dependent on that powerful and subjecting official apparatus his interpretation seeks to master. In a section Kafka deleted from his final manuscript, the mayor tells K. that the "control" office exists not to resolve questions about the scope of the official will, but rather to prevent such a question from ever reaching decision: "Und gibt es denn überhaupt eine schliessliche Entscheidung? Um sie nicht aufkommen zu lassen, sind ja die Kontrollämter da" (And is there ever a final determination? In order to prevent it, that's why the control authorities are there).[62] The need to establish the difference between the official and the unofficial has the paradoxical effect of collapsing the difference between the two. To adjudicate the question is already to have entered the sphere and sway of official process.

If the desire to establish the difference between the person and the office integrates the person into official procedures, it also allows the power of the official to be integrated into the intimate sphere. The landlady is sure of nothing more than the difference between the official Klamm and the lover who once visited her in the village. The villagers as a group share the belief that nothing could be more different than the Castle and the village Klamm. In the village, Olga tells K., Klamm's appearance is subject to myriad variations. But in the Castle he is, they believe, fundamentally different:

Er soll ganz anders aussehn, wenn er ins Dorf kommt und anders wenn er es verläßt, anders ehe er Bier getrunken hat, anders nachher, anders im Wachen,

anders im Schlafen, anders allein, anders im Gespräch und, was hienach verständlich ist, fast grundverschieden oben im Schloß. (He's reported as having
one appearance when he comes into the village and another on leaving it,
after having his beer he looks different from how he does before it, when he's
awake he's different from when he's asleep, when he's alone he's different
from when he's talking to people, and—what makes sense after all that—he's
almost a different person up in the Castle.) (278)

Thus when Klamm withdraws his affections from the landlady, she
concludes that his motivations must come from some completely other
sphere. She is convinced he has entered another realm fundamentally
different from her own: "Den welchen man vergessen hat, kann man
ja wieder kennen lernen. Bei Klamm ist das nicht möglich. Wen er
nicht mehr rufen läßt, den hat er nicht nur für die Vergangenheit völlig
vergessen, sondern förmlich auch für alle Zukunft" (He whom one
has forgotten, one can of course get to know again. But with Klamm
this is impossible. Whomever he no longer allows to be called to him
he forgets not only completely for the past, but for all the future)
(133). The "Gründe" of that withdrawal, the landlady insists, "waren
dunkel, in denen durfte ich forschen aber unglücklich hätte ich nicht
sein dürfen" (The reasons were dark, I was allowed to examine them,
but I would not have been allowed to be unhappy) (130). With this
prohibition internalized, research into Klamm's public meaning comes
to dominate her private life. The search for this absolute other—official
power removed from the private sphere—turns the landlady's marriage into a version of official bureaucratic inquiry: "Jahrelang drehten
sich unsere nächtlichen Gespräche nur um Klamm und die Gründe
seiner Sinnesänderung. Und wenn mein Mann bei diesen Unterhal-
tungen einschlief, weckte ich ihn und wir sprachen weiter" (For years
our evening talks turned only on Klamm and on the possible reasons
for his change of heart. And when my husband would fall asleep during these conversations, I awoke him, and we talked some more) (129).
These discussions resemble precisely the interminable official "night
interviews" held at the Herrenhof later in the novel. The quest for
the "Gründe," or grounds, of the Castle's difference from the village
turns the landlady's marriage into a duplicate of the Castle's official
procedures.

The collective activity of Castle definition disperses social power
everywhere, while estranging the collective from awareness of its role
in that dispersal: "Nirgends noch hatte K. Amt und Leben so ver-
flochten gesehen wie hier" (Never had K. seen work and home so
closely woven together as here) (94). Yet every time official power

enters the private sphere, the boundary in which the villagers so firmly believe can merely be redrawn. In the schoolhouse where K. accepts a position as janitor, one room of the school is to be his workplace, and the other his home. He must be willing at any moment, however, to change their places. When the boundary between *Amt* and *Leben* (work and home) so dear to K. has been crossed, it is simply sought elsewhere and temporarily redrawn: "doch müssen Sie, wenn nicht gleichzeitig in beiden Zimmern unterrichtet wird und Sie gerade in dem Zimmer, in welchem unterrichtet wird, wohnen, natürlich in das andere Zimmer übersiedeln" (But of course, if lessons are not being held simultaneously in both rooms, and you are living in that room where lessons are to be held, you must naturally move over into the other room) (151).

Construing the boundary between the official and the unofficial thus engages the critic of Castle authority in a process of perpetual construction and erasure. The moment private life is contaminated by the official sphere, the boundary which has been erased is reconstructed elsewhere. The need to draw such a boundary, and the impossibility of maintaining it, are irreconcilable alternatives which end up working together in repressive harmony. They allow for the dissolution of the Castle's authority and its continual reconstruction in new and changing realms. With the belief in the difference between Castle and village intact, the power the villagers enact against themselves will always reappear.

The attempt to define power is thus able to obliterate what is involved in the process of definition: the interpreter's agency in the system of power his or her interpretation helps to construct. The attempt to reach a clear definition necessarily confuses, as the landlady tells K.: "Unsinn, völliger Unsinn, man verwirrt sich selbst, wenn man mit solchem Unsinn spielt" (Nonsense, utter nonsense! You'll confuse yourself when you play with this nonsense) (133). The confused, however, grab eagerly for a determining sign which would clarify their confusion; her conclusion is not to reject Klamm's nonsense, but to wait eagerly for any sign of his she might obey: "Wo wäre der Mann, der mich hindern könnte, zu Klamm zu laufen, wenn mir Klamm ein Zeichen gibt?" (Where is the man who could stop me from running to Klamm, if he only gave me a sign?) (133).

Amalia's Secret: Silence and Ethnicity

Amalia's specific ethnic background remains shrouded in uncertainty. Yet her actions create an uncertainty particularly her own. For her community, and the modern reader, she poses a common problem: what is the social and political meaning of her rejection of the Castle? In declining to define her identity in public terms, and in her lack of interest in such a grounded identity, Amalia differs from the rest of the villagers. The "Unentschlossenheit" (indecision) of her political status, while clearly that of a pariah, never resolves into the "Geschlossenheit" or closure of identity, even the anxiety over self-definition that serves the powers of the *Schloß* so well. Her rebellion raises the radical hope of opposing the Castle's law, while her ambiguity remains a central example of the very indeterminacy upon which the novel's system of control depends. Is the refusal to identify as a bureaucratic citizen, or as an ethnic as well as feminine outsider, already a choice subject to power?

On the surface, this containment reading seems to hold. Though Sortini's sexual summons is said to be written in "den gemeinsten Ausdrücken" (the coarsest expressions) (302), and presumably the clearest ones as well, Amalia's subjection does not depend on sex: it is the Castle community's subjective construction of the Castle's directive that gives Sortini's command its political effect. The letter ends with the threat of a power which might exert itself anywhere and in any form—" 'Daß Du also gleich kommst, oder—!' " (that you come right away, or—!) (303)—but depends for its effectiveness upon Amalia's own interpretive filling of that gap. Amalia refuses representation in Castle terms: the border ground of the letter as a social "Zeichen" (sign) is rejected. But in tearing up the letter as she does, Amalia herself becomes a sign. Fearing the dramatic openness of her action, the villagers stigmatize Amalia with gossip, placing her securely back within the dynamic of power from which she seemed to have withdrawn.

The ground of the Castle's power, Olga believes when confronted by her sister face-to-face, is revealed in this act of rejection: "Aug in Aug mit der Wahrheit stand sie und lebte und ertrug dieses Leben damals wie heute" (Face to face with the truth she stood and lived and bore this life then, just as now) (331). What Amalia has seen, however, she steadfastly refuses to define, and reproaches K. and Olga when, as she puts it, "Schloßgeschichten werden erzählt" (323) (Castle stories are told) about her fate, calling such oral narrative the

"Einfluß des Schloßes" (influence of the Castle). Amalia recognizes that interpretation of her refusal results in a narrative reproduction of the very Castle authority she herself has refused to construe. Instead, silence governs her resistance. "Ohne besondere Veranstaltungen, ohne Befehle, ohne Bitten, fast nur durch Schweigen" (without special arrangements, without orders, or begging, almost through silence alone) (330) she takes on the leadership of her family when the community engages in what the title of chapter 18 calls "Amalia's Strafe" (Amalia's Punishment). The village community interprets her silent rejection, replacing it with critical, shunning whispers that the family has a powerful means of enforcing Sortini's threat: "es war ein fortwährendes Flüstern vom Morgen bis zum Abend und manchmal rief mich der Vater in plötzlicher Beängstigung zu sich" (There was continual whispering from morning to evening, and sometimes father, in sudden agitation, would call me to him) (330).

To interpret Amalia's silence as contained, however, places the critic in a curious position. No sooner have we imagined the textual moment that might stand outside the Castle's subjecting sway than we have filled in that *Schweigen*, or silenced it ourselves, showing its implication in the repressive system of power that is Castle construction. What we have done, in other words, is exactly what Amalia herself in that textual moment refused to do: we have *filled in a gap*, her silence, and by so doing, yielded to the hegemony of Castle power. Nothing in the novel, we might say, cements the Castle's hold on the village more firmly than the invitation Amalia's silence offers for its exercise. More than the "Lücke," or gap, in Sortini's "that you come right away, or—", the "Lücke" or gap of her silence is filled in a way that makes her subject to Sortini's oppression of her as a woman and its subjecting categories.

Wilhelm Emrich, for instance, sees Amalia's "absolute Distanz" from Sortini as cutting her off from "der empirische Grund ihres Lebens, Beruf und Arbeit" (the empirical ground of her life, her calling and work), when in fact what she has done is refuse to prostitute her sexuality to his will.[63] A similar reduction of Amalia to Sortini's terms occurs in Marthe Robert's otherwise subtle analysis: "Amalia's act is an absolute negation, a destruction of the very basis of existence, a challenge to the forces of nature."[64] When filling in the "Lücke" or gap of her silent response, the critics often castigate her for her lack of "Beruf" (profession), or desire for "procreation," in Richard Shepherd's interpretation, and thus replicate the middle-class categories that objectify her as a woman, and which allow the village community to make her a pariah for not following their social norms.[65] The unfillable gap in the Castle's hegemony—Amalia's silent refusal—is used to ensure "Lückenlosigkeit," the seamlessness of interpretation, as critical language carries out the "Lückenlosigkeit der amtlichen Organisation" (the seamlessness of the official organization) (417) of which K. is told, and folds even negative assertions of identity into the dominant categories of the novel's bureaucratic state.

Another effect of such conformity, however, is to cancel any sense of Amalia's ethnicity or relation to the questions of nationalism Kafka and his contemporaries faced. The fact that the villagers avoid such questions, while every aspect of the Castle's contradictory signs are pursued, should make critics at least consider differentiating themselves from their interpretive model in this regard. Whatever reasons of style can be adduced, Kafka himself seems to have participated in silencing her ethnic sources, giving no clues to her background himself. Formal effects aside, her social background remains obscure, inviting the existential and religious readings of her meaning in the text.[66] The signs that make Amalia a pariah in no way brand her a Jew in strict terms, a Czech nationalist, or even a feminist. The silence that ennobles her rebellion also seems to censor the concrete social meaning of her act.

Yet before one is tempted to make Kafka's text complicit in the operations of modern bureaucracy, it is worth placing Amalia's story in its cultural context in order to see what signs of ethnicity and politics her story might conspire to erase. Amalia's silence distinguishes her from Pepi, whose florid speech remains unmarked by accent or ethnic marks. But both characters contrast boldly with the overtly political representations of Jewish culture and the nationalist question which flourished in the political communities of Prague. Suppression of the markers of ethnic and historical struggle are obvious—no glaring keys give away Amalia's position, or that of Pepi, the maid with whom K. associates once Amalia's story is done. Instead, Kafka questions the roles of everyday experience in ethnic suppression: the stories of both show the importance of sexuality, gossip, and middle-class prejudice in creating the conformist culture in which ethnic repression and resistance are lived.

Pepi, for instance, was the name of the central character of Max Brod's novel *Ein Tschechisches Dienstmädchen* (1909), which aroused the ire of Czech nationalists and Zionists alike. The circumstances of Brod's novel connected it to Kafka's narrative: a troubled German bachelor falls in love with Pepi, a Czech maid in the rooming house

where he temporarily resides. As in Kafka's *Schloß*, the male protagonist is not explicitly figured as a Prague Jew, though Brod's contemporaries had little trouble in placing him as the assimilated, Jewish
son of a successful middle-class family. In a political context charged
by questions of nationalism, Pepi's heavily accented German, and the
protagonist's longing for the beauties of Czech culture, were read
as a stereotypic and disturbing political allegory. Ruzena Jesenská, a
Czech writer who was also the aunt of Kafka's Milena, attacked the
novel for representing Czech culture simplistically, while Germans
read the romance as a charter for incipient revolt.[67] The reaction in
Czech culture bore similarities to Amalia's ostracism, though the differences are also clear. While Brod was punished for representing
political relations between a Jew and a Czech to the latter's disadvan-
tage, Amalia is held to account—in an ironic political inversion—for
refusing to bed down with a representative of bureaucratic power.
Brod was nonetheless excluded from popular culture in ways that resemble Amalia's story. By representing an interethnic romance, Brod
had also exposed the charged emotions that fueled nationalist politics. Some German papers accused him of treason and branded him
an "Erbfeind" (hereditary enemy). In a fashion similar to the treatment Kafka's villagers give Amalia, they refused to give utterance to
his name.[68]

Yet it was the Zionist reaction to Brod's novel that was the most telling. As the key event in Brod's conversion to Zionism, it would hardly
have escaped Kafka's notice, and its terms indicate the highly politi-
cized context that informed Kafka's own representation of erotic affairs. Leo Hermann's critical review of Brod's novel is indignant at the
prospect that sexual relations—apparently private affairs—would be
used to solve Prague's pressing national conflicts. Brod's protagonist
seeks his Pepi in "Dienstmädchenasyl" (maid's quarters), much as K.'s
Pepi would ask him to visit him in the "Mädchenzimmer" (maid's
room) where, she promises him after his break with Frieda, a bed
would be ready for him and where he might reside.[69] Hermann complained about the depoliticizing effects of making political struggles
erotic. What was at stake for Kafka's Prague readers in K.'s use of
sex to get close to Klamm and the Castle is apparent in Hermann's
complaint against Brod's simpler and more openly political text:

Does Brod really know the German people? If so, he must surely know that
the German and Czech people are not going to be brought together through
individual, erotic relations. . . . Perhaps Max Brod will come to find a context

that will lift him out of the realm of the individual and will permit him to arrive at a solution [to such questions], which has a better foundation than a hotel bed.[70]

While Hermann's suggested "context" for politicizing the personal was Zionism, his critique has relevance beyond its immediate purpose of encouraging Brod and others to join the Zionist cause. In that end Hermann succeeded, as Brod himself relates. Yet the controversy over Brod's book is relevant beyond this narrow ideological context: Hermann's remarks make clear that Prague's Jewish readers were immediately capable, like their Czech counterparts, of reading erotic relations as suppressive symbols of overtly political and national struggles. Kafka's own response as a reader to Brod's novel is not documented: Hermann's review appeared in the Jewish newspaper *Selbstwehr* in 1909, two years before it can be ascertained with relative certainty that Kafka was a regular reader.[71] But since the incident galvanized Brod's turn to Zionism—a frequent topic of conversation with the similarly inclined Kafka—it may be assumed with relative certainty to have been an item they discussed. Regardless of this biographical dimension, the cultural context it establishes for K.'s sexual relations, devoid of such blatant political markers, is clear. The thematics of what Hermann called the "hotel bed"—so prominent in K.'s dealings with the Castle throughout relates Kafka's novel directly to Hermann's complaint. Erotic relations in *The Castle*, while devoid of Brod's signs of ethnic and national identity, examine sex as a means of enforcing the dictates of conformist culture, offering readers the chance to subject the novel's sexual politics to stringent cultural critique.

The politics of *reading* becomes the focus of K.'s relation to Amalia: in characterizing her rejection of Castle authority and its sexual summons, the best and most sympathetic readers of her character simultaneously deprive it of any ethnic and historical ground on which it might stand. "Her resistance takes no definable form," as Anne Hoffman puts it, agreeing with Heinz Politzer's earlier reading that its meaning can only be regarded as "negative."[72] Most positively, when she is seen by Marjanne Goozé as "an exception to all the assumptions made within [the novel's] society," she is emptied of significance, regarded only as "silence" ineffective against the "domination" of the novel's world.[73] In refusing to sleep with Sortini, to be sure, Amalia is still represented as his sexual subject by the villagers who tell her tale. Yet unlike Brod's heroine, Amalia rejects sex, and with it the kind of popular representation reflected in his text. Whatever her ethnic identity, Amalia succeeds in preventing its social objectification, obtaining a kind of independence she is denied through popular representations of sex.

Amalia, in other words, obtains more cultural autonomy than the alternatives of blank silence or gender subjugation suggest. The false but unavoidable choices for reading her story—as sexual submission, or heroic abstinence—are faulty precisely because of this cultural fixity they impose: the absence of a middle term reflects limiting concepts of feminine identity. Amalia appears to be offered only a "marriage" of sexual submission, or a sainthood of sexual abstinence. The same false choices apply to her ethnic definition, as if a "yes" to Sortini meant assimilation to bureaucratic culture, and a "no" signified a silent reservoir of ethnic culture that is separatist and virtuously withheld. As a woman and perhaps a Jew in Kafka's historical world, Amalia can either submit to this system of *representation*—for it is the letter of Sortini that is always at issue—or, along with her family, remain deprived of speech and concrete ethnic identity within the Castle's realm.

It is this capacity to represent Amalia and her family that constitutes the actual object of her resistance: the sexual power she rejects is far less important than the symbolic power of language to command obedience that her independence holds at bay. Power in bureaucracy, as Kafka understood, thrives on its ability to represent citizens in terms of subjection: Castle officials, explains Olga, appear listless in public, preferring to deny the public functions of such power.[74] Sortini himself is described as the most "withdrawn," or "zurückgezogen," of Castle officials (309). Amalia's resistance objectifies the representation that constitutes his power: pawning off most of his "Repräsentationspflichten," or "official representations," on "Sordini," and taking advantage of the confusion, Sortini is for the first time exposed by Amalia's inattention, and represented in a politically vulnerable way. Injustice is objectified when Amalia achieves the position of *representing* political authority herself: the potential for power she represents is contingent on objectifying power, rather than settling for its terms. As Olga puts it, "Sortini hat nicht Amalia bloßgestellt, sondern sich selbst. Vor Sortini also schrecke ich zurück, vor der Möglichkeit, daß es einen solchen Mißbrauch der Macht gibt" (It was himself that Sortini exposed, not Amalia. It is from Sortini that I draw back in horror, from the possibility of such an abuse of power) (304). For Olga, Amalia's story means that the Castle has been "bloßgestellt" (laid bare): as the self-subjection of the villagers to social signs she rejects.

Amalia's story in this way recognizes the "negative" status minorities achieve by rejecting dominant representations. But Kafka also points far more to the positive, oppositional cultural achievements of Amalia, and later Pepi, than adherents of the "negative" reading of Amalia suggest. Amalia's action is similarly effective in revealing the radical potential for criticism and social change contained within an otherwise dominant discourse. Heinz Politzer long ago traced the meaning of the German name to its root, "labor," a crucial association.[75] Above all, the villagers are the Castle's laborers, and the Castle, as we have seen, exerts its power only insofar as the villagers remain willing to do its work. Even through the screen of Kafka's "traumhaft" (dreamlike) and unrealistic vision, Walter Sokel was able to recognize in the Castle the figurative "Allianz vom österreichischen Adel und österreichischen Bürokratie, die das Bauernland der Böhmen regierte" (alliance of the Austrian aristocracy and Austrian bureaucracy, that ruled over the peasants of [Czech] Bohemia).[76] Amalia's refusal to do an official's bidding is impossible to ground with such historical specificity, but it can be explained in a way that identifies the potential for action and political change within any situation of self-subjection; the telling of her story shows that opposition is available in the village's own subjecting terms. The meaning of her name as labor, and its potential for transformation, are present in the very "Castle stories" Olga tells: "und tatsächlich sollen, was Wohlleben betrifft, die Diener die eigentlichen Herren im Schloß sein" (and as far as prosperity goes, the servants seem to be the real masters in the castle) (348).

Nor is Amalia's story bereft of Jewish culture, despite the "negative" representation of minorities Kafka strives to project. The potential for social transformation in Kafka's novel centers on Amalia *and* the archaic symbols of Jewish scripture she motivates, against the representational command of her father and the Castle's explicit rules. The most powerful scene of resistance of the novel occurs when Amalia rejects Sortini's gaze and the fire engine, the image of the social mechanism adored by her father. Crucial to the ethnic and revolutionary subtext of the *Fest* is its date—"am 3. Juli" (on the third of July) (295)— which is both the day before the Independence Day, as the author of *Amerika* would likely have known, and also charged with a sense of familial origin, since it was also Kafka's birthday. Kafka's remark that his writing might be considered to be constructing a new "Kabbalah," or book of Jewish mystical lore, fits well with the coded meanings that structure the fire engine scene.[77] While her father, in the fashion of assimilation, demands obedience to the symbol of social solidarity offered the village by a bureaucratized culture, Amalia evokes images from the Jewish tradition which, while conservative, prophetically encourage resistance to the abuses of dominant power:

"Gerade um uns, vielleicht hatte sie Amalia angelockt, waren einige solche Bläser, es war schwer die Sinne dabei zusammenzuhalten und wenn man nun auch noch nach dem Gebot des Vaters Aufmerksamkeit für die Spritze haben sollte, so war das das Äußerste was man leisten konnte, und so entging uns Sortini." (Right around us were several of these trumpeters—perhaps Amalia had attracted them; and even though father's order commanded us to pay attention to the engine and the hose, that was the last thing we could do—and thus Sortini escaped us.) (299)

What "escapes" the crowd is the institutional power Sortini exerts, replaced by ethnic associations at first not readily perceptible to the villagers or to readers who take their reactions as a guide. For the guiding irony of the scene pits the family romance against revolutionary political rhetoric. The figure of the father, for Kafka, was no source of ethnic identity to oppose in contradictory fashion to institutional power. For the writer, the contrary case obtained, as the paternal will to ethnic assimilation was precisely the danger: "Weg vom Judentum, meist mit unklarer Zustimmung der Väter," Kafka wrote to Brod: "diese Unklarheit war das Empörende" (most young Jews wanted to leave Jewishness behind them, and their fathers approved of this, but vaguely . . . this vagueness was what was outrageous to them).[78]

Obedience to the father is here mocked at the same time the oedipal problematic is recast: Amalia's reticent silence is simultaneously productive of the wildest "tones," sounds foreign to the father, though perhaps—given his relation to the villagers—the sounds of his native tongue. "Spritze" mocks the father's centrality, much as Kafka rejected psychology when discussing Jewishness as a public and political affair: "Besser als die Psychoanalyse gefällt mir in diesem Fall die Erkenntnis, daß dieser Vaterkomplex, von dem sich mancher geistig nährt, nicht den unschuldigen Vater, sondern das Judentum des Vaters betrifft" (Psychoanalysis lays stress on the father complex and many find the concepts intellectually fruitful. In this case I prefer another version, where the issue revolves not around the innocent father but around the father's Jewishness).[79] The filial rebellion central to the castle *Fest* turns on a similar issue: Amalia stages and thereby threatens paternal centrality. Much in Kafka's relation to his father, including the latter's assimilationist conformity, against which the son rebels, also characterizes Amalia's relation to fatherhood. Obedience to bureaucratic authority is enforced through her father's command, and the sexual submission he orders makes its social exploitation concrete.

It is the father's fascination with the "Spritze" of symbolic authority that enforces submission, Olga recalls: "mußten wir uns alle bücken und fast unter die Spritze kriechen" (we all had to bow down, and almost crawl under the nozzle [to look at it]) with the subordinate position of assimilation represented as sexual compliance on demand. Amalia breaks with this socially constructed fantasy of origins, and Kafka, by representing the father's "Spritze" as part of the bureaucratic machine, makes the darkly comic point about assimilation that the (Jewish) father's most intimate symbol of religious and social authority is in fact alien, its power given over to the Castle's institutional hands. While the trumpets herald the "Spritze," Amalia has no "Aufmerksamkeit" (attention) for it: instead, the representational force of the trumpets is removed from the father—"perhaps Amalia had attracted them" and given an antipatriarchal command: "Nur Amalia kümmerte sich um die Spritze nicht" (Amalia was the only one who wasn't concerned with the nozzle at all) (298–99).

The father's fascination with the fire engine, on the other hand, suggests for Kafka, who worked in insurance, the culture of Jewish assimilation he feared. In a dream recorded on 9 November 1911, in the midst of his arrangements for the Yiddish theater to perform in Prague, Kafka imagined storming the city in terms that evoke the Castle *Fest* and its revolutionary potential. Hartmut Binder points out that the fire truck incident was based on events Kafka observed as a youngster, and that the fire engine as symbol represented the public life of Prague and its institutional facts: the Palais der Prager städtischen Versicherungsanstalt, built in 1900, had allegorical images of firemen built into its gabled facades.[80] The dream itself portrays a scene of mass rebellion, where *Schloß*—clearly figured in the dream as the institutions of Prague themselves—is seized:

Die Revolution war so groß, mit riesigen den Platz aufwärts und abwärts geschickten Volksmengen, wie sie wahrscheinlich in Prag niemals stattgefunden hatte . . . vom Fest sah man zuerst nichts, der Hof war jedenfalls zu einem Feste ausgefahren, inzwischen war die Revolution losgebrochen, das Volk war ins Schloß eingedrungen, ich selbst lief gerade über die Vorsprünge der Brunnen im Vorhof ins Freie. (The revolution was so immense, with the square filled with gigantic crowds surging up and down, as never had occurred in Prague. . . . At first you saw nothing, the court, in any case, had ridden off to a *Fest*, and in the meantime the revolution had broken out, people surged into the castle, I myself ran out over the ledges of the fountain into the open.[81]

Kafka's dream insists on a potential revolution and seizure of the *Schloß*, a hope transformed into cultural criticism in the novel that bears that name. Analysis replaces the immature fantasy of revolt: rather than imagining the storming of Prague's bastions, Kafka depicts Amalia's father as helping to operate its conformist engines, and opposes the social stasis to which the father's culture gives force. Revolution consists—to emphasize Adorno's accurate point once more—in incorporating the "power of the adversary," taking hold of an assimilationist identity and using it to challenge bureaucratic power. Kafka's fictional fire engine, modeled after the institutional facade of Prague, represents power only through the support of its subjects: yet the same trumpets produced by the Castle to fete its engines, Kafka points out, are capable of resisting assimilation by asserting the different sounds and claims of minority culture. Like the latent revolutionary power of cultures suppressed by a bureaucratic order, Amalia's trumpets were "besondere Instrumente, auf denen man mit der kleinsten Kraftanstrengung, ein Kind könnte das, die wildesten Töne hervorbringen konnte; wenn man das hörte, glaubte man, die Türken seien schon da" (extraordinary instruments on which, with the smallest effort—a child could do it—one could produce the wildest blasts; to hear them was enough to make one think the Turks were there) (299).

Though the fire of ethnic uprising never breaks out in Amalia's story, the linguistic and political material for such a revolt is rendered in the kind of sounds she attracts. The "wildest blasts" of the trumpets correspond to utterances charged with ethnic undertones, emerging with power from dominant discourse. Kafka's own interest in such sounds was recorded in a diary entry just before his dream of assaulting the *Schloß*. While attached to the Yiddish theater, Kafka's romantic fascination with Mania Tschissik, a leading actress, expressed itself in attraction to the linguistic resonance of her name: "Frau Tschissik (ich schreibe den Namen so gerne auf) neigt bei Tisch auch während des Gansbratenessens gern den Kopf" (Mrs. Tschissik—I enjoy writing the name so much—likes to bow her head at the table even while eating roast goose).[82] Yiddish resonance here strikes a contradictory tone of self-assertion to the bowed head of submission, a trope that Deleuze and Guattari trace throughout Kafka's narrative work.[83] As in the *Fest* scene, the sound and staging of the Yiddish theater represent a form of popular culture that resists the controls of mass culture as well as the limits of high art.

The "wildesten Töne" sounded on the castle trumpets in *Das Schloß* parallel Kafka's diary comments of 26 October 1911 on the Yiddish play *Der Wilde Mensch* precisely in this regard. For while "concessions" are made to a popular audience—"es werden allerdings dem Publikum Koncessionen gemacht und manchmal glaubt man sich recken zu müssen um über die Köpfe des Newyorcker jüdischen Theaterpublikums weg das Stück zu sehn" (concessions are made to the public, and sometimes you must stretch to see the play over the heads of the Jewish theatergoers of New York)—to Kafka, however, high-cultural pretensions were more harmful: "schlimmer aber ist daß auch irgendeiner geahnten Kunst greifbare Koncessionen gemacht werden" (worse is the fact that palpable concessions are made to some vaguely felt art). In between popular pandering and high-cultural pretension, however, the "Töne" of the castle *Fest* resemble the sounding of the name "Tschissik" and Yiddish to Kafka: bowed by the constraints of "Castle" culture, the popular event releases oppositional linguistic energy that challenges political and linguistic bounds.

Amalia's influence, of course, remains indirect, never defined as specifically ethnic. The attention she gains may resemble that paid to the popular theater of Yitzchak Löwy, but like Kafka, Amalia is a critical observer rather than a popular performer. Resistance to the Castle in Kafka's novel consists of her explicit act of sexual refusal, but the critical importance of her act is the consistent attention it draws to the latent energy that resides in all social codes, regardless of the ethnic group or dominant bureaucracy involved. Amalia's act occurs at a popular *Fest* because Kafka recognized the dual potential of such popular rituals. Like the "engine" of mass-produced obedience, popular culture can enforce social submission, or objectify the suppressed energy of marginalized "villagers" and their groups. Amalia's function in *Das Schloß* works self-critically, representing both ethnic assimilation and the resistant cultural power it holds. The blare of the trumpets is Kafka's parable: transformed by Amalia from a modern herald of social assimilation into symbols of an archaic Jewish tradition, whose conservatism, like the Kabbalah, evokes revolutionary energies and ends. Conformist heraldry here also evokes the startling sound of the Jewish shofar, which called ancient Israel to revolt against its oppressors; the Book of Ezekiel describes such trumpets sounding in the service of a solitary watchman who, like Amalia, summons the country to battle against the enemy: "its people choose one of themselves to be a watchman. When he sees the enemy approaching and blows his trumpet, to warn the people, then if anyone does not heed the warning and is overtaken by the enemy, he is responsible for his own fate." [84]

Such cultural undertones, moreover, are more than apparent to the Castle officials. Fire in the novel is both a real and a symbolic threat: Castle bureaucracy establishes its dominance through the "Akten" or the bureaucratic paper language it encourages the villagers to exchange. Paperwork, like the monumental buildings of the Prague insurance industry, bearing the fire engine as symbols, masks the smoldering tensions of social as well as ethnic unrest. To "put out the fire" in Kafka's novel is more than a useful social function; Amalia's father had distinguished himself by rescuing a Castle official whom the mere mention of fire was enough to panic into helplessness: "Es war zwar keine Feuersgefahr, nur das trockene Holz neben einem Ofen fing zu rauchen an, aber Galater [the official] bekam Angst, rief aus dem Fenster um Hilfe, die Feuerwehr kam und mein Vater mußte ihn hinaustragen" (There was no danger of fire. Only the dry wood by the stove began to smoke, but Galater became anxious, the firemen came and my father had to carry him out) (297). Like the "papiernes Deutsch" (paper German), as Klaus Wagenbach puts it, which the Austrian monarchy imposed on Czech and Jewish Bohemia, bureaucratic power in Kafka's novel is more fragile than it seems. Kafka himself referred to the bureaucratic society by which Jews were subjected as "Papierdeutsch[e]."[85] Fire represents a challenge to the similarly imposed speech of political domination in *Das Schloß*. Wagenbach's central assertion deserves repeating: "Kafka worked against the historical denaturing of language in Prague."[86] The "wildeste Töne" Kafka centered around Amalia draw attention away from the fire engine and toward a fiery linguistic potential which, like an uncontrolled popular dialect, creates a powerful social threat.

For the "tones" of language, as Kafka suggested in his speech on the Yiddish theater, possessed a frightening as well as critical cultural power. The relative atonality of Kafka's language itself, as Wagenbach remarks, was itself a historical fact, signifying the language of imperial assimilation to the subject nations of the Hapsburg empire. Sounds that are increasingly familiar in Kafka's last works break the frame of such seemingly neutral language: the "piping" of the mouse folk in *Josephine* resounds in the manner of the village trumpets, simultaneously powerful and silent, like the voice of ethnic minorities struggling to be heard. Because of this liminal quality, minority speech for Kafka was a model for political resistance in general, always threatened with modern culture's mechanisms of control while never surrendering its oppositional force. The *Fest* trumpets break normative perceptions without producing a new political order, or even an identifiably ethnic or different speech. By Olga's folkloric suggestion that the "Turks" might be there, Kafka suggests the realistic sense in which the foreign "Other" presents totalitarian social control with a threat.

Thus *Das Schloß* never names or hails any particular minority. As in Kafka's diaries, minority culture is valued as a model for the kind of self-criticism which a genuinely popular culture might someday attain. Far from a source of popular speech in assimilated Prague, in which Yiddish was never learned or forgotten, Jewish culture for Kafka symbolized the alternative potential of ethnic inheritance for critically changing the patterns of dominant culture. Hence Jewish culture is particularized, but also compared with the language of subjugated ethnic groups in general. The "uninterrupted tradition of national struggle that determines every work" in Yiddish was a position which "keine Litteratur, auch nicht die des unterdrückten Volkes, in dieser durchgängigen Weise hat" (pervades no other literature, not even that of the most oppressed people).[87]

The model Yiddish established, however, relates to the productions of every minority speaking through a dominant culture. Amalia is therefore no hero in the tradition of nationalist literature. Unlike Němcová's Czech novel *The Grandmother,* where a similar young heroine marries at a traditional *Fest,* with the blessing of the castle, Amalia refuses her spouse. Kafka, retaining the split between village and castle, refuses the consoling images of cultural accommodation that close Němcová's patriotic work.[88] Instead, silence augurs resistance to the incorporation of ethnic tradition by political authority. For Kafka always argued for a self-critical concept of cultural heroism, particularly where ethnic self-promotion was concerned. In reading Graetz's *History of the Jews,* Kafka remarked its "strangeness" to him precisely because of this critical quality; the heroes of popular ethnic tradition were subject to criticism from within:

es [war] mir zuerst fremder als ich dachte und ich mußte hie und da einhalten, um durch Ruhe mein Judentum sich sammeln zu lassen. Gegen Schluß ergriff mich aber schon die Unvollkommenheit der ersten Ansiedlungen im neu eroberten Kanaan und die treue Überlieferung der Unvollkommenheit der Volksmänner (Josuas, der Richter, Elis). (it was at first stranger to me than I thought, and I had to stop here and there in order by resting to allow my Jewishness to collect itself. Toward the end, however, I was already gripped by the imperfection of the first settlements in the newly conquered Canaan and the faithful handing down of the imperfections of the popular heroes— Joshua, the Judges, Elijah).[89]

"Popular heroes," in Kafka's view, are not to be celebrated as much as examined for their "imperfections." The act of such historical self-reflection he models in these reflections is exemplary for cultural criticism, and not without effect on his novels themselves. Ethnic tradition for Kafka thus meant historical self-criticism, not any jingoistic celebration of nationhood or conquest. Ethnic sources of ideological nationalism are not so much absent in *Das Schloß* as transformed into self-critical models of the struggle for individual and critical autonomy. Traces of Jewish and Czech sources make themselves felt, paradoxically, when overt gestures of resistance are at a narrative minimum; they emerge as crucially critical "imperfections" within a containing narrative point of view.

The conflagration that might liberate the villagers from political subjection is nonetheless present toward the conclusion of *Das Schloß*. Amalia's silence gives way to Pepi's anarchism, as Pepi encourages K. toward the goal of apocalyptic liberation. Fire threatens the "paper" forms practiced at the Herrenhof, promising to free Pepi and her fellow workers from the domination of the "Herren" (gentlemen, masters) they serve. A critical attitude toward ethnic liberation never held Kafka back from articulating the hope that subject peoples might be free. Pepi's plea to K. speaks beyond Amalia's silence, to the commitment to political struggle Kafka shared: ". . . und wer die Kraft hätte, den ganzen Herrenhof anzuzünden und zu verbrennen, aber vollständig, daß keine Spur zurückbleibt, verbrennen wie ein Papier im Ofen, der wäre heute Pepis Auserwählter" (Whoever had the strength to torch the whole Herrenhof, to burn it down, so that no trace remained, to burn like paper in a stove, he would today be Pepi's redeemer) (455).

No political or ethnic redeemer arrives in Kafka's novel. Yet its silence about ethnicity and politics is not necessarily pessimistic. "Sie mißdeuten alles," K. is told early in the novel, "auch das Schweigen" (you misunderstand everything—silence too). If the critic cannot be silent in attempting to define the ethnic and nationalist dilemmas behind Kafka's fiction, it is because, paradoxically, Kafka's novel resonates so fully with contemporary dilemmas of assimilation and ethnicity. The difficulty of defining Amalia and Pepi, or the meaning of their resistance, itself defines the dilemma of articulating ethnic identity in a suppressive bureaucratic world. For silence was not without meaning in the Jewish tradition Kafka studied. According to a Talmudic legend, the ministering angels sing praises at night, but remain silent during the day, so that prayers for justice uttered by an exiled people might be heard. If we listen carefully to the silence of Kafka's novel on ethnic questions, no such definitive silence emerges. But in Pepi's desire for freedom, Olga's outrage at injustice, and the sound of the trumpets at the *Fest*, the ground of a reading without Kafka's Jewish tradition begins to shift. While these are not the sounds of social upheaval, Kafka's modernism suggests that suppressed ethnicity, like the reticence of the oppressed, is never mute in mass society, but replete with the energy that brings social change. For as another Talmudic saying puts it, the world returns to primordial silence for seven days only as a prelude to its creation anew.

Coda: The Fire and the Book

Kafka's parable on revolution cautions against any fervor for sudden revolution. Radical transformation is seen as continuous, rather than ruptural, and at work in moments of apparent inaction: "der entscheidende Augenblick der menschlichen Entwicklung ist immerwährend. Darum sind die revolutionären geistigen Bewegungen, welche alles Frühere für nichtig erklären, im Recht, denn es ist noch nichts geschehen" (The decisive moment in human development is a continuous one. For this reason, revolutionary intellectual movements which declare everything before them to be null and void are in the right, for nothing has yet happened).[90] Radical social change, Kafka suggests, is a continuous process. Reading, as the act is represented in his novel, may serve the purposes of domination in modern bureaucracy, but may also find sources for political action, by locating the oppositional force of cultural tradition within the suppressive power of social ritual and its signs.

The ending of *Das Schloß* argues that reading itself opens forms of political practice. Unlike the villagers, who close Amalia's silence down into subjection, Kafka concludes his novel in an open fashion, challenging the reader to imagine new forms of political action and speech. Max Brod, who edited the first version of Kafka's novel, ends it at chapter 20, as it appears in the usual English edition. But he also indicated that "the manuscript of the novel continues with a few lines . . . that break off in the middle of a manuscript page."[91] These lines were not included in the first or second editions. The new critical edition rightfully restores them to a concluding place, as the narrator brings the novel's protagonist to a darkened room, lit only by a fire, where Gerstäcker's mother reads "in einem Buche" (in a book).[92] This act of reading takes place within the novel's system of containment, in which political power thrives on producing openings that foster control. Yet the novel ends in the middle of an unfinished sentence, with K. gazing at an open book whose meaning remains undetermined. Modeled in the scene is a freedom that only the novel's reader can foreclose.[93]

This is the postmodern challenge of Kafka's novel: its insistent link between textuality and effective political action. In a world increasingly controlled by bureaucratic codes, *Das Schloß* finally insists that language, while controlling experience in modernity, is also the boundary zone where commitment to social change begins. The final entry in Kafka's diary therefore stresses the openness inherent in textual limits. Reflection on language, he concedes, can lead to self-containment, rather than commitment. Kafka recognized writing as an abyssal form of self-reflection that could cancel the will to act: "Immer ängstlicher im Niederschreiben. Es ist begreiflich. Jedes Wort, gewendet in der Hand der Geister—dieser Schwung der Hand ist ihre charakteristische Bewegung—wird zum Spieß, gekehrt gegen den Sprecher. Eine Bemerkung wie diese ganz besonders" (More and more fearful as I write. It is understandable. Every word, twisted in the hands of the spirits—this twist of the hand is their characteristic gesture—becomes a spear turned against the speaker. Most especially a remark like this).[94] But the self-cancellation of the subject in language—"Und was Du willst, hilft nur unmerklich wenig" (And what you want is of infinitesimally little help)—was for Kafka impossible to see without also seeing its political content, the potential for literature to grasp the language of subjugation and turn it into the instrument of action and cultural critique. As a reminder of the potentially empowering social force of language, the final words of Kafka's diary provide the fitting ending to Kafka's narrative work. "More than consolation is," Kafka's diary concludes: "you too have weapons."

Afterword

I have argued throughout this book that mass culture is a crucial element in the cultural criticism that Dickens, Melville, and Kafka produced. Each chapter has traced the mass-cultural engagements of one of these novelists, arguing that the conformist pressures of commodity culture were opposed by a critical use of popular culture in their works. Cold war cultural theory, as I argued in Chapter 1, concerned itself with a liberal-modernist novel of subversion or a mass-cultural narrative of containment, and thus offered a limited view of such mass-cultural criticism in the social novel. The Frankfurt School's emphasis on both cultural domination and critical reflection illuminates the contradictory mode of the redemptive cultural criticism these authors pursued.

Dickens, to be sure, helped to transform the novel into a mass-market commodity, yet his style embodies the conflicting forms of speech that writing for a mass audience could produce.[1] Melville's angry response to popular fiction in America relates him to Dickens's most self-conscious novels, but also created innovative forms of cultural criticism that both capitulated to the conformist pressure of an expansionist society and challenged its narrative tastes. With Kafka, it becomes clear that the modernist tradition can neither be defined by aesthetic skepticism nor separated from mass culture, whose popular sources lend his most abstract fiction a resistant ethnic and political force. These writers demonstrate that a self-conscious criticism of mass culture should be considered an important element of narrative modernism: far from contained, the works I have studied in this book define an important chapter in the oppositional cultural history of the novel.

With the end of the cold war, however, the limitations of New Historicism's "containment" emphasis seem less significant than before. Anxieties over mass culture have diminished, and the New Historicist concern with the devices of "subversion" and "containment" has helped found the broader view of popular culture taken by cultural studies. No longer the "repressed" of modernism, as Andreas Huyssen has described it, mass culture can no longer be ignored as a formative influence of modern culture.[2] It is not enough, however, to include mass culture as a subject for serious analysis. Modern media society has strengthened the dominating power of mass culture, making any celebration of postmodern pluralism a premature hope at best.[3] The social containment identified by New Historicist critics remains a fact of contemporary culture, though the cold war cultural pressures that produced the critical model have passed.

Cold war cultural politics, moreover, continue to shape positions in contemporary cultural criticism. In response to the post-Vietnam resurgence of the cultural right, John Carlos Rowe has recently argued the need for a new "liberal consensus," as if the danger of "containment" had finally disappeared.[4] In an effort to counter conservative opposition to an increasingly political and engaged literary scholarship, Rowe maintains that critics must forge an alliance between postmodern developments in literary theory and the larger liberal community. Richard Rorty advocates a similar vision of cultural criticism, in which modern narrative plays an educational role in constructing a progressively liberal culture for democratic society.[5] To borrow Linda Hutcheon's apt phrase, the same exponents of theory who could once be defined by their commitment to "interrogating the notion of consensus," now seek to ground cultural criticism, like Trilling, in the liberal center once more.[6]

This hope for a new liberal consensus, however, runs the risk of producing, in the name of irony, only homogenized inclusion at best.[7] Attempts to found a renewed liberalism in the irony of the modern novel lack perspective on the culture industry and the commodification of resistance which, since Melville's time, has become a permanent feature of modern political culture. For the "weapons" of criticism, to borrow the conclusion of Kafka's diary, can only be diluted by a cultural criticism that emphasizes the kind of fictional self-creation that Rorty's liberal vision suggests. The ideal of "consensus" always runs the risk of becoming a false consensus, in which the emergent voices of oppositional culture lose their culturally critical force. What Benjamin called the "homogenous, empty time" figured by mass culture is always capable of emptying progressive political gestures of their challenging power, thus affirming the social status quo.[8]

For it is not the cultural center but cultural difference that fans the sparks of political and cultural redemption, and it is attention to such

differences that directs the most progressive social impulses present
in these novelists' work. Even Dickens, whose novels' totalizing pic-
tures of society were shaped by the Victorian marketplace and its
demands, wrote for readers whose interests were split by gender and
class. Liberal inclusivity was challenged by the differences in that
audience, and their contestation made his fiction, for all its popularity,
both self-critical and complex. Not consensus, but participation in the
most oppressive and homogenizing aspects of Victorian culture, gives
Dickens' most critical insights their force. Social progress, Dickens
suggests, is better attained through a rigorous criticism of social control than by rhetorically touting the social inclusion that fiction effects.

Kafka's austerity in referring explicitly to Jewish culture, for instance, must also be noted as a narrative register of assimilationist
pressure. Late stories such as *Josephine* represent the power of minority culture as a sounding silence: Josephine sings, and her voice
cannot be heard, just as commodification of minority culture often
cancels its oppositional force.[9] Students can learn about cultural difference from reading such a narrative, but only by first recognizing
the domination that mass culture effects through the act of inclusion
itself. It is not modernist complexity that gives Josephine's singing
the still moving power that Kafka's story represents: its silent sound
stands for the self-cancellation of ethnicity in modern society that she
conforms with, but also struggles to break.

No model of "consensus" speaks to the self-division of ethnic subjects, struggling for identity against assimilation, and who, like Kafka,
have created works that were far from silent in their critical power.
Such a cancellation of ethnicity, however, is still promoted by Arthur
Schlesinger, a representative of the old liberal consensus.[10] Many
taboos of cold war liberalism are still intact, and these novelists, I
hope, provide sources for a cultural criticism that looks beyond the
nostalgic wish of cultural conservatives to return to the suppressions
of the past. For there is no position "beyond" mass-cultural containment, nor any "consensus" on cultural diversity in these authors that
frees their work from repressive power. Domination cannot be romanticized or wished away: no hope for an inclusive liberalism is possible
without a complete working-through of mass cultural containment
and a recovery of the cultural voices it suppressed.[11]

Beyond "containment," however, is the critical task of analyzing the
oppositional cultures that liberal modernism contained. In the task
of recovering the critical dimension of an increasingly commodified
culture, neither liberal-modernist nostalgia for a novel immune to the

sway of mass culture, nor theories of totalizing cultural domination will suffice. Attention to the dominating power of signs, to be sure, is a crucial element in this critical project. Important new perspectives on mass culture, such as Baudrillard's simulacrum, or new readings of technological culture, will surely influence readings of Melville's technologism in *Moby-Dick*, or Dickens' salable Victorian icons, and produce different readings of their texts.[12] Yet it is the redemptive dimension of Adorno and Benjamin, I believe, that best fits the needs of cultural criticism at the present time. What is contained in the increasingly commodified objects of modern culture, Benjamin argued, could be redeemed and recovered as part of the historical suppressed. Feminist recoveries of women's histories from nineteenth-century fiction can be aided, not opposed, by a reading of narrative's mass-cultural reductions of the feminine voice. "Nothing that has ever happened," as Benjamin put it, "should be regarded as lost for history."[13]

This messianic task of Benjamin's, of course, was unfulfillable. "Only a redeemed mankind receives the fullness of its past," he wrote, "—which is to say, only for a redeemed mankind has the past become citable in all its moments."[14] Yet the cultural criticism of mass society in Dickens, Melville, and Kafka partakes of that spirit of messianic hope. With perspectives that were different but equally distanced from false populism, each writer confronted mass culture and its domination, while recovering its oppositional dimensions, thus preserving the hope of a transformed social world. In the postcontainment era, both confrontation and recovery remain necessary. Cultural criticism should address the novel and its cultures with a similarly messianic commitment to recovering those historical voices that have been moved to the margins of the historical mind.

Traditional narrative offers models for such an ethnically engaged contemporary criticism. In the paradoxes of change that arise from basing cultural criticism in memory, moreover, one finds the hope of utopian thought that critical theory implies. "We know that the Jews were prohibited from investigating the future," Benjamin wrote in his final "Thesis on the Philosophy of History": "the Torah and the prayers instruct them in remembrance, however."[15] This linkage between the emergent and the traditional is part of the heritage of dialectical thought, which Theodor Adorno defined as "the attempt to see the new in the old."[16] Preserved in such narratives are the grounds for a cultural criticism committed to reading cultural memory, and the catastrophic continuity it represents, for the redemptive signs of social change.

Notes
Index

Notes

Introduction

1. Debates between American liberals during the cold war over mass culture were formative, I believe, of both the contribution and limits of the New Historicist position on mass culture. Catherine Gallagher also provides a longer inheritance for New Historicism in "Marxism and New Historicism," in H. Aram Veeser, ed., *The New Historicism* (New York and London: Routledge, 1989), 37–48, but, like most critics, concentrates on "American radicalism of the sixties and seventies" (38). Carolyn Porter's lengthy critique of largely Renaissance New Historicism does not address the cold war modernism that made "history," for American criticism, a containing and compelling term. The same could be said of Brook Thomas' book-length work which, while discussing the relevance of the American Progressives, centers its discussion on poststructuralism rather than on the cold war cultural situation in which New Historicism arose. See Carolyn Porter, "Are We Being Historical Yet," in David Carroll, ed., *The States of "Theory:" History, Art and Critical Discourse* (New York: Columbia University Press, 1990), and Brook Thomas, *The New Historicism and Other Old-Fashioned Topics* (Princeton: Princeton University Press, 1990).

2. I have in mind here the similar separation from mass culture accorded modernist fiction in works as disparate in outlook as Georg Lukács's *The Meaning of Contemporary Realism*, trans. John Mander and Necke Mander (London: Merlin Press, 1963), Edmund Wilson's *Axel's Castle: A Study in the Imaginative Literature of 1870–1930* (New York: C. Scribner's Sons, 1931), and more recent accounts such as Robert Alter's *Partial Magic: The Novel as Self-Conscious Genre* (Berkeley and Los Angeles: University of California Press, 1975).

3. Theodor W. Adorno, "Television and the Patterns of Mass Culture," in Bernard Rosenberg and David Manning White, eds., *Mass Culture: The Popular Arts in America* (Glencoe, IL: Free Press, 1957), 474–88. The often false interpretation of Adorno as a cultural "mandarin" has been given trenchant critique by Martin Jay: "the very same criticisms [Adorno] leveled against mass culture were often directed as well against elite culture, which he refused to fetishize as inherently superior." See Martin Jay, "Culture as Manipulation, Culture as Redemption," in his *Adorno* (Cambridge: Harvard University Press, 1984), esp. 119ff.

4. The most balanced account of Adorno's significance for contemporary

approaches to mass culture is Andreas Huyssen, "The Vanishing Other: Mass Culture," and "Adorno in Reverse: From Hollywood to Richard Wagner," in *After the Great Divide: Modernism, Mass Culture, Postmodernism* (Bloomington and Indianapolis: University of Indiana Press, 1986), 3–65. For an account of Benjamin's formative influence on Adorno, see Susan Buck-Morss, *The Origins of Negative Dialectics: Theodor Adorno, Walter Benjamin, and the Frankfurt Institute* (New York: Macmillan, 1977).

5. I borrow this phrase from the title of Richard Wolin's excellent *Walter Benjamin: An Aesthetic of Redemption* (New York: Columbia University Press, 1982).

6. Franz Kafka, Aphorism 17, in *The Great Wall of China: Stories and Reflections*, trans. Willa Muir and Edna Muir (New York: Schocken Books, 1946), 165.

7. See Regina Gagnier, *Subjectivities: A History of Self-Representation in Britain, 1832–1920* (New York: Oxford University Press, 1991), and Janice A. Radway, *Reading the Romance: Women, Patriarchy, and Popular literature* (Chapel Hill: University of North Carolina Press, 1984), and the explicitly anticontainment populism of Andrew Ross articulated in his *No Respect: Intellectuals and Popular Culture* (London, Routledge, 1989), 47–49ff.

8. See David Reynolds, *Beneath the American Renaissance: The Subversive Imagination in the Age of Emerson and Melville* (New York: Alfred A. Knopf, 1988).

9. The canonical definition of the historical/textual criticism divide is Frank Lentricchia, *After the New Criticism* (Chicago: University of Chicago Press, 1980), 12.

10. The divide between historical and textual criticism was discussed in a different form by Adorno and Benjamin in their treatment of commodity culture in the 1930s, particularly in relation to the latter's Arcades Project. For the relevant correspondence in English, see *Aesthetics and Politics: Ernst Bloch, Georg Lukács, Bertolt Brecht, Walter Benjamin, Theodor Adorno* (London: NLB, 1977), 100–142. I discuss the historical/textual divide in relation to my own practice and to contemporary criticism at different points in this book.

11. See Theodor Adorno, "Cultural Criticism and Society," in *Prisms*, trans. Samuel Weber and Shierry Weber (Cambridge: MIT Press, 1981), 21ff.

12. Dialectical cultural criticism, as he puts it, does not "stop at a general recognition of the servitude of the objective mind, but seeks rather to transform this knowledge into a heightened perception of the thing itself." Theodor Adorno, "Cultural Criticism and Society," in *Prisms* 32.

13. Max Horkheimer and Theodor W. Adorno, Preface to the New Edition, *The Dialectic of Enlightenment*, trans. John Cumming (New York: Continuum, 1986), x.

Chapter 1. Cold War Cultural Theory:
Modernism, Socialism, and Subversion

1. See Frank Lentricchia, *After the New Criticism* (Chicago: University of Chicago Press, 1980) 12.

2. Adorno's legendary pessimism also played a role in obscuring the redemptive dimension of his thought. On the pluralist reception of Adorno, see
Martin Jay, "Adorno in America," in his *Permanent Exiles: Essays on the Intellectual Migration from Germany to America* (New York: Columbia University Press,
1985) 121ff.

3. Adorno disclaimed the work, first published in 1947, as the Hollywood
blacklist and its effects took hold. See Miriam Hansen, "Introduction to
Adorno's 'Transparencies on Film,'" *New German Critique* 24–25 (Fall/Winter
1981–82): 186–98, 188.

4. Frank Lentricchia notes this isolation of both Adorno and Benjamin from
questions that have shaped current American criticism in *After the New Criticism* xii–xiii.

5. See Lionel Trilling, "Hemingway and His Critics," in Diana Trilling, ed.,
Speaking of Literature and Society, The Works of Lionel Trilling, Uniform Edition
(New York and London: Harcourt Brace Jovanovich, 1980), 134: "the relation
of an artist to his culture, whether that culture be national or the culture of
a relatively small and recusant group, is a complex and contradictory relation . . . in removing from art a burden of messianic responsibility which
it never has discharged and cannot discharge we may leave it free to do
whatever it actually can do."

6. According to John Lewis Gaddis, Kennan's article of 1947, "The Sources
of Soviet Conduct," which I will discuss below, "introduced the term 'containment' to the world." See John Lewis Gaddis, "George F. Kennan and the
Strategy of Containment," in his *Strategies of Containment: Critical Appraisal of
Postwar American National Security Policy* (New York: Oxford University Press,
1982), 25–26.

7. Frank Lentricchia, *Criticism and Social Change* (Chicago: University of Chicago Press, 1983).

8. See Lionel Trilling, "Freud: Within and Beyond Culture," in *Beyond Cul-
ture, The Works of Lionel Trilling, Uniform Edition* (Oxford: Oxford University
Press, 1980), 102. The linkage between Dickens and Kafka as oppositional
modernists is made in Trilling's "The Dickens of Our Day," in *A Gathering of
Fugitives* (Boston: Beacon Press, 1956). A useful summary of the influence of
Trilling's formulation on readings of Dickens as well as of Kafka can be found
in George Ford's *Dickens and His Readers: Aspects of Novel-Criticism since 1836*
(New York: Gordian Press, 1955).

9. J. Hillis Miller, *Charles Dickens: The World of His Novels* (Cambridge: Harvard University Press, 1958), 233–34.

10. James's major work, *The Black Jacobins: Toussaint L'Ouverture and the San
Domingo Revolution* (1938), is still the standard account of its subject. For a
selection of his essays, see "Essays and Lectures by C. L. R. James: A Tribute,"
special issue of *CQ: Caribbean Quarterly* 35, no. 4 (December 1989).

11. Franklin's essay appeared in an important New Left collection, along
with a contribution by Jameson, entitled *Weapons of Criticism*, ed. Norman
Rudich (Palo Alto, CA: Ramparts Press, 1967). See H. Bruce Franklin, "The

Worker as Criminal and Artist: Herman Melville," in H. Bruce Franklin, *The Victim as Criminal and Artist: Literature from the American Prison* (New York: Oxford University Press, 1978), 31–72.

12. For a short account of his career, see "The Politics of Literary Criticism," in Alan M. Wald, *The New York Intellectuals: The Rise and Decline of the Anti-Stalinist Left from the 1930s to the 1980s* (Chapel Hill: University of North Carolina Press, 1987), 223–25.

13. For the sources of that revival and its debt to the American Progressives, see Hershel Parker, ed., *The Recognition of Herman Melville: Selected Criticism since 1846* (Ann Arbor: University of Michigan Press, 1967).

14. Lionel Trilling, Preface to *The Liberal Imagination: Essays on Literature and Society* (New York: Doubleday Anchor Books, 1950), xii.

15. Lionel Trilling, "On the Teaching of Modern Literature," in *Beyond Culture* 22.

16. See Daniel Bell, *The End of Ideology: On the Exhaustion of Political Ideas in the Fifties* (Glencoe, IL: Free Press, 1960).

17. See Richard Hofstadter, "Conflict and Consensus in American History," in his *The Progressive Historians: Turner, Beard, Parrington* (New York: Alfred A. Knopf, 1969), 437–66.

18. Lionel Trilling, "Reality in America," in *Liberal Imagination* 20.

19. For an account of the Popular Front and its role in shaping American liberal culture, see Frank A. Warren III, "Liberalism Reconsidered, 1930–1935" and "Behind the Popular Front," in *Liberals and Communism: The Red Decade Revisited* (Bloomington: Indiana University Press, 1966), 6–33, 103–26.

20. Van Wyck Brooks, "Primary Literature and Coterie Literature," in Jack Salzman, ed., *The Survival Years: A Collection of American Writings of the 1940s* (New York: Pegasus, 1969), 185–203, here 188.

21. Lionel Trilling, *Partisan Review* 9 (Jan.–Feb. 1942): 46.

22. Trilling, "On the Teaching of Modern Literature" 19.

23. See Alan M. Wald, "Introduction: Political Amnesia," in *New York Intellectuals* 3–24, here 8. See also Lary May, ed., *Recasting America: Culture and Politics in the Age of Cold War* (Chicago: University of Chicago Press, 1989), 2–4ff.

24. George F. Kennan, "The Sources of Soviet Conduct," *Foreign Affairs* 25 (July 1947): 566–82.

25. David Horowitz, ed., *Containment and Revolution*, with a Preface by Bertrand Russell (Boston: Beacon Press, 1967), 9. The late cold war brought the covert exercise of state power into public discussion in the Iran/Contra Affair. See Alex Whiting, *Covert Operations and the Democratic Process: The Implications of the Iran/Contra Affair* (Washington, D.C.: Center for National Security Studies, 1987).

26. For an account of contemporary uses of subversion in American politics, see Kenneth O'Reilly, "The FBI, HUAC, and Cold War Liberalism," in *Hoover and the Un-Americans: The FBI, HUAC, and the Red Menace* (Philadelphia: Temple University Press, 1983), 168–93.

27. Geraldine Murphy, "Romancing the Center: Cold War Politics and Classic American Literature," *Poetics Today* 9, no. 4 (1988): 737–47, here 745.

28. See *America and the Intellectuals: A Symposium, Partisan Review*, ser. no. 4 (New York: Partisan Review, 1953).

29. Mailer's response to "Our Country and Our Culture," with additional comments, was reprinted in his *Advertisements for Myself* (New York: New American Library, 1959), 169–72.

30. Terry A. Cooney, *The Rise of the New York Intellectuals: Partisan Review and Its Circle, 1934–1945* (Madison: University of Wisconsin Press, 1986), 206.

31. See Van Wyck Brooks, *The Times of Melville and Whitman* (New York: E. P. Dutton, 1947), 173, 278.

32. Philip Rahv, "Notes on the Decline of Naturalism," in John W. Aldridge, ed., *Critiques and Essays on Modern Fiction, 1920–1951* (New York: Ronald Press, 1952), 416–17.

33. Lionel Trilling, "Art and Fortune," in *Critiques and Essays on Modern Fiction* 530–31.

34. Geraldine Murphy discusses the roles of Chase and Trilling in the formation of "centrist, anti-Communist liberalism" in "The Politics of Reading *Billy Budd*," *American Literary History* 1, no. 2 (Summer 1989): 361–62ff.

35. See Mary Sperling McAuliffe, "A New Liberalism," in *Crisis on the Left: Cold War Politics and American Liberals, 1947–1954* (Amherst: University of Massachusetts Press, 1978), 63.

36. Lionel Trilling, "Reality in America" 7–8.

37. Lionel Trilling, "The Dickens of Our Day," in *A Gathering of Fugitives* 41, and "On the Teaching of Modern Literature" 7.

38. Irving Howe, "The Culture of Modernism," in *The Decline of the New* (New York: Harcourt, Brace, and World, 1963), 16.

39. See Alan Liu, "Local Transcendence: Cultural Criticism, Postmodernism, and the Romanticism of Detail," *Representations* 32 (Fall 1990): 98, and Stephen Greenblatt, "Invisible Bullets: Renaissance Authority and Its Subversion," *Glyph* 8 (1981): 40–61, here 57.

40. Stephen Greenblatt, "The Improvisation of Power," in *Renaissance Self-Fashioning: From More to Shakespeare* (Chicago: University of Chicago Press, 1980), 253–54.

41. Theodor Adorno and Max Horkheimer, "The Culture Industry," in *The Dialectic of Enlightenment*, trans. John Cumming (New York: Continuum, 1986), 151.

42. Jonathan Arac, Introduction, in Arac, ed., *Postmodernism and Politics*, Theory and History of Literature, Vol. 28 (Minneapolis: University of Minnesota Press, 1986), xxxiv.

43. Gerald Graff, "American Criticism Left and Right," in Sacvan Bercovitch and Myra Jehlen, eds., *Ideology and Classic American Literature* (Cambridge: Cambridge University Press, 1986), 95.

44. Greenblatt, *Renaissance Self-Fashioning* 253.

45. F. R. Leavis, "Mass Civilization and Minority Culture," in Leavis, *For Continuity* (Cambridge: Minority Press, 1933), 38.

46. See Christopher Lasch, "The Cultural Cold War: A Short History of the Congress for Cultural Freedom," in his *The Agony of the American Left* (New York: Alfred A. Knopf, 1969), 61–114.

47. Jonathan Dollimore and Alan Sinfield, eds., *Political Shakespeare: New Essays in Cultural Materialism* (Ithaca: Cornell University Press, 1985), 10–15.

48. See Raymond Williams, "Beyond Liberalism," rev. of *Beyond Culture, Manchester Guardian*, April 15, 1966. For a discussion, see Mark Krupnick, *Lionel Trilling and the Fate of Cultural Criticism* (Evanston, IL: Northwestern University Press, 1986), 137.

49. See "Structuralism and Poststructuralism: An Interview with Michel Foucault," *Telos* 55 (Spring 1983): 200.

50. Lentricchia, Afterword to *After the New Criticism* 350–51.

51. See Michael Rogin, "Billy Budd: In the Penal Colony," in *Subversive Genealogy: The Politics and Art of Herman Melville* (New York: Alfred Knopf, 1983), xiff.

52. See D. A. Miller, "Discipline in Different Voices: Bureaucracy, Police, Family, and *Bleak House*," in *The Novel and the Police* (Berkeley: University of California Press, 1988), 58–106 and x–xii.

53. Trilling, "Reality in America" 9.

54. Mark Selzer, *Henry James and the Art of Power* (Ithaca: Cornell University Press, 1984).

55. See Catherine Gallagher, *The Industrial Reformation of English Fiction: Social Discourse and Narrative Form, 1832–1867* (Chicago: University of Chicago Press, 1985).

56. See, for instance, Richard Hofstadter, "Pseudo-Conservative Revolt, Pseudo-Conservatism Revisited," and Seymour Martin Lipset, "The Sources of the Radical Right," in Daniel Bell, ed., *The Radical Right* (Garden City, NY: Doubleday, 1962).

57. See Michael Rogin, *The Intellectuals and McCarthy: The Radical Specter* (Cambridge: MIT Press, 1967).

58. See Michael Rogin, *Ronald Reagan, "The Movie"* (Berkeley: University of California Press, 1987), xii–xiii.

59. See Jane Tompkins, "The Other American Renaissance," in Walter Benn Michaels and Donald Pease, eds., *The American Renaissance Reconsidered: Selected Papers from the English Institute, 1982–83* (Baltimore: Johns Hopkins University Press, 1985), 34–57.

60. Fredric Jameson, *The Political Unconscious: Narrative as a Socially Symbolic Act* (Ithaca: Cornell University Press, 1981), 52–53.

61. See Fredric Jameson, *Marxism and Form: Twentieth-Century Dialectical Theories of Literature* (Princeton: Princeton University Press, 1971, and "Modernism and Its Repressed; or, Robbe-Grillet as Anti-Colonialist," in Jameson, *The Ideologies of Theory: Essays 1971–1986*, Vol. 1: *Situations of Theory*, Theory

and History of Literature, Vol. 48 (Minneapolis: University of Minnesota Press, 1988), 167–80.

62. For Jameson's critique of the "ideology" implicit in Walter Michael's New Historicist work, see his "Immanence and the New Historicism," in *Postmodernism, or, The Cultural Logic of Late Capitalism* (Durham, NC: Duke University Press, 1991), 181–217.

63. Sacvan Bercovitch, "The Ideological Context of the American Renaissance," in Winfred Fluck, Jürgen Pepper, and Willi Paul Adams, eds., *Forms and Functions of History in American Literature: Essays in Honor of Ursula Brumm* (Berlin, 1981), 1.

64. See Sacvan Bercovitch, "Hawthorne's A-Morality of Compromise," *Representations*, no. 24 (Fall 1988): 11, 18ff., and his "Emerson, Individualism, and American Dissent," manuscript.

65. Jonathan Arac, "The Politics of the *Scarlet Letter*," in *Ideology and Classic American Literature* 249 and 257.

66. See "Traditions of Democracy," in Arthur M. Schlesinger, *The Age of Jackson* (Boston: Little and Brown, 1945), 505.

67. Arac, "Politics of the *Scarlet Letter*" 455.

68. Irving Howe, *Politics and the Novel* (New York: Horizon Press, 1957), 19.

69. See Nancy Armstrong, "The Rise of Female Authority in the Novel," in *Desire and Domestic Fiction: A Political History of the Novel* (New York and Oxford: Oxford University Press, 1987), 30 and 3–58.

70. Judith Lowder Newton, noting this tension, has pointed out the complexities that have accompanied the recovery of a suppressed feminine literature and history. See Judith Lowder Newton, "History as Usual? Feminism and the New Historicism," in H. Aram Veeser, ed., *The New Historicism* (New York and London: Routledge, 1989), 152–67.

71. New Historicist method, as Dominic LaCapra has pointed out, worked through an anecdotal method of juxtaposition and produced a concept of power, as well as cultural opposition, that was inspecific. See Dominic LaCapra, "Intellectual History and Critical Theory," in *Soundings in Critical Theory* (Ithaca: Cornell University Press, 1989), 190.

72. See "Visionary Compacts and the Cold War Consensus," in Donald Pease, *Visionary Compacts: American Renaissance Writings in Cultural Context* (Madison: University of Wisconsin Press, 1987), 3–48, here 12.

73. Lentricchia, *After the New Criticism* 350.

74. Theodor Adorno, "On Dickens' *The Old Curiosity Shop*: A Lecture," in *Notes to Literature*, ed. Rolf Tiedemann, trans. Shierry Weber Nicholsen (New York: Columbia University Press, 1992), 2:171.

75. Theodor W. Adorno, *Negative Dialectics*, trans. E.B. Ashton (New York: Continuum, 1983), 298: "Neuroses are pillars of society; they thwart the better potential of men, and thus the objectively better condition which men might bring about."

76. See Theodor Adorno, "Subject and Object," in *The Essential Frankfurt*

School Reader, ed. Andrew Arato & Eike Gebhardt (New York: Continuum, 1982), 499.

77. Adorno, *Negative Dialectics* 221.

78. Adorno, "Extorted Reconciliation: On Georg Lukács' *Realism in Our Time*," in *Notes to Literature* 1:225.

79. Ibid.: "The great avant-garde works of art cut through this illusion of subjectivity both by throwing the frailty of the individual into relief and by grasping the totality in the individual, who is a moment in the totality and yet can know nothing about it."

80. See Peter Uwe Hohendahl, "A Return to History? New Historicism and Its Agenda," *New German Critique*, no. 55 (Winter 1992): 87–104, here 104.

81. Adorno, "On Dickens' *The Old Curiosity Shop*" 171–72.

82. Theodor Adorno, "Rede über den 'Räritatenladen' von Charles Dickens," in *Noten zur Literatur, Gesammelte Schriften*, Vol. 2 (Frankfurt, 1974), 515–22, here 522.

83. Walter Benjamin, "Theses on the Philosophy of History," Thesis IX, in *Illuminations*, ed. Hannah Arendt trans. Harry Zohn (New York: Schocken Books, 1969), 258.

84. Ibid. 256.

85. Ibid. 257.

86. Jürgen Habermas, "Consciousness-Raising or Rescuing Critique," in Gary Smith, ed., *On Walter Benjamin: Critical Essays and Recollections* (Cambridge: MIT Press, 1988), 98.

87. Susan Buck-Morss, *The Dialectics of Seeing: Walter Benjamin and the Arcades Project* (Cambridge: MIT Press, 1989), 55.

88. See Richard Wolin, "The Adorno-Benjamin Dispute," in *Walter Benjamin: An Aesthetic of Redemption* (New York: Columbia University Press, 1982), 205, and Theodor Adorno to Walter Benjamin, August 2, 1935, in *Aesthetics and Politics: Ernst Bloch*, Georg Lukács, Bertolt Brecht, Walter Benjamin, Theodor Adorno (London: NLB, 1977), 115–16. For an account of the debate from Adorno's point of view, see Susan Buck-Morss, *The Origins of Negative Dialectics: Theodor Adorno, Walter Benjamin, and the Frankfurt Institute* (New York: Macmillan, 1977), 27–32.

89. Theodor Adorno and Max Horkheimer, "Elements of Anti-Semitism," in *Dialectic of Enlightenment* 185, 187.

90. Walter Benjamin, "The Storyteller: Reflections on the Works of Nikolai Leskov," in *Illuminations* 89.

91. Walter Benjamin, "IMPERIAL PANORAMA: A Tour of German Inflation," *One-Way Street*, in Peter Demetz, ed., *Reflections: Essays, Aphorisms, Autobiographic Writings*, trans. Edmund Jephcott (New York and London: Harcourt Brace Jovanovich, 1978), 74–75.

92. See Stéphane Moses, "Walter Benjamin and Franz Rosenzweig," in Gary Smith, ed., *Benjamin: Philosophy, Aesthetics, Politics* (Chicago: University of Chicago Press, 1989), 228–46.

93. "Wenn Adorno von dem 'rein der Sache sich Überlassen' spricht, geht es ihm um die Rettung des Einzelwerks in seiner Besonderheit." See Peter Bürger, "Das Vermittlungsproblem in der Kunstsoziologie Adornos," in Burkhardt Lindner und W. Martin Lüdke, eds., *Materialien zur Ästhetischen Theorie: Theodor W. Adornos Konstruktion der Moderne* (Frankfurt, 1980), 171.

94. See Eugene Lunn, "Benjamin and Adorno: The Development of Their Thought," in his *Marxism and Modernism: An Historical Study of Lukács, Brecht, Benjamin, and Adorno* (Berkeley: University of California Press, 1982), 173–214, esp. 197–201. For an interpretation of Benjamin's messianism that splits it from his Marxist concerns, see Gershom Scholem, *Walter Benjamin: The Story of a Friendship,* trans. Harry Zohn (Philadelphia: Jewish Publication Society of America, 1981).

95. Theodor Adorno, *Aesthetic Theory,* trans. C. Lenhardt, ed. Gretel Adorno and Rolf Tiedemann (London and New York: Routledge & Kegan Paul, 1984), 26, and Theodor Adorno, "On the Fetish Character in Music and the Regression of Listening," in *The Essential Frankfurt School Reader* 270.

96. Jauss's objection, that Adorno's aesthetic had to "ignore the dialogic process between work, public and author," can be found in his "Negativität und ästhetische Erfahrung: Adorno's Ästhetische Theorie in der Retrospektive," in *Materialien zur Asthetischen Theorie* 147ff.

97. See Leo Lowenthal, "Historical Perspectives on Popular Culture," in Bernard Rosenberg and David Manning White, eds., *Mass Culture: The Popular Arts in America* (Glencoe, IL: Free Press, 1957).

98. Michael McKeon, *The Origins of the English Novel, 1600–1740* (Baltimore: Johns Hopkins University Press, 1987), 1–25 and 205–11.

99. Alexis de Tocqueville, *Democracy in America,* 2 vols., trans. Henry Reeve (New York: Alfred A. Knopf, 1945), 2:61.

100. Walter Benjamin, "Theses on the Philosophy of History" 256.

101. "Commodity fetishes," Adorno wrote, "are not merely the projection of opaque human relations onto the world of things. They are also the chimerical deities which originate in the primacy of the exchange process but nevertheless represent something not entirely absorbed in it." See Adorno, "Veblen's Attack on Culture," in *Prisms* 85.

102. Adorno, "Extorted Reconciliation: On Georg Lukács's Realism in Our Time" 225.

103. Ibid., 225.

104. See Adorno, *Aesthetic Theory* 332. Fetishization was linked to art by the historical division between mental and material labor in Adorno's view, and was not a trait to be attributed to modernism alone, as Lukács had suggested.

105. Ibid. 329.

106. Georg Lukács, "The Ideology of Modernism," in *Realism in Our Time,* trans. John Mander and Necke Mander (New York: Harper and Row, 1971), 35–36.

107. See Robert Alter, *Partial Magic: The Novel as Self-Conscious Genre* (Berke-

ley and Los Angeles: University of California Press, 1975), 127–37, 137; Robert Weisbuch, *Atlantic Double-Cross: American Literature and British Influence in the Age of Emerson* (Chicago: University of Chicago Press, 1986), 45–48; and Nina Baym, "Melville's Quarrel with Fiction," *PMLA* 94, no. 5 (Oct. 1979): 909–23.

108. Charles Feidelson, *Symbolism and American Literature* (Chicago: University of Chicago Press, 1953), 2.

109. Hans Mayer, "Walter Benjamin and Franz Kafka: Report on a Constellation," in *On Walter Benjamin* 185–209.

110. Adorno, "Extorted Reconciliation: On Georg Lukács's Realism in Our Time" 227–28.

111. These two examples will be discussed in detail in Chapters 2 and 3, respectively.

112. Theodor Adorno, "The Antinomy of Modern Music," in his *The Philosophy of Modern Music*, trans. Anne G. Mitchell and Wesley V. Blomster (New York: Continuum, 1973), 19–20.

113. Adorno, *Aesthetic Theory* 327.

114. Adorno and Horkheimer, *Dialectic of Enlightenment* 157.

115. Rainer Nägele, "The Scene of the Other: Theodor W. Adorno's Negative Dialectic in the Context of Poststructuralism," in *Postmodernism and Politics* 91–111.

116. Michel Foucault, "What Is an Author," in Donald F. Bouchard, ed., *Language, Counter-Memory, Practice: Selected Essays and Interviews by Michel Foucault*, trans. Donald F. Bouchard and Sherry Simon (Ithaca: Cornell University Press, 1977), 113–38, here 124.

117. "The resistance of thought to mere things in being, the commanding freedom of the subject, intends in the object even that of which the object was deprived by objectification." Adorno, *Negative Dialectics* 19.

118. Theodor Adorno, "Education for Autonomy," Interview, broadcast August 6, 1969, seven days after Adorno's death. Reprinted in Russell Berman, ed., "Adorno's Radicalism," *Telos*, no. 56 (Summer 1983): 103–10, here 107.

119. Walter Benjamin, "Theses on the Philosophy of History" 256.

120. Theodor Adorno, "Reading Balzac," in *Notes to Literature* 1:128.

121. Adorno to Benjamin, November 10, 1938, in *Aesthetics and Politics* 129.

122. Adorno, "Reading Balzac" 128–29.

123. Adorno to Benjamin, March 18, 1936, in *Aesthetics and Politics* 123.

Chapter 2. Dickens: The Radical Novel and Its Public

1. Charles Dickens, September 27, 1869, Speech to the Birmingham and Midland Institute Inaugural Meeting, in K. J. Fielding, ed., *The Speeches of Charles Dickens* (Oxford: Clarendon Press, 1960), 407.

2. Portions of the letter, as well as Dickens' subsequent response in his speech of January 6, 1870, at Birmingham, are reprinted in *Speeches of Charles Dickens* 407–12.

3. See Myron Magnet, *Dickens and the Social Order* (Philadelphia: University

of Pennsylvania Press, 1985), and David Musselwhite's argument for the coercion of the radical anarchism of Dickens' early work by commodity culture in "Dickens: The Commodification of the Novelist," in *Partings Welded Together: Politics and Desire in the Nineteenth-Century Novel* (London: Methuen, 1988), 143–226.

4. J. A. Sutherland, *Victorian Novelists and Publishers* (London: Athlone Press, 1976), 166.

5. John Butt and Kathleen Tillotson, "Dickens as a Serial Novelist," in their *Dickens at Work* (London: Methuen, 1957), 14–16.

6. Charles Dickens to James T. Fields, January 14, 1870, in Walter Dexter, ed., *The Letters of Charles Dickens,* (Bloomsbury: Nonesuch Press, 1938), 3:760. Hereafter cited as *Letters* (1938).

7. See D. A. Miller, *The Novel and the Police* (Berkeley: University of California Press, 1988), xi; Magnet, *Dickens and the Social Order* 12ff.; and Musselwhite, *Partings Welded Together* 178.

8. On the contemporary popularity of *Dombey and Son* in nineteenth-century middle-class households, see Amy Cruse, *The Victorians and Their Books* (Boston and New York: Houghton and Mifflin, 1936), 157–58.

9. Raymond Williams, *The Country and the City* (New York: Oxford University Press, 1973), 161.

10. Charles Dickens, *Dombey and Son,* ed. Alan Horsman (Oxford: Clarendon Press, 1974), 65.

11. Theodor Adorno, "Cultural Criticism and Society," *Prisms,* trans. Samuel Weber and Shierry Weber (Cambridge: MIT Press, 1981), 27.

12. See Christopher Hibbert, ed., *Queen Victoria in Her Letters and Journals: A Selection* (London: John Murray, 1984), 218.

13. Theodor Adorno, "The Economic Crisis as Idyll," *Notes to Literature,* ed. Rolf Tiedemann, trans. Shierry Weber Nicholsen (New York: Columbia University Press, 1991), 2:283.

14. Quotations in this section are from *Dombey and Son* 20, n. 1; this particular deletion is discussed by the editor on xvi–xvii as an unfortunate one. The passage is restored to the continuous text in the more commonly used Penguin edition of *Dombey and Son.,* ed. Peter Fairclough, with an Introduction by Raymond Williams (London and New York: Penguin Books, 1970), 70.

15. On the politics and economics of the body in the novel, see Jeff Nunokawa, "For Your Eyes Only: Private Property and the Oriental Body in *Dombey and Son,*" in Jonathan Arac and Harriet Ritvo, eds., *Macropolitics of Nineteenth-Century Literature: Nationalism, Exoticism, Imperialism* (Philadelphia: University of Pennsylvania Press, 1991), 138–58.

16. See John Stuart Mill, *Autobiography,* ed. Jack Stillinger (Boston: Houghton Mifflin, 1969), 174–76. For an account of Dickens' involvement in the Governor Eyre affair and the India mutiny, see Patrick Brantlinger, *Rule of Darkness: British Literature and Imperialism, 1830–1914* (Ithaca: Cornell University Press, 1988), 124–26ff.

17. See Charles Dickens, "A Bundle of Emigrants' Letters," *Household Words,*

March 30, 1850, reprinted in Harry Stone, ed., *Charles Dickens' Uncollected Writings from Household Words* (Bloomington: Indiana University Press, 1968), 1:85–96, and "The Noble Savage," in *The Commercial Traveler and Reprinted Pieces, Etc.*, ed. Leslie Staples (London: Oxford University Press, 1958), 467.

18. Dickens, December 2, 1855, to Bradbury and Evans, quoted in Charles Dickens, *Little Dorrit*, ed. Harvey Peter Sucksmith (Oxford: Clarendon Press, 1979), xxiii.

19. Ibid. 556–57. All further references to the text of *Little Dorrit* will cite page numbers from this edition parenthetically in the text. When another edition is used, page numbers will be given in a note.

20. Dickens to Forster, April 1856, *Letters* (1938), 2:765. Nationalist propaganda and its reception by the Victorian working classes of *Little Dorrit* is discussed in P. J. Keating, *The Working Classes in Victorian Fiction* (London: Routledge and Kegan Paul, 1971), 225–26.

21. Charles Dickens, *Great Expectations*, ed. Angus Calder (London: Penguin Books, 1965), 221.

22. Charles Dickens, "A Preliminary Word," in *Household Words*, March 30, 1950, quoted in *Charles Dickens' Uncollected Writings from Household Words* 13.

23. Charles Dickens, Preface to the First Edition, 1853, in *Bleak House*, ed. Norman Page (London: Penguin Books, 1971), 41.

24. George Henry Lewes, "Dickens in Relation to Criticism," in George H. Ford and Lauriat Lane, Jr., *The Dickens Critics* (Ithaca: Cornell University Press, 1961), 58. On the relation of the novel to mid-Victorian social debate, see John Butt and Kathleen Tillotson, "The Topicality of *Bleak House*," in *Dickens at Work* 177–200.

25. Dickens to Mrs. Watson, August 27, 1853, in *The Letters of Charles Dickens*, (London: Chapman and Hall, 1880), 1:309. Hereafter cited as *Letters* (1880).

26. Dickens to W. C. Macready, October 4, 1855, in *Letters*, (1938), 2:695.

27. The political events surrounding the novel's composition are usefully surveyed in John Butt, "The Topicality of *Little Dorrit*," *University of Toronto Quarterly* 29 (Oct.–July 1959–60): 4–5, 1–10. For a reading of Tennyson's poem in its social and historical context, see Jerome McGann, "Tennyson and the Histories of Criticism," in *The Beauty of Inflections: Literary Investigations in Historical Method and Theory* (Oxford: Oxford University Press, 1985), 190–201.

28. Dickens to Austen H. Layard, April 10, 1855, in *Letters* (1880), 1:391–93.

29. Dickens to Macready, Oct. 4, 1855, *Letters* (1938), 2:695.

30. Important contemporary reevaluations of Mayhew's work include Regina Gagnier, "Henry Mayhew's Rich World of Poverty," in her *Subjectivities: A History of Self-Representation in Britain, 1832–1920* (New York and Oxford, 1991), 62–92, and Catherine Gallagher, "The Body Versus the Body Social in the Works of Thomas Malthus and Henry Mayhew," in Catherine Gallagher and Thomas Laqueur, eds., *Sexuality and Society in the Nineteenth Century* (Berkeley: University of California Press, 1987), 83–106.

31. Raymond Williams, *The English Novel from Dickens to Lawrence* (London: Hogarth Press, 1984), 30–32.

32. Theodor Adorno, *Introduction to the Sociology of Music*, trans. E. B. Ashton (New York: Continuum, 1976), 208.

33. See Lionel Trilling, Introduction to Charles Dickens, *Little Dorrit*, (London: Oxford University Press, 1953), xiiiff.

34. Prisons in the novel, he argued, were "not accidental and exterior, but inner and permanent" states of mind. See J. Hillis Miller, *Charles Dickens: The World of His Novels* (Cambridge: Harvard University Press, 1958), 231.

35. See Janice Carlisle, *"Little Dorrit:* Necessary Fictions," *Studies in the Novel* 7 (Summer 1975): 201, 211ff. Victorian critical taste for realism, its didacticism, as well as their internal conflicts, can be explored in Richard Stang, *The Theory of the Novel in England, 1850–1870* (New York: Oxford University Press, 1959).

36. See Martha Vicinus, ed., *Suffer and Be Still: Women in the Victorian Age* (Bloomington: Indiana University Press, 1972), xiiff.

37. A brief account of Dickens' plans for religious instruction at Urania Cottage, and his later letters to Miss Coutts on class conflict, can be found in Edgar Johnson, *Charles Dickens: His Tragedy and Triumph,* (New York: Simon and Schuster, 1952), 2:593–94, 611, 621, and 840–41. For a fuller account of their collaboration, and its influence on the novel, see K. J. Fielding's two essays, "Dickens's Work with Miss Coutts I: 'Nova Scotia Gardens and What Grew There,'" and "Dickens's Work with Miss Coutts II: Casby and the Westminster Landlords," *Dickensian* 61 (Spring 1965): 112–19 and 155–60, and Charles Osborne, eds., *Letters of Charles Dickens to the Baroness Burdett-Coutts* (London: John Murray, 1931).

38. Shaw's remarks are reprinted in Alan Shelston, ed., *Dombey and Son and Little Dorrit: A Casebook* (London: Macmillan, 1985), 140–41.

39. Sadoff's reading follows the novel's reconstruction of the "paternal metaphor" in "Storytelling and the Figure of the Father in *Little Dorrit,*" *PMLA* 95, no. 2 (March 1980): 241.

40. *Lancet,* 1885. For a discussion of this passage and its implications, see Anthony S. Wohl, "Sex and the Single Room: Incest among the Victorians," in Wohl, ed., *The Victorian Family: Structure and Stresses* (New York: St. Martin's Press, 1978), 197–216.

41. Viktor Shklovskij, "The Mystery Novel: Dickens's *Little Dorrit,*" in Ladislav Matejka and Krystyna Pomorska, eds., *Readings in Russian Poetics* (Cambridge: MIT Press, 1971), 273–80.

42. See Avrom Fleischman, "Master and Servant in *Little Dorrit,*" *Studies in English Literature* 14 (Autumn 1974): 580ff.

43. On the social history of sexual violence in Victorian culture and the fictional conventions for its representation, see Regina Barreca, ed., *Sex and Death in Victorian Literature* (Bloomington: Indiana University Press, 1990); Ian Gibson, *The English Vice: Beating, Sex, and Shame in Victorian England and After* (London: Duckworth, 1978); Steven Marcus, *The Other Victorians: A Study of Sexuality and Pornography in Mid-Nineteenth-Century England* (New York: Basic Books, 1966); and Judith Walkowitz, *Prostitution in Victorian Society:*

Women, Class and the State (Cambridge and New York: Cambridge University Press, 1980).

44. Juliet Swindells, *Victorian Writing and Working Women: the Other Side of Silence* (Minneapolis: University of Minnesota Press, 1985), 84.

45. Unsigned Review, *Leader*, June 27, 1857, reprinted in Philip Collins, ed., *Dickens: The Critical Heritage* (London: Routledge and Kegan Paul, 1971), 363.

46. E. B. Hamley, "Remonstrance with Dickens," *Blackwood's Magazine*, April 1857, in *Dickens: The Critical Heritage* 360.

47. See James Fitzjames Stephens, "The License of Modern Novelists," *Edinburgh Review*, July 1857, and Dickens's response, "A Curious Misprint in the *Edinburgh Review*," *Household Words*, August 1, 1857, in *Dombey and Son and Little Dorrit: A Casebook* 119–23.

48. Trilling, Introduction to Charles Dickens, *Little Dorrit* xvi.

49. "The narrator of Little Dorrit," a group of critics writes, "exalts Amy for the very self-mortifying virtues that are the novel's chief examples of outrageous oppression." See Richard Barrickman, Susan MacDonald, Myra Stark, *Corrupt Relations: Dickens, Thackeray, Trollope, Collins and the Victorian Sexual System* (New York: Columbia University Press, 1983), 111ff.

50. Johnson, *Charles Dickens: His Tragedy and Triumph* 1:35.

51. "In the *flaneur*," Benjamin writes, "the intelligentsia pays a visit to the marketplace, ostensibly to look around, yet in reality finds a buyer." See Walter Benjamin, "Paris, Capital of the Nineteenth Century," in *Reflections: Essays, Aphorisms, Autobiographical Writings*, ed. Peter Demetz, trans. Edmund Jephcott (New York: Harcourt Brace Jovanovich, 1978), 156–58.

52. Benjamin, "Paris, Capital of the Nineteenth Century" 157.

53. Alexander Welsh, *The City of Dickens* (Oxford: Clarendon Press, 1971), 142.

54. Janice Carlisle, "*Little Dorrit*: Necessary Fictions" 195–96.

55. Barbara Hardy, "Dickens's Storytellers," *Dickensian* 69, no. 370, (May 1973): 77.

56. Garrett Stewart, *Death Sentences: Styles of Dying in British Fiction* (Cambridge: Harvard University Press, 1984), 70.

57. Flora's allusive history of her own marital relations and the cultural criticism of Victorian institutions it offers deserve further study. On the socially satiric content of her speeches, see Martin Price, "Dickens: Selves and Systems," in *Forms of Life: Character and Moral Imagination in the Novel* (New Haven: Yale University Press, 1983), 132ff. For an account of the resistant hostility of these scenes, see Alan Wilde, "Mr. F's Aunt and the Analogical Structure of *Little Dorrit*," *Nineteenth Century Fiction* 19 (1964): 33ff.

58. Swindells, *Victorian Writing and Working Women* 86.

59. See Eve Kosofsky Sedgwick, *Between Men: English Literature and Male Homosocial Desire* (New York: Columbia University Press, 1985).

60. On the confrontation with sexual stigma in Dickens and its social dimensions, see Rosemarie Bodenheimer, *The Politics of Story in Victorian Social Fiction* (Ithaca: Cornell University Press, 1988), 128–29.

61. See John Forster, The *Life of Charles Dickens*, chap. 1, book VII, quoted in *Dombey and Son and Little Dorrit: A Casebook* 125.

62. Benjamin, "Paris, Capital of the Nineteenth Century" 157.

63. On the prostitute in Benjamin, see Susan Buck-Morss, *The Dialectics of Seeing: Walter Benjamin and the Arcades Project* (Cambridge: MIT Press, 1989), 184–85.

64. Theodor Adorno and Max Horkheimer, *The Dialectic of Enlightenment* trans. John Cumming (New York: Continuum, 1986), 49: "sacrifice . . . appears as the magical pattern of rational exchange, a device of men by which the gods may be mastered: the gods are overthrown by the very system by which they are honored."

65. See *Little Dorrit*, ed. John Holloway (London: Penguin Books, 1967), 531. In the earlier Oxford Illustrated Dickens (1953), this title is given as "Mr. Dorrit is Habitually Hurt," dropping the question of Amy's agency.

66. The critical uses of theater in Dickens are explored in Joseph Litvak, *Caught in the Act : Theatricality in the Nineteenth-Century English Novel* (Berkeley: University of California Press, 1992).

67. Adorno and Horkheimer, *Dialectic of Enlightenment* 230.

68. See Suvendrini Perera, "All the Girls Say Serve Him Right: The Multiple Anxieties of *Edwin Drood*," in her *Reaches of Empire: the English Novel from Edgeworth to Dickens* (New York: Columbia University Press, 1991), 103–22.

69. See M. E. Chamberlain, *British Foreign Policy in the Age of Palmerston* (London: Longman, 1980), 42–44 and 75–77.

70. Charles Dickens, *Dickens' Working Notes for His Novels*, edited and with an introduction by Harry Stone (Chicago: University of Chicago Press, 1987), 311.

71. Anthony Trollope, *The Warden* (London: Elkin Mathews & Marrot, 1926), 187.

72. Advertisement for the Works of George Sand, translated by Mathilda M. Hays, from *Dombey and Son*, reprinted in Bernard Darwin, ed., *The Dickens Advertiser: A Collection of the Advertisements in the Original Parts of the Novels of Charles Dickens* (New York: Macmillan, 1930), 87.

73. On the class and cultural differences forged into the mass public for Victorian fiction, see Jon P. Klancher, "From Crowd to Mass Audience," in his *The Making of English Reading Audiences, 1790–1832* (Madison: University of Wisconsin Press, 1987), 76–97.

74. See Elaine Showalter, "Guilt, Authority, and the Shadows of *Little Dorrit*," *Nineteenth-Century Fiction* 19 (1964): 23.

75. Theodor Adorno, "The Stars Down to Earth: The *Los Angeles Times* Astrology Column," in Theodor Adorno, *Gesammelte Schriften*, Vol. 9:2, (Frankfurt, 1975), 48.

76. Miller, *Charles Dickens: The World of His Novels* 231. For twentieth-century criticism, emphasis on the prison-as-society motif in the novel begins earlier, with T. A. Jackson's *Charles Dickens: The Progress of a Radical* (New York: International, 1938), 164–69, and Edmund Wilson's "Dickens: The Two Scrooges,"

in *The Wound and the Bow: Seven Studies in Literature* (Boston: Houghton Mifflin, 1941), 46–51.

77. Marcus, *Other Victorians* 109, 139–40.

78. The topic of feminine friendship in Victorian fiction is explored in Nina Auerbach, *Communities of Women: An Idea in Fiction* (Cambridge: Harvard University Press, 1978).

79. See Frances Winwar, *The Rossettis and Their Circle* (London: Hurst & Blackett, 1934), 224–25: "London's celebrated bon vivants now frequented Tudor House, provided their tales could spice an evening and they could listen as well as tell. Those were the days of Charles Augustus Howell the prodigious, and Sala, and Sandys, raconteurs of Munchausen propensities and Casanovan zest."

80. Marcus, *Other Victorians* 222.

81. See, for instance, Michael R. Booth, "Melodrama and the Working Class," in Carol Hanberry McKay, ed., *Dramatic Dickens* (New York: St. Martin's Press, 1989), 96–109: "because melodrama was always in touch with the social concerns and cultural tastes of its audience, it quickly absorbed the new industrial proletariat into its structure" (101).

82. Melodrama, as Peter Brooks argues, is the mode of dramatic excess, whose extremities point out the limits of representation per se. In Rigaud's example, however, the limits of representation dramatized are not universal but cultural and ideological, see Peter Brooks, *The Melodramatic Imagination: Balzac, Henry James, Melodrama, and the Mode of Excess* (New Haven: Yale University Press, 1976).

83. See John Forster, *The Life of Charles Dickens*, quoted in *Dombey and Son and Little Dorrit: A Casebook* 128.

84. Trilling, Introduction to Charles Dickens, *Little Dorrit* xi.

85. See, for instance, Don Richard Cox, ed., *Sexuality and Victorian Literature* (Knoxville: University of Tennessee Press, 1984), 144: "In Miss Wade, Esther's latent sadistic lesbianism is made overt. Tattycoram, the rebellious maid she persuades to come and live with her, is always seen as a sexual object."

86. See Lilian Faderman, *Surpassing the Love of Man: Romantic Friendship and Love between Women from the Renaissance to the Present* (New York: Morrow, 1981).

87. See Pauline Nestor, "The Popular Debate over Female Friendships and Communities," in her *Female Friendships and Communities: Charlotte Brontë, George Eliot, Elizabeth Gaskell* (Oxford: Clarendon Press, 1985), 7–27.

88. Trilling, Introduction to Charles Dickens, *Little Dorrit* xi.

89. On Tattycoram and the Victorian servant class in Dickens, see William Myers, "The Radicalism of *Little Dorrit*," in John Lucas, ed., *Literature and Politics in the Nineteenth-Century: Essays* (London: Methuen, 1971), 85.

90. Quoted in M. Jeanne Peterson, "The Victorian Governess: Status Incongruence in Family and Society," in *Suffer and Be Still* 3.

91. Sadoff, "Storytelling and the Figure of the Father in *Little Dorrit* 239.

92. William Axton, "The Trouble with Esther," *Modern Language Quarterly* 26, no. 4 (Dec. 1965): 545.

93. *Blackwood's Magazine*, 1855, quoted in James M. Brown, *Dickens: The Novelist in the Marketplace* (Totowa, NJ: Barnes & Noble Books, 1982), 38.

94. Walter Bagehot, "Charles Dickens," 1858, reprinted in *Dickens: The Critical Heritage* 390.

95. Theodor Adorno, *Aesthetic Theory*, trans. C. Lenhardt, ed. Gretel Adorno and Rolf Tiedemann (London and New York: Routledge & Kegan Paul, 1984), 5: "the dialectic of art resembles the social dialectic without consciously imitating it. The productive force of useful labour and of art are the same . . . the aesthetic relations of production . . . are sedimentations of social relations of production, bearing the imprint of the latter."

96. See John Holloway, "Appendix A: The Denouement of *Little Dorrit*," in *Little Dorrit*, ed. Holloway, 896–97. Holloway claims that "Arthur's father had dictated the codicil." In fact, it was Gilbert Clennam, the father's uncle, who "dictated to me," as Mrs. Clennam asserts, the terms of the codicil and its "imaginary relenting" (847, Holloway ed.).

97. Sadoff, "Storytelling and the Figure of the Father in *Little Dorrit*" 241.

98. Shklovskij, "The Mystery Novel: Dickens's *Little Dorrit*" 220–21.

99. Sigmund Freud, "Fragment of an Analysis of a Case of Hysteria," in James Strachey, ed., *The Standard Edition of the Complete Psychological Works of Sigmund Freud*, Vol. 7 (London: Hogarth Press, 1953), 70, 108–9.

100. Michael Slater, *Dickens and Women* (Stanford: Stanford University Press, 1983), 258.

Chapter 3. Melville: Ironic Democracy

1. Herman Melville to Nathaniel Hawthorne, June 1?, 1851, in *The Letters of Herman Melville*, ed. Merrell R. Davis and William H. Gilman (New Haven: Yale University Press, 1960), 127.

2. See "The Author as Subject," Dimmock's reading of *Redburn* and *White-Jacket*, in *Empire for Liberty: Melville and the Poetics of Individualism* (Princeton: Princeton University Press, 1989), 76–108. For a less sophisticated and convincing New Historicist reading of *Moby-Dick*'s perpetuation of the "exclusive religious and racial assumptions" of Manifest Destiny, see James Duban's "Nationalism and Providence in Ishmael's White World," in his *Melville's Major Fiction: Politics, Theology, and Imagination:* (Dekalb: Northern Illinois University Press, 1983), 82–148.

3. See Theodor Adorno, "The Culture Industry," in Theodor Adorno and Max Horkheimer, *The Dialectic of Enlightenment* trans. John Cumming (New York: Continuum, 1986), 143. "The ideology of the culture industry," Adorno wrote later, "contains the antidote to its own lie." See Theodor Adorno, "Transparencies on Film," *New German Critique*, nos. 24–25 (Fall/Winter 1981–82): 202.

4. William Charvat, "Melville and the Common Reader," *Studies in Bibliography* 12 (1959): 42, 45, and 42–57ff.

5. See Michael Gilmore, "Hawthorne, Melville, and the Democratic Public," and "Selling One's Head: *Moby-Dick*," in his *American Romanticism and the Marketplace* (Chicago: University of Chicago Press, 1985), 52–70 and 113–31.

6. See Richard Chase, *Herman Melville: A Critical Study* (New York: Macmillan, 1949), x.

7. See Mentor Williams, "Some Notices and Reviews of Melville's Novels in American Religious Periodicals," *American Literature* 22 (May 1950): 119–27, and Hugh Heatherington, *Melville's Reviewers: British and American, 1846–1891* (Chapel Hill: University of North Carolina Press, 1961), 20–65.

8. Melville to John Murray, July 15, 1846, in *Letters* 37–41.

9. Evert (and George?) Duyckinck, "Mr. Melville's *White-Jacket*," *New York Literary World* 6 (March 16, 1850): 272 and (March 23, 1850): 297–99, reprinted in Hershel Parker, ed., *The Recognition of Herman Melville: Selected Criticism since 1846* (Ann Arbor: University of Michigan Press, 1967), 37–41.

10. Herman Melville, "A Thought on Book-Binding," in *The Piazza Tales and Other Prose Pieces, 1839–1860* (Evanston and Chicago: Northwestern University Press and the Newberry Library, 1987), 237–38.

11. Herman Melville, *Redburn: His First Voyage* (Evanston and Chicago: Northwestern University Press and the Newberry Library, 1969), 8. Michael Davitt Bell sees the containment of Melvillean "aggression against authority" in the scene; the moment illustrates the "passive enervation" that appears to replace "rebellious defiance" throughout Melville's work. See Michael Davitt Bell, *The Development of American Romance: The Sacrifice of Relation* (Chicago: University of Chicago Press, 1980), 207–9, 213.

12. Melville to Richard Henry Dana, Jr., Oct. 6, 1849, in *Letters* 92–93.

13. See Walter Benjamin, "The Work of Art in the Age of Mechanical Reproduction," in *Illuminations*, ed. Hannah Arendt, trans. Harry Zohn (New York: Schocken Books, 1969), 217–51.

14. Herman Melville, "Hawthorne and His Mosses, by a Virginian Spending July in Vermont," in *Piazza Tales and Other Prose Pieces* 245.

15. Melville to Evert Duyckinck, March 3, 1849, in *Letters* 79–80. Donald Pease offers a useful reading of the "Hawthorne" essay as Melville's exploration of "conflicting opinions within a reading public," and historicizes the cultural politics behind Melville's interest in Shakespeare, as well as F. O. Matthiessen's reception of it. See Donald Pease, "Melville and Cultural Persuasion," in *Visionary Compacts: American Renaissance Writings in Cultural Context* (Madison: University of Wisconsin Press, 1987), 267 and 270–74.

16. For Melville, Shakespeare could appear as a symbol of the writer subject to mass-cultural control as well as an opponent of commodity culture, and thus as an ambivalent image of Hawthorne as well. For a reading of *The House of the Seven Gables* and its concerns with burgeoning forms of American consumer society, see Susan L. Mizruchi's "From History to Gingerbread:

Manufacturing a Republic in *The House of the Seven Gables*," in her *The Power of Historical Knowledge: Narrating the Past in Hawthorne, James, and Dreiser* (Princeton: Princeton University Press, 1988), 83–134.

17. Melville to Dana, May 1, 1850, in *Letters* 108.

18. William Charvat, *The Profession of Authorship in America*, ed. Matthew J. Bruccoli (Columbus: Ohio State University Press, 1968), 240.

19. See Hershel Parker, "Why *Pierre* Went Wrong," *Studies in the Novel* 8 (Spring 1976): 7–23, and Brian Higgins and Hershel Parker, "The Flawed Grandeur of Melville's *Pierre*," in Higgins and Parker, eds., *Critical Essays on Herman Melville's Pierre, or, the Ambiguities* (Boston: G. K. Hall, 1983), 240–66. Emory Elliott argues against this "failed" reading of *Pierre*, and the attempt to read it psychologically, interpreting it as Melville's novel most concerned with "ideology," in the sense of the "system of beliefs" of the "dominant culture" in which Melville wrote. See Emory Elliott, "The Problem of Authority in *Pierre*," in Sacvan Bercovitch and Myra Jehlen, eds., *Ideology and Classic American Literature* (Cambridge: Cambridge University Press, 1986), 337–38ff.

20. Herman Melville, *Pierre, or, The Ambiguities* (Evanston and Chicago: Northwestern University Press, 1971), 351, 356.

21. Sacvan Bercovitch offers a rich account of the novel's contemporary cultural and political satire in "How to Read Melville's Pierre," *Amerikastudien* 31 (1986): 31–48.

22. See Ann Douglas, *The Feminization of American Culture* (New York: Alfred Knopf, 1977), 288–326.

23. Melville to Lemuel Shaw, October 6, 1849, in *Letters* 91–92.

24. See Perry Miller, *The Raven and the Whale: The War of Words and Wits in the Era of Poe and Melville* (New York: Harcourt, Brace, 1956), 283ff. Miller's claim that the essay supported expansionist "nationalism" ignores Melville's irony, and has been corrected in John Gerlach, "Messianic Nationalism in the Early Works of Melville: Against Perry Miller," *Arizona Quarterly* 28 (Spring 1972): 5–26. Weisbuch gives a far more subtle account of Melville's relation to Dickens, as well as nationalist politics, in his *Atlantic Double-Cross: American Literature and British Influence in the Age of Emerson* (Chicago: University of Chicago Press, 1986), 36–54, here 47.

25. Weisbuch, *Atlantic Double-Cross* 45.

26. See James D. Hart, *The Popular Book: A History of America's Literary Taste* (New York: Oxford University Press, 1950), 91–92.

27. Melville to Hawthorne, June 1?, 1851, and November 17?, 1851, in *Letters* 128 and 142.

28. Melville to Dana, Oct. 6, 1849, in *Letters* 92–93.

29. Nathaniel Hawthorne, *The English Notebooks*, ed. Randall Stewart (London: Oxford University Press, 1941, 432–33.

30. See Paul Brodtkorb, Jr., *Ishmael's White World: A Phenomenological Reading of Moby Dick* (New Haven: Yale University Press, 1965), 136–37. John Seelye's *Melville: The Ironic Diagram* (Evanston, IL: Northwestern University Press,

1966) is considered the standard treatment of Melville's irony, and takes its approach specifically from Hawthorne's comments, covering the question in Melville as largely one of skeptical epistemology.

31. Carolyn Porter, "Call Me Ishmael, or How to Make Double-Talk Speak," in Richard Brodhead, ed., *New Essays on Moby-Dick* (Cambridge: Cambridge University Press, 1986), 93ff.

32. Herman Melville, *Moby-Dick, or, The Whale,* ed. Harrison Hayford, Hershel Parker, G. Thomas Tanselle (Evanston and Chicago: Northwestern University Press and the Newberry Library, 1988), 331. All subsequent references to *Moby-Dick* will be from this edition, and will be given parenthetically in the text.

33. See Charles H. Foster, "Something in Emblems: A Reinterpretation of *Moby-Dick*," *New England Quarterly* 34 (March 1961): 3–35, and T. Walter Herbert, "Calvinist Earthquake: *Moby-Dick* and the Calvinist Tradition," in *New Essays on Moby-Dick* 116–19ff.

34. Herman Melville, *White-Jacket, or, The World in a Man-of-War* (Evanston and Chicago: Northwestern University Press and the Newberry Library, 1970), 3.

35. David Reynolds, *Beneath the American Renaissance: The Subversive Imagination in the Age of Emerson and Melville* (New York: Alfred A. Knopf, 1988), 149ff. Reynolds' work, and its characterization of popular culture as "Subversive" with a capital *S*, fails to take into account any of the limitations Melville understood as part of popular culture, and thus misses almost all of Melville's satire in *White-Jacket* on his audience and their potential to be manipulated by such radical works.

36. Dimmock, *Empire for Liberty* 100–101ff.

37. Melville to Dana, May 1, 1850, in *Letters* 106.

38. See Samuel Shapiro in *Richard Henry Dana, Jr. 1815–1882* (East Lansing: Michigan State University Press, 1961), 190–92. On the relation between *Moby-Dick* and the Buffalo Free Soil Convention of 1848 at which Dana spoke, see Alan Heimert, "*Moby-Dick* and American Political Symbolism," *American Quarterly* 15 (Winter 1963): 529–30.

39. See Eric Foner, *Free Soil, Free Labor, Free Men: The Origins of the Republican Party before the Civil War* (London: Oxford University Press, 1970), 60–61; on Dana, see 67–68.

40. Quoted in Foner, *Free Soil, Free Labor, Free Men* 67–68.

41. On the novel's racial satire, see Carolyn Karcher, *Shadow over the Promised Land: Slavery, Race, and Violence in Melville's America* (Baton Rouge: Louisiana State University Press, 1980), 40–47ff. Karcher argues that Melville's "subversive mode" of "extended parallels between black and white character types . . . did not fulfill its purpose," but does not consider its relation to Free Soil ideology.

42. Melville, *Redburn* 202. On Melville's handling of African and African-American figures in *Redburn*, see Eleanor E. Simpson, "Melville and the

Negro: From *Typee* to *Benito Cereno*," *American Literature* 41, (March 1969): 22–25.

43. Richard Henry Dana, Speech at the Free Soil Meeting, July 7, 1848, at Boston, in Richard Henry Dana, Jr., *Speeches in Stirring Times and Letters to a Son*, ed. Richard Henry Dana III (Boston and New York: Houghton Mifflin, 1910), 148.

44. Herman Melville, "Authentic Anecdotes of 'Old Zack,'" in *Piazza Tales and Other Prose Pieces* 212–29. As Richard Herskowitz has argued, P. T. Barnum's "contribution to modern advertising" was his means of making such "misrepresentation tolerable to the consumer." See Richard Herskowitz, "P. T. Barnum's Double Bind," *Social Text* 2 (Summer 1979): 134.

45. See Henry Louis Gates, Jr., "Figures of Signification," in his *The Signifying Monkey: A Theory of African-American Literary Criticism* (New York and London: Oxford University Press, 1988), here 94.

46. John Van Buren, son of Martin Van Buren, the Barnburner candidate who began the Free Soil movement in "Buffalo" (244), Steelkilt's home, would declare in 1848: "you can not induce a laboring man to work beside a black slave." John Van Buren, Proceedings of the Utica Convention of Feb. 16, 1848, quoted in Eric Foner, *Free Soil Free Labor, Free Men* 61.

47. Peter Bailey, "Making Sense of Music Hall," in Peter Bailey, ed., *Music Hall: The Business of Pleasure* (Milton Keynes and Philadelphia: Open University Press, 1986), xvii.

48. Shaw refused Dana's request for a writ of habeas corpus, and Shadrach, as he was also called, was helped in the interim by other blacks to escape, in a case that was a prologue to the Sims affair. See Shapiro, *Richard Henry Dana, Jr.*, 58–59.

49. Dana to Daniel Lord, Jan. 26, 1854, quoted in Charles Francis Adams, *Richard Henry Dana: A Biography* (Boston and New York: Houghton, Mifflin, 1890), 124–26.

50. See "*Moby-Dick*, Napoleon, and Workers of the World," in Larry Reynolds, *European Revolutions and the American Literary Renaissance* (New Haven: Yale University Press, 1988), 108–24.

51. Benjamin, "Work of Art in the Age of Mechanical Reproduction" 232.

52. Theodor Adorno, "Perennial Fashion—Jazz," in *Prisms*, trans. Samuel Weber and Shierry Weber (Cambridge: MIT Press, 1981), 126.

53. See Guy Debord, *Society of the Spectacle* (Detroit, 1977).

54. The marginalia is mentioned in Charles Robert Anderson, *Melville in the South Seas* (New York: Columbia University Press, 1939), 399.

55. Susan Buck-Morss, *The Dialectics of Seeing: Walter Benjamin and the Arcades Project* (Cambridge: MIT Press, 1989), 34.

56. See Howard P. Vincent, *The Tailoring of Melville's White-Jacket* (Evanston: Northwestern University Press, 1970), 183.

57. Walter Benjamin, "The Author as Producer," in *Reflections*, ed. Peter Demetz, trans. Edmund Jephcott (New York and London: Harcourt Brace Jovanovich, 1978), 232.

58. Ibid. 233.

59. See Reynolds, *European Revolutions* 108 and 122; "Antidemocratic Emphasis in *White-Jacket*," *American Literature* 5 no. 48 (March 1976): 13–28. On the symbol of the hammer in the American labor movement of the nineteenth century, see Sean Wilentz, *Chants Democratic: New York City and the Rise of the American Working Class, 1788–1850* (New York: Oxford University Press, 1984), 345, and plate 4.

60. Robert Caserio, *Plot, Story, and the Novel* (Princeton: Princeton University Press, 1979), 166.

61. See Sacvan Bercovitch, *The American Jeremiad* (Madison: University of Wisconsin Press, 1978), 192–94.

62. See Murray Krieger, *The Tragic Vision* (Chicago: University of Chicago Press, 1960), 254–55.

63. Pease, *Visionary Compacts* 274.

64. Melville to Duyckinck, December 14, 1949, in *Letters* 95–96.

65. F. O. Matthiessen, *American Renaissance: Art and Expression in the Age of Emerson and Whitman* (London and New York: Oxford University Press, 1941), 452–53ff. For an analysis of Matthiessen's relation to Popular Front literary criticism, see Jonathan Arac, "F. O. Matthiessen: Authorizing an American Renaissance," in Walter Benn Michaels and Donald Pease, eds., *The American Renaissance Reconsidered: Selected Papers from the English Institute, 1982–1983* (Baltimore: Johns Hopkins University Press, 1985), 101–2ff.

66. Theodor Adorno, *Aesthetic Theory*, trans. C. Lenhardt, ed. Gretel Adorno and Rolf Tiedemann (London and New York: Routledge & Kegan Paul, 1984), 340.

67. George Fitzhugh, *Sociology for the South, or the Failure of a Free Society* (New York: B. Franklin, 1965), 26.

68. In the memorable phrase of John William Ward, "Manifest Destiny was Janus-Faced." See "Extending the Area of Freedom," in John William Ward, *Andrew Jackson: Symbol for an Age* (London: Oxford University Press, 1953), 133–49, here 144.

69. Theodor Adorno, "Reading Balzac," in *Notes to Literature*, ed. Rolf Tiedemann, trans. Shierry Weber Nicholsen (New York: Columbia University Press, 1992), 1: 122–23.

70. Donald Pease, "Melville and the Cultural Persuasion," in *Visionary Compacts* 272: "the endless proliferation of possible deeds displaces the need for any definitive action."

71. Larzer Ziff, *Literary Democracy: The Declaration of Cultural Independence in America* (New York: Viking Press, 1981), 284.

72. Eric Sundquist, *Home as Found: Authority and Genealogy in Nineteenth-Century American Literature* (Baltimore: Johns Hopkins University Press, 1979), 146.

73. Melville to Hawthorne, June 1?, 1851, in *Letters* 130.

74. See Paul Royster, "Melville's Economy of Language," in *Ideology and Classic American Literature* 321–22: "Ishmael, squeezing spermacetti on the deck of

the *Pequod*, burlesques the idea of universal brotherhood . . . the sexual implications of 'milk and sperm' are hardly accidental." See Wilson Cary McWilliams, *The Idea of Fraternity in America* (Berkeley: University of California Press, 1973), 334–35.

75. Theodor Adorno, "Critique of the Notion of Catharsis; Kitsch and Vulgarity," in *Aesthetic Theory* 337–43.

76. Walter Benjamin, "Theses on the Philosophy of History," in *Illuminations* 256.

77. Henry Louis Gates, Jr., *Figures in Black: Words, Signs and the Racial Self* (New York: Oxford University Press, 1987), 85.

78. O'Sullivan's position in American letters is usefully presented in John Stafford, *The Literary Criticism of "Young America:" A Study in the Relationship of Politics and Literature, 1837–1850* (New York: Russell & Russell, 1952), 5–9.

79. John Gerlach, "Messianic Nationalism in the Early Works of Herman Melville," *Arizona Quarterly* 28, (Spring 1972): 5–26, here 14.

80. Karl Marx, "The Fetishism of the Commodity and the Secret Thereof," in *Capital: A Critique of Political Economy* (New York: Modern Library, 1906), 83. My interpretation of Melville here, and sense of his relation as a critical mass-cultural novelist to Dickens, have been influenced by David Simpson's *Fetishism and the Imagination: Dickens, Melville, Conrad* (Baltimore: Johns Hopkins University Press, 1982).

81. The significance of Melville and Dickens in the philosophic tradition of the novel has been well explored by Edwin Eigner, in *The Metaphysical Novel in England and America: Dickens, Bulwer, Melville, and Hawthorne* (Berkeley: University of California Press, 1978).

82. Jonathan Cobb and Richard Sennett explore the internalization of work as psychological limitation in *The Hidden Injuries Class* (New York: Vintage, 1973).

83. Walter Benjamin, "The Storyteller: Reflections on the Works of Nikolai Leskov," in *Illuminations* 94, 101: "Death is the sanction of everything that the storyteller can tell. He has borrowed his authority from death . . . what draws the reader to the novel is the hope of warming his shivering life with a death he reads about."

84. See Dimmock, "The Author as Subject," in *Empire for Liberty* 76–108.

85. Henry Nash Smith, "The Madness of Ahab," *Yale Review* 66 (Autumn 1976): 32.

86. Adorno and Horkheimer, *Dialectic of Enlightenment* 9.

87. Theodor Adorno, "Veblen's Attack on Culture," in *Prisms* 87.

88. See Victor Turner, *The Ritual Process: Structure and Anti-Structure* (Chicago: Aldine, 1969).

89. Adorno and Horkheimer, *Dialectic of Enlightenment* 51.

90. Adorno, *Aesthetic Theory* 369.

91. Review of *Moby-Dick, United States Magazine and Democratic Review*, January 1852, reprinted in Hershel Parker, and Harrison Hayford, eds., *Moby-Dick as Doubloon: Essays and Extracts, 1851–1970* (New York: Norton, 1970), 83.

92. See Heimert, "*Moby-Dick* and American Political Symbolism" 509–11, and David Potter, *The Impending Crisis, 1848–1861* (New York: Harper and Row, 1976), 114.

93. Melville, "Hawthorne and His Mosses" 242–43.

94. Melville, "Hawthorne and His Mosses" 242, and Walter Benjamin, "Allegory and Trauerspiel," in *The Origin of German Tragic Drama*, trans. John Osborne (London: Verso, 1977), 185.

95. See Gilmore, *American Romanticism and the Marketplace* 129–30.

96. For an account of the relations between kitsch and modern art, see "Kitsch," in Matei Calinescu, *Five Faces of Modernity: Modernism, Avant-Garde, Decadence, Kitsch, Postmodernism* (Durham, NC: Duke University Press, 1987), 225–59.

97. "To go down to posterity is bad enough, anyway," he wrote, "but to go down as a man who 'lived among the cannibals!' " Melville to Hawthorne, June 1?, 1851, in *Letters* 130.

98. Herman Melville, "Mr. Parkman's Tour," *Piazza Tales and Other Prose Pieces* 231.

99. See Julia Kristeva, *Powers of Horror: An Essay on Abjection*, trans. Leon S. Roudiez (New York: Columbia University Press, 1982).

Chapter 4. Kafka: Criticism and Social Change

1. Theodor Adorno, "Notes on Kafka," in *Prisms*, trans. Samuel Weber and Shierry Weber (Cambridge: MIT Press, 1967), 265.

2. Mark Spilka, *Dickens and Kafka: A Mutual Interpretation* (Bloomington: Indiana University Press, 1963), 242. For a useful summary of these connections, see George Ford, *Dickens and His Readers: Aspects of Novel-Criticism since 1836* (New York: Gordian Press, 1955), 144.

3. Marthe Robert has placed *The Castle* in the tradition of the novel of social challenge, as a revision of its inheritance, in "Momus, or the Last Messenger," in her *The Old and the New: From Don Quixote to Franz Kafka*, trans. Carol Cosman (Berkeley: University of California Press, 1977).

4. Franz Kafka, Diary Entry of October 8, 1917, in *Tagebücher*, ed. Hans-Gerd Koch, Michael Müller, and Malcolm Pasley, *Franz Kafka: Schriften Tägebücher Briefe, Kritische Ausgabe* (Frankfurt, 1990), 841. Translations of the diaries are from *The Diaries of Franz Kafka 1914–1923*, ed. Max Brod, trans. Martin Greenberg (New York: Schocken Books, 1965). I have modified Greenberg's translation at different points.

5. Theodor Adorno, "Notes on Kafka," in *Prisms* 255. For an excellent treatment of Adorno's method, see Willi Goetschel, "Kafka's Negative Dialectics" *Journal of the Kafka Society of America* 9 (1985): 83–106.

6. Sabina Kienlechner, for instance, links Adorno and Kafka as practitioners of an "ethisch-moralischen Reflexion auf Erkennen" (ethical-moral epistemology critique), but questions the political content Adorno finds in his work.

See "Aus der Perspektive der Erlösung: Eine Parallel im Denken Kafkas und Adornos," in her *Negativität der Erkenntnis im Werk Franz Kafkas* (Tübingen: Max Niemeyer Verlag, 1981), 148–53.

7. Kafka, Diary Entry of December 13, 1911, in *Tagebücher* 291.

8. Harry Zohn, for instance, points out that *Josephine* is legible as an allegory of diaspora Judaism and its ambiguous forms of self-identification. See Harry Zohn, "Participation in German Literature," in *The Jews of Czechoslovakia: Historical Studies and Surveys*, Vol. 1 (Philadelphia and New York: Jewish Publication Society of America, 1968), 488.

9. Franz Kafka, [Rede über die jiddische Sprache], Jewish Town Hall, Prague, February 18, 1912, in *Gesammelte Werke*, ed. Max Brod, Vol. 6 (Frankfurt, 1976), 306–9. English translation, "An Introductory Talk on the Yiddish Language," in Mark Anderson, ed., *Reading Kafka: Prague Politics and the Fin de Siècle* (New York: Schocken Books, 1989), 263–66.

10. Franz Kafka, [Rede über die jiddische Sprache] 309.

11. Klaus Wagenbach, *Franz Kafka: Eine Biographie seiner Jugend* (Berne: Francke, 1958), 94.

12. Kafka to Max Brod and Felix Weltsch, April 10, 1920, in Franz Kafka, *Briefe 1902–1924*, ed. Max Brod (Frankfurt: S. Fischer Verlag, 1958), 270–71. Translation from Franz Kafka, *Letters to Friends, Family, and Editors*, trans. Richard Winston and Clara Winston (New York: Schocken Books, 1977), 233. I have modified the Winstons' translation at certain points.

13. Kafka, Diary Entry of January 16, 1922, in *Tagebücher* 878.

14. See Gershom Scholem, "Kabbalah and Myth," in his *On the Kabbalah and Its Symbolism*, trans. Ralph Mannheim (New York: Schocken Books, 1969), 112, Evelyn Torton Beck, *Kafka and the Yiddish Theater: Its Impact on His Work* (Madison: University of Wisconsin Press, 1971), 195. This same pun is also noticed by Ritchie Robertson in *Kafka: Judaism, Politics, and Literature* (Oxford: Clarendon Press, 1985), 228 and 232–33, who discusses the relation of messianism to the novel, as does W. G. Sebald, in "The Law of Ignominy: Authority, Messianism, and Exile in *The Castle*," in Franz Kuna, ed., *On Kafka: Semi-Centenary Perspectives* (New York: Harper and Row, 1976), 42–58.

15. Franz Kafka, *Hochzeitsvorbereitungen auf dem Lande und andere Prosa aus dem Nachlaß*, *Gesammelte Werke* 6:30.

16. See Max Brod, "New Aspects of Kafka," in *Franz Kafka: A Biography*, 2d ed. trans. G. Humphreys Robert (New York: Schocken Books, 1960), 219, 221–23.

17. Adorno, "Notes on Kafka" 287.

18. Franz Kafka, Aphorism 20, in *Hochzeitsvorbereitungen* 31, and *The Great Wall of China: Stories and Reflections*, trans. Willa Muir and Edwin Muir (New York: Schocken Books, 1946), 163.

19. This postcard is described in the best account of Kafka's political involvements, "Interessen und Aktivitäten: Politik," in Hartmut Binder, ed., *Kafka-Handbuch in Zwei Bänden* (Stuttgart, 1979), 1:361–67ff. Most historical ac-

counts of Kafka's political affiliations with anarchism and socialism, nonetheless, lack an appreciation of such irony. See Lee Baxandall, "Kafka as Radical," in Angel Flores, ed., *The Kafka Debate: New Perspectives for Our Time* (New York: Gordian Press, 1977), 120–26.

20. Adorno, "Notes on Kafka" 252. For a discussion of Kafka's political interests in the context of German expressionism, see Walter Sokel, *The Writer in Extremis: Expressionism in Twentieth Century German Literature* (Stanford: Stanford University Press, 1959), 160–61.

21. Theodor Adorno, "Subject and Object," in Andrew Arato and Eike Gebhardt, eds., *The Essential Frankfurt School Reader*, (New York: Continuum, 1982), 499, Adorno, "Extorted Reconciliation: On Georg Lukacs' *Realism in Our Time*, trans. Shierry Weber Nicholson (New York: Columbia University Press, 1991), 1:225, and "Notes on Kafka" 252.

22. Kafka, Aphorism 93, in *Gesammelte Werke* 6:38, and Adorno, "Notes on Kafka" 252.

23. Adorno, "Notes on Kafka" 252.

24. Kafka, Diary Entry of December 25, 1911, in *Tagebücher* 312–19, 321–22.

25. Kafka, *Tagebücher* 313, 315. The passage as a whole has been read by Gilles Deleuze and Felix Guattari as a program for a postmodern and postnational writing, in chap. 2 of their *Kafka: Toward a Minor Literature*, trans. Dana Polan (Minneapolis: University of Minnesota Press, 1986). 16–27.

26. Charles Bernheimer, *Flaubert and Kafka: Studies in Psychopoetic Structure* (New Haven: Yale University Press, 1982), 150–51.

27. Franz Kafka, *Brief an den Vater, Gesammelte Werke* 6:129.

28. Ritchie Robertson, *Kafka: Judaism, Politics, and Literature* (Oxford: Clarendon Press, 1985), 44ff.

29. See Judith Ryan, "Our Trial: Kafka's Challenge to Literary Theory," *Novel* 18, no. 3 (Spring 1985): 257–66, here 260.

30. Margaret Walter-Schneider, in particular, revises the work of Beissner as well as Jörgen Kobs, and the principle that "Kafkas Menschen sind gefangen in ihrer Subjektivität" (Kafka's individuals are imprisoned in their subjectivity), arguing that "objektive Wahrnehmung nicht unmöglich ist" (objective perception is not impossible) in his novels (7, 13), in her *Denken als Verdacht: Untersuchungen zum Problem der Wahrnehmung im Werk Franz Kafkas* (München und Zürich: Artemis Verlag, 1980). Sabina Kienlechner's *Negativität der Erkenntnis im Werk Franz Kafkas* (Tübingen: Max Niemeyer Verlag, 1981) makes use of Adorno's critical theory directly. On the issue of critical subjectivity in Kafka, see Jörgen Kobs, *Kafka: Untersuchungen zu Bewusstsein und Sprache seiner Gestalten* (Bad Hamburg, 1970), and Friedrich Beissner, *Kafkas Darstellung des Traumhaften innern Lebens* (Bebenhausen, 1972).

31. See, for instance, Winfried Kudszus, "Erzählhaltung und Zeitverschiebung in Kafka's *Prozess* und *Schloß*," *Deutsche Vierteljahrsschrift für Literaturwissenschaft und Geistesgeschichte* 38 (1964): 192–207.

32. The best biographical source for such material is part 3 of his *Kafka in neuer Sicht* (Stuttgart, 1976). A shorter and more social-historical approach is

usefully taken in Christoph Stölzl's *Kafka's Böses Böhmen: Zur Sozialgeschichte eines Prager Juden* (München, 1975).

33. Russell Berman, *The Rise of the Modern German Novel: Crisis and Charisma* (Cambridge: Harvard University Press, 1986), 262.

34. Walter Benjamin, "Some Reflections on Kafka," in *Illuminations*, ed. Hannah Arendt, trans. Harry Zohn (New York: Schocken Books, 1969), 142–43.

35. Benjamin, "Some Reflections on Kafka" 144.

36. Kafka, Diary Entry of March 9, 1922, in *Tagebücher* 910.

37. Benjamin, "Some Reflections on Kafka" 143.

38. Franz Kafka, *Das Schloß*, ed. Malcolm Pasley, *Franz Kafka: Schriften Tagebücher Briefe, Kritische Ausgabe*, ed. Jürgen Born, Gerhard Neumann, Malcolm Pasley und Jost Schillemeit (Frankfurt, 1982), 7. References to this novel will hereafter be given parenthetically in the text.

39. Kafka, Diary Entry of November 20, 1911, in *Tagebücher* 259.

40. Gary Cohen, *The Politics of Ethnic Survival in Prague: Germans in Prague, 1861–1914* (Princeton, NJ: Princeton University Press, 1981), 262.

41. Kafka to Max Brod, June 1921, in *Briefe* 337.

42. See Hans Tramer, "Prague—City of Three Peoples," *Leo Baeck Institute Year Book*, (1964), 305–39. Prague's population in 1900 was 450,000 including 25,000 Jews and 10,000 non-Jewish German-speaking Hapsburg subjects; 14,000 Jews declared Czech to be their everyday language.

43. Quoted by Wilhelm Emrich, *Franz Kafka* (Frankfurt, 1964), 199.

44. See Michel Foucault, *The History of Sexuality*, trans. Robert Hurley (New York: Pantheon Books, 1978).

45. Henry Sussman provides the best account of the boundary in Kafka's novel as a paradox of epistemology: "perhaps the most enigmatic paradox of *The Castle* is that the powers imputed to the Castle, making it a superior and exclusive realm, do not prevent the border separating it from the village from being penetrated almost at will, as the literal intercourse between the officials and villagers most concretely attests. Conversely, the manifold penetrations of the border do not weaken the belief, on both sides, in its efficacy and the prevalence of the ontological and normative categories for which it serves as a point of reference. K.'s doubled *Blick* into the Castle encompasses the contradictory thrusts of this paradox and thus prefigures the overall movements of the novel." See Henry Sussman, *Franz Kafka: Geometrician of Metaphor* (Madison, WI: Coda Press, 1979), 117.

46. The same pattern also holds for deconstructive allegorization of the novel's interpretive mystery. See Marjanne Goozé, "Texts, Textuality, and Silence in Kafka's *Das Schloß*," Modern Language Notes 98, no. 3 (April 1983): 346–47.

47. See Margaret Buber-Neumann, *Milena*, trans. Ralph Mannheim (New York: Seaver Books, 1988), 49. See also Wagenbach, *Franz Kafka: Eine Biographie seiner Jugend* 73.

48. Theodor Herzl, "Die Juden Prags zwischen den Nationen" (1897), reprinted in *Das Jüdische Prag: Eine Sammelschrift* (Prague, 1917), 7.

49. *Das Judische Prag: Eine Sammelschrift* 39.

50. Leo Hermann, "Aus Tägebuchblättern," *Der Jude, Sonderheft zu Martin Bubers 50. Geburtstag* (Berlin, 1928), 159–64.

51. Kafka to Felice Bauer, January 19, 1913, in *Briefe an Felice und andere Korrespondenz aus der Verlobungszeit*, ed. Erich Heller and Jürgen Born (Frankfurt, 1967), 257, translation from Franz Kafka, *Letters to Felice*, ed. Erich Heller and J. Born (New York: Schocken Books, 1967), 161.

52. Kafka to Felice Bauer, January 16, 1913, in *Briefe an Felice* 252.

53. Hermann, "Aus Tagebuchblättern" 160.

54. Kafka remarked of Balzac's narrative description: "diese Generalisierung ist falsch." See Willy Haas, *Die literarische Welt: Erinnerungen* (München, 1960), 32–36, reprinted as "Erinnerungen an die Prager Literarische Welt," in Wilma Iggers, ed. *Die Juden in Böhmen und Mähren: ein Historisches Lesebuch* (München: Verlag C. H. Beck, 1986), 280.

55. The dissolution of realist representation into produced images in Balzac, however, is discussed as anticipatory, skeptical modernism in Claudia Brodsky, *The Imposition of Form: Studies in Narrative Representation and Knowledge* (Princeton, NJ: Princeton University Press, 1987), 188–209ff.

56. Marthe Robert, *As Lonely as Franz Kafka*, trans. Ralph Mannheim (New York: Schocken Books, 1986), 73.

57. Kafka, Diary Entry of October 24, 1911, *Tagebücher* 102.

58. Kafka to Brod, June 1921, in *Briefe* 334–38.

59. Kafka, Diary Entry of October 29, 1921, *Tagebücher* 871.

60. Kafka, Diary Entry of December 25, 1911, *Tagebücher* 321.

61. Ritchie Robertson in *Kafka: Judaism, Politics and Literature* gives an example of the public situation Kafka faced as well: "He became one of the few Jews employed in the public service when he left a private insurance company . . . some years later Kafka informed Brod that there was not the remotest chance of any more Jews being taken on" (9).

62. Franz Kafka, *Das Schloß*, ed. Malcolm Pasley (Frankfurt, 1982), 2:211.

63. Emrich, *Franz Kafka* 365.

64. Robert, *Old and the New: From Don Quixote to Franz Kafka* 293.

65. Richard Sheppard, *On Kafka's Castle: A Critical Study* (London: Croom/ Helm, 1973), 157.

66. Brod's reading, for instance, emphasized Kierkegaard's significance for Amalia's character. See Kafka, Diary Entry of August 21, 1913, and Max Brod, "Nachwort zur dritten Ausgabe" (Afterword to the Third Edition), *Das Schloß*, in Franz Kafka, *Gesammelte Werke*, Vol. 3 (Frankfurt, 1976).

67. I draw throughout this section on Hillel J. Kieval, *The Making of Czech Jewry: National Conflict and Jewish Society in Bohemia, 1870–1918* (New York and Oxford: Oxford University Press, 1988), 138–39.

68. See Max Brod, *Streitbares Leben: Autobiographie* (München: Kindler Verlag, 1960), 343–44.

69. Max Brod, *Ein Tschechisches Dienstmädchen*, 2d ed. (Berlin: Axel Junger Verlag, n.d.), 66.

70. Leo Hermann, Review of Max Brod, *Ein Tschechisches Dienstmädchen*, *Selbstwehr*, April 1909, quoted in Kieval, *Making of Czech Jewry* 139.

71. Hartmut Binder, "Franz Kafka and the Weekly Paper *Selbstwehr*," *Leo Baeck Institute Yearbook XII* (1967), 135–48, here 140.

72. Anne Golomb Hoffman, "Plotting the Landscape: Stories and Story-tellers in *The Castle*," *Twentieth Century Literature* 27 (Fall 1981): 296, and Heinz Politzer, *Franz Kafka: Parable and Paradox* (Ithaca: Cornell University Press, 1962), 271–72.

73. Goozé, "Texts, Textuality, and Silence" 344, 349.

74. "Es war das keine Eigenheit Sortinis, die meisten Beamten scheinen in der Öffentlichkeit teilnahmslos" (It was no characteristic peculiar to Sortini. Most officials seem in public as if they had nothing to do) (300).

75. Politzer, *Franz Kafka: Parable and Paradox* 272.

76. Walter Sokel, *Franz Kafka—Tragik und Ironie: Zur Struktur Seiner Kunst* (München, 1965), 396–97.

77. Kafka, Diary Entry of January 16, 1922, in *Tagebücher* 878.

78. Kafka to Brod, June 1921, in *Briefe* 337.

79. Ibid. 337.

80. See Hartmut Binder, "Prag in Bildvorstellungen Kafkas unter besonderer Berücksichtigung seines Traumes vom 7./8. November 1911," in Hartmut Binder, ed., *Franz Kafka und die Prager Deutsche Literatur* (Bonn: Kulturstiftung der Deutschen Vertriebenen, 1988), 17.

81. Kafka, Diary Entry of November 9, 1911, in *Tagebücher* 240–41.

82. Kafka, Diary Entry of October 22, 1911, in *Tagebücher* 96–97. On Kafka's relations with Mania Tschissik, see Evelyn Torton Beck, *Kafka and the Yiddish Theater* 19–20.

83. See Gilles Deleuze and Felix Guattari, "Content and Expression," in *Kafka: Toward a Minor Literature* 1–8.

84. Ezekiel 33:1–6, *New English Bible with the Apocrypha* (New York: Oxford University Press, 1971).

85. Kafka to Brod, June 1921, *Briefe* 336.

86. Wagenbach, *Franz Kafka: Eine Biographie seiner Jugend* 50. For an interpretation of the cultural politics of Prague German in Kafka that relies on Wagenbach, see Gilles Deleuze and Felix Guattari, "Content and Expression," in *Kafka: Toward a Minor Literature* 22–24ff.

87. Kafka, Diary Entry of October 6, 1911, in *Tagebücher* 68.

88. As Peter Demetz points out, Kafka's novel, insisting on the split between village and castle, differs from the consoling image of cultural accommodation that closes Němcóva's novel. See Peter Demetz, Afterword, *Die Grossmutter*, trans. and afterword by Hanna Demetz und Peter Demetz (Zürich: Manesse Verlag, 1959), 441.

89. Kafka, Diary Entry of November 1, 1911, in *Tagebücher* 215.

90. Kafka, Aphorism 7, *Gesammelte Werke* 6:30, and *Great Wall of China* 163.

91. Brod reproduces these lines in his Afterword to the Third Edition of *Das Schloß*, in *Gesammelte Werke*, Vol. 3: "Die Erzählung ist im Manuscript noch um einige Zeilen weiter geführt, als die zweite Ausgabe des Romans dies wiedergibt . . . Schlußzeilen des Romans, die unvermittelt in der Mitte der Seite abbrechen . . ." (The manuscript continues several lines farther than the Second Edition indicates . . . concluding lines that abruptly break off in the middle of the page) (355).

92. Kafka, *Das Schloß* 2:495.

93. The concluding passage reads as follows: "Sie reichte K. die zitternde Hand und ließ ihn neben sich niedersetzen, mühselig sprach sie, man hatte Mühe sie zu verstehn, aber was sie sagte" (She offered K. her trembling hand and had him sit next to her, she was difficult to understand, but what she said) (495).

94. Kafka, Diary Entry of June 12, 1923, in *Tagebücher* 926.

Afterword

1. For a persuasive reading of voice in Dickens in these terms, see Patrick O'Donnell, *Echo Chambers: Figuring Voice in Modern Narrative* (Iowa City: University of Iowa Press, 1992).

2. Andreas Huyssen, "The Vanishing Other: Mass Culture," in *After the Great Divide: Modernism, Mass Culture, Postmodernism* (Bloomington and Indianapolis: University of Indiana Press, 1986), 3–20ff.

3. On the critical weakness of postmodern theory, see Russell A. Berman, Introduction, *Modern Culture and Critical Theory: Art, Politics, and the Legacy of the Frankfurt School* (Madison: University of Wisconsin Press, 1989).

4. This position on literary theory is articulated by John Carlos Rowe in his essay, "The New Pedagogy," *South Atlantic Quarterly* 91, no. 3 (Summer 1992): 765–84, which begins: "The time has come for progressive teachers to reconstruct a liberal consensus."

5. See Richard Rorty, "Private Irony and Liberal Hope," as well as the later chapters of his *Contingency, Irony, and Solidarity* (Cambridge: Cambridge University Press, 1989), 73–96 and 141–88ff.

6. Linda Hutcheon, *A Poetics of Postmodernism: History, Theory, Fiction* (New York: Routledge, 1988), 7.

7. The "jargon of authenticity," as Adorno suggested, can easily turn such difference into conformity; his critique of the rhetoric of authenticity, moreover, is directed primarily at Heidegger, whose thought provides a model for Rorty's practice. See Theodor Adorno, *The Jargon of Authenticity*, trans. Knut Tarnowski and Frederic Will (Evanston, IL: Northwestern University Press, 1973).

8. Walter Benjamin, "Theses on the Philosophy of History," in *Illuminations*, ed. Hannah Arendt, trans. Harry Zohn (New York: Schocken Books, 1969), 261: "The concept of the historical progression of mankind cannot be sundered from the concept of its progression through a homogenous, empty time. A

critique of such a progression must be the basis of any criticism of the concept of progress itself."

9. Mark Anderson, moreover, demonstrates the links between Josephine's silence and Kafka's engagement with contemporary anti-Semitic writing on Jewish music. See Mark M. Anderson, " 'Jewish' Music? Otto Weininger and 'Josefine the Singer,' " in *Kafka's Clothes: Ornament and Aestheticism in the Hapsburg Fin de Siècle* (Oxford: Clarendon Press, 1992), 194–216.

10. Schlesinger's critique of contemporary multiculturalism is articulated in *The Disuniting of America* (New York: Norton, 1992).

11. Kitsch, as Saul Friedländer has argued, bears a strong relation to twentieth-century totalitarianism, and is well deserving of the kind of analysis Melville gave to popular culture. See Saul Friedländer, *Reflections of Nazism: An Essay on Kitsch and Death*, trans. Thomas Weyr (New York: Harper and Row, 1984).

12. See Jean Baudrillard, *La Société de Consommation* (Paris, 1970), and *Selected Writings*, edited and with an introduction by Mark Poster (Stanford: Stanford University Press, 1988). On new approaches to technology and culture, see Andrew Ross, *Strange Weather: Culture, Science, and Technology in the Age of Limits* (London and New York: Verso, 1991).

13. Walter Benjamin, "Theses on the Philosophy of History," in *Illuminations* 254.

14. Ibid 254.

15. Walter Benjamin, "Theses on the Philosophy of History," in *Illuminations* 256ff.

16. Theodor Adorno, *Zur Metakritik der Erkenntnistheorie: Drei Studien zu Hegel, Gesammelte Schriften*, Vol. 5 (Frankfurt, 1970), 46.

Index